Britain Pre-eminent

Each volume in this series is designed to make available to students important new work on key historical problems and periods that they encounter in their courses. Every volume is devoted to a central topic or theme, and the most important aspects of this are dealt with by specially commissioned essays from specialists in the period. The editorial Introduction reviews the problem or period as a whole, and each essay provides a balanced assessment of the particular aspect, pointing out the areas of development and controversy and indicating where conclusions can be drawn or where further work is necessary. An annotated bibliography serves as an up-to-date guide to further reading.

PROBLEMS IN FOCUS SERIES

Britain after the Glorious Revolution 1689–1714 edited by Geoffrey Holmes

Britain Pre-eminent: Studies of British world influence in the nineteenth century edited by C. J. Bartlett

FORTHCOMING TITLES

Great Politicians and Their Electoral Appeal 1860–1920 edited by Donald Southgate

Aspects of Victorian Liberalism edited by Leyland Lyons

Popular Movements 1830–50 edited by John Ward

The Interregnum edited by Gerald Aylmer

The Republic and the Civil War in Spain edited by Raymond Carr

Urban Studies edited by A. M. Everett

The Hundred Years War edited by Kenneth Fowler

Development Finance in Latin America edited by K. B. Griffin

Industrial Revolutions edited by R. M. Hartwell

Sweden 1632–1718 edited by Michael Roberts

Britain Pre-eminent

Studies of British world influence
in the nineteenth century

EDITED BY

C. J. BARTLETT

Macmillan
St Martin's Press

© C. J. Bartlett, Peter N. Stearns, S. G. E. Lythe,
D. F. Macdonald, Kenneth Fielden, D. R. Watson,
Oliver Furley, Donald Southgate 1969

First published 1969 by
MACMILLAN AND CO LTD
Little Essex Street London WC2
and also at Bombay Calcutta and Madras
Macmillan South Africa (Publishers) Pty Ltd Johannesburg
The Macmillan Company of Australia Pty Ltd Melbourne
The Macmillan Company of Canada Ltd Toronto
St Martin's Press Inc New York
Gill and Macmillan Ltd Dublin

Library of Congress catalog card no. 75-93447

Printed in Great Britain by
RICHARD CLAY (THE CHAUCER PRESS), LTD
Bungay, Suffolk

Contents

Introduction

THE era of British pre-eminence has too often been thought of in terms of the Empire on which the sun never set, of those vast tracts of red sprawling across Mercator projections of the world, or those millions of Africans and Asians benevolently ruled by proconsuls and district officers. This limited view is all too evident in such assertions as 'the British Empire can now be seen to have been so brief in duration, so slight in its impact, so inchoate in its shape, that it scarcely rates Gibbonian treatment . . .' (Malcolm Muggeridge). But Gibbon wrote of an empire whose influence was largely coterminous with the extent of its sovereign power, and one should rather argue that no Gibbon has yet come forth to analyse British influence in the world at its peak, for the simple reason that it spread so far and took so many forms that many lesser scholars will be needed to provide the foundations before a polyhistor can erect an adequate monument to this 'empire'. The present volume can be no more than an interim assessment of some of the most notable ways in which Britain influenced the nineteenth-century world, introducing qualifications where the British impact may already have been exaggerated or misunderstood, but above all striving to transcend the artificial limits that are so often imposed on the study of this fascinating subject by conventional textbooks on British imperial, foreign or economic history, each a speciality in itself, and so failing to provide an overall picture. To attempt this task with eight authors may seem to introduce further fragmentation, but although each chapter is complete in itself, each is also complementary to the others.

In 1781 Horace Walpole wrote with some dismay of 'the moment of the fall of an Empire'. Many in Europe rejoiced at Britain's discomfiture in the War of American Independence, and prophesied that she would become a second-rate power. Yet posterity was to note that 1776 was not only the year of the Declaration of American Independence, but also of the publication of Adam Smith's *Wealth of Nations:* that in 1781 a British army may have capitulated at Yorktown, but that James Watt perfected the rotary motion in the same year: and that 1783 witnessed both the Peace of Versailles and Cort's construction of a puddling furnace. With prophetic insight the British negotiator at Versailles, Lord Shelburne, claimed: 'We prefer trade to dominion.' Barely a generation later, at another peace conference in Vienna in 1814–15, the now victorious British could disdain preferential commercial treaties, as they were convinced of their own economic strength and persuaded that privileged treatment could lead to ill-will and recoil against them in the long run. It was a remarkable advance, in part expressed in terms of new territory in India, the Caribbean and elsewhere, but even more so in the colossal industrial lead which Britain had built up over all others. For more than half a century anti-imperial sentiment was to run strongly in Britain, though not with overwhelming force, as two prime ministers showed in 1838 and 1849, when first Melbourne and then Russell argued in favour of retaining current colonies, if only for reasons of prestige.

Although Britain was to be the world's leading trading nation for roughly two hundred years, her period of greatest dominance was in the nineteenth century, when she was involved in between one-fifth and one-quarter of all trade. For much of this period she owned between one-third and two-fifths of the world's shipping. As a financier, carrier, insurer and commercial agent she was involved in up to one-half of all commerce. In 1898 Albert Beveridge of Indiana, contemplating the growing power of his country, remarked: 'The trade of the world must and shall be ours . . . And we will get it as our mother England has told us how.' As the first two chapters of this book set out to show, the British were the main propelling force behind an economic revolution that was transforming much of the world. Britain was not only the world's leading manufacturing nation until the late nineteenth century – as late as 1870 she produced about one-third of the world's manufactures – but she was also contributing to the industrialisation of Europe and the United States. If one would be rash to speculate on the outcome of industrialisation without the British example and impact, one can nevertheless see clearly the very large debt of others to British machinery, skills and general know-how. Similarly in the provision of capital to lubricate, enlarge and transform the world economy Britain contributed the lion's share, nearly half of all foreign investment being in her hands in mid-century, while throughout the century her nearest rival, France, rarely contributed half as much, and often a good deal less. If British industry and capital sometimes had a devastating effect – on countries such as India, Turkey and Egypt – for good or ill their role as the pace-makers to a new economic environment is undisputed.

Another British export in the nineteenth century – and later – was that of people. Between 1850 and 1900 possibly 10 million souls left the British Isles, out of a grand total of about 23 million for the whole of Europe. This was one of the great migrations in human history which helped to build the United States into the world's strongest power, and which transformed the wildernesses of Canada and Australia into new and thriving states. By 1900 two-thirds of the English-speaking people in the world lived outside Europe. Bismarck described the common language of Britain and the United States as one of the most significant political facts of the time – as his countrymen were to discover in 1917–18, and again in 1941–5. This remarkable exodus is examined in the third chapter, together with its impact on two such different regions as the United States and Australia. But Britons abroad contributed as individuals as well as *en masse*, ranging from the exploits of Lord Cochrane in aid of the liberation of Latin America to those of General Gordon against Taiping rebels in China. Professor Stearns (in Chapter 1) highlights the contribution of British entrepreneurs and skilled artisans to the spread of mechanisation throughout the world, whether at the level of the vast undertakings of the railway magnate, Thomas Brassey, or of the nameless engine-drivers who drove the first locomotives in France and Japan.

Not all Britons, however, were content that they should be famed as the 'nation of shopkeepers', mere hard-faced businessmen, or pain and pleasure calculators. Sydney Smith lamented: 'The great object for which the Anglo-Saxon race appears to have been created is the making of calico.' Lord Elgin, in the midst of the Second China War, asserted: 'Neither our own conscience nor the judgement of mankind will acquit us if, when we are asked to what use we have turned our opportunities, we can only say that we have filled our pockets from among the ruins which we have found or made.' In the quest for a better world three British contributions stand out, and are examined in Chapters 4–6. These include the British belief that in Free Trade the world would discover not only the path to greater prosperity, but also perhaps to better international understanding and even world peace. Secondly there was the British faith in their parliamentary institutions, which were held up as a model for others to copy. And thirdly there were the diverse elements who made up the Humanitarian movement, with their great struggle against the slave trade and slavery, and their endeavour to Christianise and even to civilise the black and brown millions of the world.

All three had much less impact than British capital and industry, and were frequently frustrated by unpropitious circumstances. Even so, for a time in mid-century it seemed as if the world was beginning to understand and implement the doctrines of the Manchester School. Equally in the eighteenth and early nineteenth centuries British political institutions and ideas had inspired and in some ways acted as a model for European constitution-makers. If the precise contribution cannot always be measured, the existence of so successful an example cannot be ignored. Even in strife-ridden Spain, torn by extremist parties, a politician could still be found seeking in the speeches of Gladstone and Disraeli a guide to a more stable and generous political environment. This was Cánovas del Castillo, who was to give his country a measure of calm, if little progress, in the later nineteenth century. The achievement of the Humanitarians is more concrete, though the final abolition of the slave trade owed much to changes in the internal environment of, for instance, both the United States and Brazil. Similarly native enthusiasm for Christianity could in reality be inspired by a quest for more practical elements in western learning, or from the desire to better their lot in their own society by enlisting the protection of these obviously influential foreigners. Nevertheless these British offerings to the world, whether accepted only in part or in a distorted form, represented a new – and often a better – way of ordering certain aspects of human affairs.

Meanwhile fewer than 40 million Britons were steadily accumulating the world's largest empire. As Gladstone was to remark in 1879: 'Why, gentlemen, there is not a country in the history of the world that has undertaken what we have undertaken . . . a small island at one extremity of the globe peoples the whole earth with its colonies . . . We have undertaken to settle the affairs of about one-fourth of the entire human race scattered over all the world.' Even then British enthusiasm for the Empire had yet to reach its peak, and was in fact to postdate the period of British pre-eminence in the world. In many ways this later enthusiasm seemed a defensive reaction – a retreat from the optimistic universalism of the earlier part of the century, a substitute for lost ascendancy. True, there had existed what some historians term 'the Imperialism of Free Trade', but most thinking concerning empire had remained vague and confused. Britain had groped her way to a new relationship with her white colonies, but had found the path towards what Macaulay had described as a class of people, 'Indian in blood and colour, but English in taste, in opinions, in morals and in intellect', far longer and more difficult than had been imagined. Indeed, from the time of the Indian Mutiny she had doubts about the wisdom of following this path at all, while efforts to pursue a paternal policy were often dismally ineffectual.

In the world of great powers and independent states Britain achieved a considerable measure of influence at this time that was often out of proportion to the strength immediately, and sometimes potentially, at her disposal. Exceptional circumstances in Europe and in the world as a whole played into her hands as never before or since. No state threatened to achieve a position of hegemony and thereby constitute a threat to Britain. No great power was sufficiently free from internal or European problems to devote much attention to the wider world before the 1870s, while outside Europe people after people showed themselves almost helpless in the face of western technology and organisation. Only in the Americas and in Japan were real power centres developing. It is no accident, therefore, that this should prove the hey-day of British diplomacy, the era of the so-called Pax Britannica and a period when, although the British navy was not unchallenged, only a lack of national will could really endanger the nation's interests down at least until the 1880s.

In a larger work space would have been devoted to other aspects of British influence in the world. One would, for instance, have liked to include some reference to the nation's cultural impact, ranging from the almost intoxicating effect that Lord Byron had upon some of the European Romantics to the British contribution to the century's craze for neo-Gothic, which owed not a little to the continentally famous Sir Walter Scott, with his mock-medieval castle at Abbotsford. Then there were the English novelists, with the fame of Dickens spreading as far as Russia, where he found a warm admirer in Tolstoy, and even the anti-western Dostoyevsky described him as 'almost a Russian force'. Macaulay boasted of the 'imperishable empire of our arts and our morals, our literature and our laws', but there were also periods of doubt when even the great Viceroy, Lord Curzon, could wonder whether the British were but writing in the sands of the East, and waiting for the next wind to erase their work.

Certainly not all were such willing imbibers of British influence as the Indian philosopher Ram Mohun Roy, who wrote: 'Conquest is very rarely an evil where the conquering people are more civilised than the conquered . . . India requires many more years of English dominion so that she may not have many things to lose while she is reclaiming her political independence.' Sir Eric Ashby's *Universities: British, Indian and African* suggests that in this respect, for one, Britain did not render good service to India. At the other extreme were the Chinese, who tried hard to ignore and exclude the revolutionary powers of the British.

Even in Europe there were many who were dismayed by Britain's industrial innovations as well as her liberal political ideas. The Spaniards were particularly fatalistic: 'God wills it. Progress is a law of Humanity, and there is nothing more to be done than to bare one's back and endure the stick.' For much of the century Britons wielded that 'stick' with enthusiasm, and more than any one people they drove humanity into a different world.

1. Britain and the Spread of the Industrial Revolution

PETER N. STEARNS

'I AM here in the centre of the most advanced industry of Europe and of the Universe.' So wrote the young French textile entrepreneur Motte-Bossut during a visit to England in 1842. He was not exaggerating. A few years later, when Britain celebrated its industrial might in the Great Exhibition at the Crystal Palace, it had no peer in any of the principal phases of mechanical production. Several European countries were superior in textile design; the United States led in some as yet minor categories, such as machine stitching. Britain could concede these few inferiorities, for she led in all the basics: in the manufacture of thread and the most widely sold kinds of cloth, in metallurgy and in the industry central to all further progress, the building of machines themselves.

The crucial fact was, of course, that Britain had been in the business of industrialisation at least forty years longer than anyone else. The steam engine, the spinning mule, the coke-using furnaces to smelt iron were being widely applied by the 1780s. Though there were isolated introductions of these techniques, often by Britons, in western Europe before 1815, it is possible to talk of a comparable extension of them, a genuine if early stage of industrialisation, only after 1820 for Belgium and France, after 1830 for the United States and after 1840 for Germany.

Britain's industrial superiority inevitably coloured the industrial revolution elsewhere. Stated quite simply, a list of causes of any industrialisation under way before 1870 has to include the example of Britain and the foreign activities of British entrepreneurs. The countries first to industrialise, aside from Britain, led above all because they were closest to Britain, geographically or, in the case of the United States, culturally. Even within a country, patterns of industrialisation followed in part from different possibilities of contact with Britain. In France the leading factory centres of cotton production were the Lille and Rouen areas, both geographically close to England, and the Mulhouse region, where the Protestantism of all the major entrepreneurs encouraged English contacts. One of the reasons for northern Italy's long lead over the South was, again, greater proximity to Britain and a tradition of closer contact.

Britain's contributions to the spread of industrialisation were in many ways quite obvious. First, there was example reinforced by competition. For governments and individual businessmen alike, Britain was proof that the mechanisation of industry was possible and profitable. Well before 1800 French and German governments were sending representatives to study the secrets of Britain's industrial advance. After 1800 imitation could be a necessity. The economic and financial might Britain displayed in the Napoleonic Wars led some statesmen to realise the implications of industrialisation for power politics. More directly, businessmen faced with mounting British competition, particularly in textiles, might see Britain not simply as an abstract example of what might be accomplished by machines, but as a rival who could be fought only on her own terms. For some businessmen, British competitive example motivated industrial innovations that would not otherwise have been undertaken. More generally, competitive example entered into a more complex set of reasons for private or governmental innovation.

British example inspired technical imitation above all, for here was where Britain's superiority patently lay. Before 1870, almost all the machines basic to industrialisation anywhere had to be initially copied from Britain. France and the United States contributed some important adaptations of British machines and some genuinely new inventions in subsidiary textile processes, but, before 1850, all the leading inventions were British.

Britain's greatest contributions to industrialisation elsewhere were, then, the provision (however grudging) of new techniques and the overwhelming example of their success. Added to this, in some industries by the 1820s and massively by the 1840s, particularly in railway development, was the provision of British capital to establish industry. Several major railway lines in France, Belgium and Austria were built by British capital, on British design, using British machines, by British contractors using largely British labour.

In some cases Britain's role in spreading industrialisation went beyond technology and capital. Britain helped shape the environment and attitudes in which industrialisation was possible. Example, again, played a role here. The fantastic magnitude and novelty of Britain's factory system could be an inspiration, as it was to the Italian manufacturer who, in the 1820s, set out (abortively) to build a 'Manchester' on the Istrian peninsula. British entrepreneurs who established themselves abroad played an even greater role. They brought new techniques, of course, but they could also bring something of the spirit which motivated their counterparts at home, and which was not always abundant in Europe. British workers could do the same. Again, they brought vital skills, but they could contribute to a 'modernisation' of attitudes as well. Finally, British economic and even political ideas, so eagerly imported during the first part of the nineteenth century, could contribute to building an environment appropriate to industry.

In any discussion of Britain's role in spreading the industrial revolution, questions of motivation are fundamental, and they are related to vital problems of assessing the industrial process in many areas. On the British side, what spurred entrepreneurs and workers to help foreigners either at home, by discussing industrial designs or by actually going abroad? Here was one of the most concrete tests of the liberal spirit, broadly defined. Some manufacturers and legislators tried to conceal Britain's secrets. Some accused their fellows of virtual treason by going abroad; and surely it is interesting to see Britons in France and in Belgium play a key role in the economy of Napoleon's empire. There were profits to be had abroad, of course, but, as we shall see, this may not have been the only motive.

Britons did not spread industrialisation in a vacuum. In every area there are questions about the relation between British example and the local or national environment. In the attitude of French manufacturers and workers towards British initiative lies part of the explanation of France's slow and uneven industrial advance. Significant British industrial activity in Spain did not produce a real Spanish industrial revolution; a probably lower level of activity helped trigger the extraordinary industrialisation of Germany.

Britain's inspiration to industrialisation elsewhere was not an unmixed blessing. We cannot know whether and how industrialisation would have proceeded had Britain somehow not been there; but without doubt Britain quickened the process immensely. Many nations profited by Britain's mistakes. The rapidity of German or American industrialisation was due in large part to the ability to use advanced techniques and business forms, which the British had more laboriously worked out. The same is true of social legislation, at least in Europe, and partly because of imitation of contemporary British laws, in the early stages of factory industry, none of the later nineteenth-century industrialisations brought the degree of human suffering that was so vivid in Britain before 1850. On the other hand, one can ask if Britain's example was not, sometimes, too compelling; if it did not encourage a growth that was too forced. This is a question most obvious in cases such as Germany, where the imitation of Britain was overwhelmingly imposed from above, from the State, on a society that was in many respects unprepared. More generally, if Britain was an example and inspiration, so she was also a threat. Every nineteenth-century industrialisation, aside from the British, operated under a sense of inferiority. Some people thought that the inferiority was permanent, that Britain could never be overtaken, while others were confident of catching up sometime. On the governmental level most obviously, but among individual businessmen as well, a feeling of rivalry and, perhaps, of insecurity grew up with industry itself.

Rising exports of manufactured goods announced British industrialisation to the world. In America, political independence seemed to be joined to an economic subservience greater than before. Cheap British imports flooded the markets after the American Revolution and overwhelmed the frail, native industrial base. Textile exports to France expanded quickly in the 1780s and again after 1815, despite generally high tariffs, and continued at a significant level until the 1860s. Massive exports of cotton and worsted goods to Germany dislocated traditional cottage production; British competition in Belgium increased rapidly after 1815. Swiss weavers began to fear the influx of British cotton goods after 1785. The point is clear: the often geometric expansion of British exports was at the very least a challenge to manufacturers elsewhere. It brought new levels of competition in the home market and in traditional export markets. In some cases British rivalry seemed overwhelming; Germany, before the annexation of Alsace in 1871, produced few textiles in factories; French manufacturers in many industries decided, even as they mechanised, that they could not compete with Britain in exports, an attitude that long persisted. Everywhere, individual manufacturers, consciously or not, surrendered to a frequent and painfully slow decline. Many putting-out manufacturers, many linen producers, to use the most obvious examples, lacked the capital, the knowledge, the will to change, yet British competition, combined with internal innovations, made change essential.

There was opportunity in British exports as well. Britain could now supply coal and machines for industrialisation elsewhere, and the fact that European imports of these products increased more rapidly than those of textiles or metallurgy showed that the opportunity was taken up. Above all, for the enterprising, British competition was a challenge that could be met, if painfully, by the imitation of British techniques.

From the late eighteenth century until the 1870s, Britain served as the world's centre for technical information. There were three principal stages in the effort to copy Britain's mechanical advances. Before 1789 most of the students of British industry were government-sponsored, as were the few, but important, British entrepreneurs abroad. In 1764 the French government sent a young scientist, Gabriel Jars, to study developments in British metallurgy; on his return he tried to spread new methods in France and did succeed in encouraging the de Wendel family to innovate. The French government also paid 12,000 *livres* to an English metallurgist, William Wilkinson, to set up a royal cannon foundry near Nantes; Wilkinson later joined de Wendel in establishing the first major modern iron foundry in France, at Le Creusot, for which he was paid another 60,000 *livres*. German governments were active also. Stein studied steam engines in England in the 1780s; the Saxon government sponsored various efforts to acquire new textile equipment for its threatened cotton and wool industries. Swiss cantons also sent observers to study British textile machines.

With the exception of Saxony and Switzerland, where town governments took the lead in reacting to British competition, interest in British technology focused at this point on metallurgy, because of its obvious importance for armaments. Prussia as well as France concentrated its investigations and subsidies in this field. Some of the early efforts were quite important. Von Reden, an agent in the Prussian mining office, became a leader in the introduction of coke smelting to Silesia after his government-sponsored visit to Britain. For the most part, however, this first stage remained rather barren of results. The French Revolution cut off many promising ventures; Le Creusot, for example, temporarily went under. Furthermore, there was a great deal of British hostility to the foreign investigators. Laws forbade the export of machinery, designs and skilled artisans, and most British entrepreneurs urged that they be enforced. A number of foreigners were arrested, as were several of the artisans they tried to hire away from their native shores. Many foreign visitors were unable to gain admission to a single factory, though obviously experiences varied in this respect. Finally, even successful investigations might have little repercussion. The initiative of governments in almost all the studies of British industry was in itself an indication of a lack of private interest. Many imported designs for machines went almost unused, as in Saxony, because of inadequate entrepreneurial and labour skill.

In the 1790s, haltingly, and more significantly between 1815 and 1840 a second wave of imitations began. It was far more important than the first wave, far more dramatic than the next. Governmental efforts continued. In 1819 the Prussian State sent a Westphalian locksmith, Egels, to study British machine-building, and he returned to establish one of the first German plants, in Berlin in 1821. Many governments, notably the French and the Dutch, subsidised English entrepreneurs such as James Jackson, one of the founders of modern steel manufacture in France. The most significant development, however, was the proliferation of private study visits to Britain.

The vanguard of visiting foreign manufacturers arrived in the war-torn decades between 1790 and 1815. One of the first Swiss machine-builders, J. C. Fischer, worked in a London engineering firm in 1794–5. Lieven Bauwens smuggled British spinning machinery into Ghent and virtually kidnapped several artisans in the 1790s. One of the first major developments in American industrialisation was the visit of Francis Cabot Lowell to Britain in 1810–12; two years after his return he set up the first power looms in the United States in the first factory anywhere that combined all spinning and weaving processes in the same plant.

The trickle of foreign visitors became a flood after 1815. Americans came in increasing numbers, though they relied less on direct visits, more on imported artisans and their own ingenuity, than did Europeans. In most continental countries almost all the dynamic entrepreneurs demonstrated and reinforced their industrial zeal by one trip or many to Britain. Fischer returned to Switzerland to urge his fellows to see British advances on the spot, and all the leading machine-builders came. Modern metallurgical manufacturers everywhere visited Britain. The Duc de Decazes, fallen from political power, came to England for a year before setting up his ambitious metallurgical plant in Decazeville in the early 1820s; his manager, François Cabrol, was a frequent visitor also. So was the manager of Fourchambault, another of the chief new centres in France. Indeed, the coal-burning forges established in France during the Restoration were called *forges à l'anglaise*. Germans were not far behind; Alfred Krupp, for example, made his visit to study British methods of steel manufacture in 1838–9. The Germans were also quick to study British railway development. Camille von Denis, the builder of the first German line (in Bavaria) had visited Britain; many Prussian mining engineers came for the same purpose.

Leading textile manufacturers travelled to Britain also. The Alsatian cotton producers visited Britain periodically to keep abreast of technical developments, and a stay in Britain was a normal part of the technical education of their sons. Many new initiatives resulted from visits of this sort. An Italian nobleman returned from England to introduce the first flying shuttle into Italy in 1838. Motte-Bossut conceived the idea for his giant cotton-spinning plant, the largest in France, during his admiring visit to Britain. The first mechanised linen-spinning in France resulted from the tours of men such as Auguste Scrive.

In sum, during the first part of the nineteenth century, hundreds, probably thousands of hopeful businessmen came to Britain, with state encouragement or entirely on their own. Their quest for technical information was not always easy. Factory doors were often still closed to them. Many of them worked for a year or more as manual labourers so that they could make their own designs of the precious machines and be able to install them once made. Many hired English workmen, which became increasingly easy, though it remained technically illegal until 1825. Many simply bought the machines they needed. A number of French entrepreneurs came to Britain whenever they needed an important new machine, taking a fresh look at British industry at the same time. But it was not always as simple as this. The British government could still prohibit the export of machinery until 1843, and though it was highly inconsistent in its licensing policies it tried to block most types of textile machinery. The result was some rather imaginative smuggling. In 1837 Auguste Scrive, soon to be one of the industrial leaders of northern France, painstakingly dismantled his English linen-spinning mules so that they would fit into the small boat he hired to take him across the Channel, and later had an exciting race with British customs officials. The rewards for the successful imitator were great, which is why so many foreigners made the pilgrimage to Britain, but it often took considerable work and ingenuity to earn them.

Foreign visits did not stop in the 1840s, but they became considerably less important. The earlier visitors had established a nucleus of modern industry in many centres, and technical advance could proceed and spread from this basis. Equally important, the final repeal of restrictions on machine exports meant that simply by placing an order one could obtain techniques that before could only be acquired on the spot. One result was that areas more remote from Britain, which had lacked sufficient interest to surmount the barriers previously surrounding British technical knowledge, now began the first halting steps towards industrialisation. Thus there was no significant modernisation of Russian textile production before 1843. Cheap servile labour and high tariffs meant that Russian manufacturers lacked any clear reason to go to the trouble of imitating British methods; but after 1843, and with the aid of British entrepreneurs in Russia, Russian cotton production began to expand rapidly. Most of the factories were filled with British-made equipment, much of it bought through the import agency of a German immigrant named Knoop, who had been a clerk in a Manchester cotton firm before going to Russia. Knoop faithfully placed all the orders that came to him in English firms, and was happy to tell any Russian entrepreneur who wanted alterations to the usual equipment, 'That is not your affair; in England they know better than you.' Many Austrian textile firms, similarly, were long based on British equipment.

In western Europe and the United States massive imports of British machinery had a significant impact too, though usually their sway was more quickly challenged by domestic imitations. The first machines in the newer textile processes, such as linen-spinning, were almost always British even after mid-century. More important, British equipment was found on almost all the first railway lines, and here there were no major impediments to export, even before the 1840s. The Belgian government began its lines with British locomotives, not surprisingly since Stephenson was its main technical adviser. The first two locomotives on the Bavarian state railway were British-built. The first Saxon line was constructed under a British adviser, and its British locomotive had a British driver. By the end of 1845 German railways had bought 237 locomotives from Britain. The United States, less dependent, nevertheless imported the locomotive that for the first time, in 1829, fully demonstrated the railway's potential, though an American engine was built the following year.

Until the 1850s, and in some cases beyond, Britain was the direct parent of technological advance all over Europe and to a lesser degree the United States. The first machines in virtually every industry were either copied from British design or directly imported, and as British restrictions on exports eased, the dependence on British equipment could last for decades. More commonly, in countries where industrialisation really took hold, domestic imitation quickly followed the British impulsion. By 1845 Germany was building its own locomotives. If some French textile entrepreneurs obstinately ignored locally built machinery in favour of British equipment that was not always so well adapted to their needs, many depended on the production of French machine-builders by the 1840s. Similarly, while almost all the steamboats on French rivers in the early 1840s were of British manufacture, French models had won the day by the end of the decade. It was in this sense that Britain spread industrialisation and not just industrial products; this was the difference between her economic impact on Europe and her role in much of the rest of the world.

Britain's long technological superiority was directly related to two of her other principal contacts with industrialisation elsewhere. British workers often followed British machines. They were needed, at the least, to help build and install new equipment, unless the entrepreneur was exceptionally adept. Often they were needed to train other workers in the use of machines, and sometimes they had to run the machines themselves for some time. British entrepreneurs frequently took the lead in setting up new factory industries abroad, for they had the knowledge that locals usually lacked. Often, too, they could buy British equipment more easily than foreigners could, if only by conveniently forgetting to mention that they were planning to export it. Though their initiative was technological above all, both manufacturers and workers from Britain could have a broader impact abroad, by giving training not only in techniques, but also in industrial organisation and attitudes.

At least a handful of British workers could be found wherever industrialisation was taking hold. The first coke blast furnace in Belgium, built during the 1820s, relied on the technical knowledge of its English operatives. Manchester labour installed the machines that were sent to Knoop's clients in Russia. British workers were found in the leading textile mills and shipbuilding establishments in Switzerland, and in the machine shops. In France there were at least 15,000 British workers employed in industry during the 1820s. During the July Monarchy a linen-spinning plant in Amiens had a hundred English mechanics; a metallurgical factory in Charenton used three to five hundred British workers each year. Railway building, particularly of course when done under British contractors such as Thomas Brassey, brought thousands of British navvies to the Continent. And throughout the nineteenth century, though in proportions that are less clear, English emigration to the United States included many workers who contributed vital skills to the emerging industrial labour force.

Certain skills were almost invariably supplied by British labour, such as puddling in iron manufacture and the driving of locomotives. But British workers were widely used in textiles, and not just to install machines. Prussian manufacturers imported labour for mechanical woollens. The need could be felt by quite modest entrepreneurs. When Narcisse Faucheur set up a lace shop near Lille, only semi-mechanical and employing only eight workers, he carefully imported an English woman to head, and hopefully train, his staff.

The demand for British labour far exceeded the supply for a time. Manufacturers offered long-term contracts, including a bonus for signing, all travel expenses and a huge bonus for completing the contract. Their visits to England often turned into recruiting trips. Above all, they paid. English workers earned wages from 25 to 100 per cent higher than those of locals in the same job. Here was a clear reflection of how essential British labour was to the spread of the industrial revolution.

Needless to say, manufacturers were eager to replace their expensive English labour with local products; in many cases British workers were used above all as teachers. According to many industrialists, only the dregs of British labour came abroad. Fischer, the Swiss engineer, summed up a not uncommon sentiment, explaining why he avoided British workers in all circumstances:

> Not only do they cost a damned lot of money, but they are often drunkards. English workers who are both efficient and well-behaved can earn a very good living at home. It is by no means uncommon to come across English workers in foreign countries who are far from thoroughly skilled in all branches of their trade. One can expect that range of skill not only from a foreman but also from the average worker. British workers seldom fulfil the sanguine expectations of their foreign employers because they are handling materials to which they are not accustomed and because they are working with different people than they would be at home.

There was, certainly, much truth in this condemnation. Undoubtedly British workers abroad were hard to handle. A German machine-builder in the Ruhr, one of the many who used British labour, longed to replace expensive foreigners with Germans, but simply could not; he sadly noted, 'one must go easy with them (English workers) since they actually talk of leaving if one fails to give them a smile'. A galling indignity for a budding manufacturer, but it suggests the other side of the picture. British workers, even possibly inferior ones, had skills and aptitudes that could be developed only with difficulty elsewhere. In large part, of course, this was simply because they had a generation or two of industrial experience behind them. But there was more than mere technical competence involved in this. British workers had also a sense of assiduousness and regularity at the job that other workers did not acquire quickly. This is why Thomas Brassey filled half his labour force with British navvies when building the Paris–Rouen railway; he needed skills in platelaying, of course, but he also needed English labour at first even for rough work. (It may be, also, that British workers were unusually strong because they were better fed; most French observers felt this to be the case at the time, citing higher rates of meat consumption.) Many French metallurgists found that it took ten years or more to train enough French puddlers to begin to displace the British. This was not because of a lack of technical intelligence, but because of lack of ambition. French workers, newly arrived from the countryside and often quite traditionalist in their expectations, simply did not feel that the prospect of earning more money was worth the effort of learning more skills. Here, too, British workers – who seemed quite entranced with high earnings – were better adapted to industrial labour. In sum, British workers brought motivations and habits as well as pure technical skill to European industrialisation; they clearly played a role in imparting all these industrial virtues to the local labour force.

Unfortunately there is no record of the precise impact of British labour abroad, either on foreign workers or on the British themselves. Certainly the British were often clannish and isolated; their high earnings could cause resentment and there were some strikes against them, such as that of French railway workers in 1848. How much and how directly they taught European workers cannot at present be known. Interestingly there seems to have been no importation of the doctrines and organisations that were agitating workers in Britain before 1848; undoubtedly British workers abroad were too remote from their European counterparts to have this sort of influence and too well paid and individualistic to be interested in a labour movement. And, in any event, the temper of European factory workers was too moderate for contemporary British radicalism. What of the experiences of British workers themselves? Some of the more enterprising individuals rose to become managers or employers on the spot, exploiting their technical abilities to the utmost. Others could have earned enough in a decade or so of work to return to Britain in some style. Some were clearly unhappy and moved frequently from job to job, or simply came home. There were a number of reports of dissatisfaction with cooking and the lack of beer in France. Again, there are far more questions than answers here. We know that the skill and strength of British labour played an important role in spreading industrialisation, perhaps in some rather subtle ways. We do not know how deeply they influenced foreign workers, either by guiding or by annoying; we do not know what happened to the British workers themselves.

By the 1850s the hey-day of British labour abroad had ended, with the vital exception of the continuing stream of emigration to the Empire and to the United States. More prosperous conditions in British industry after 1850 made it increasingly difficult to attract skilled workers abroad, and to a great extent they had done their job of training and were not so necessary. They still appeared to install machines in areas just beginning to industrialise, and the use of British foremen outlasted the use of significant numbers of workers. The foremen in many Austrian textile plants well after mid-century were from Manchester or Glasgow.

Closely related to the use of British labour, throughout the early industrial period, was the employment of British technicians. Britain's most direct contributions to early American industrialisation came in the persons of Samuel Slater, John and Arthur Scofield and a few similar individuals. Slater, an apprentice in one of the Arkwright plants, emigrated to the United States in 1789 under the sponsorship of Moses Brown, a Rhode Island merchant; he soon established the first real factory in the country. Three years later the Scofield brothers emigrated from Yorkshire and set up the first mechanical production of woollen goods. This pattern was repeated in many European countries, as skilled English workers obtained some sort of foreign sponsorship or capital and set up their own factories or served as chief technicians. The example was repeated as late as 1851, when the Sulzer Company, a Swiss engineering firm, hired a skilled British mechanic, Charles Brown, who during the next thirty years brought continuing prosperity to the company by a series of new machine tools, improved steam engines and other technical advances.

From the late eighteenth century to the mid-nineteenth an uncounted number of British entrepreneurs went beyond the role of technician and founded their own companies outright. Often they provided more than technical skill, though their technical ability was vital. They appeared all over Europe, though their impact was greatest in France and the Low Countries, and in all the industries involved in the first upsurge of machinery. The first Swiss factory with modern cotton machinery was run by two Britons. A pioneer in the South Russian iron industry, the biggest wool manufacturer on the Neva, the leading exploiters of coal mines in the Don basin were British. Thomas Ainsworth led in the improvement of Dutch cotton production after 1830 by bringing a few skilled British workers into his factory in Twente to teach mechanical weaving. The examples could be multiplied almost endlessly. In many cases British manufacturers inspired an entire national or regional industry. The production of tulles, a lace net that could be worked on machines, was begun in the Calais region after 1817 by a number of Englishmen who smuggled in bobbinet machines, and it long remained largely in British hands. In at least nine regions of France, between 1815 and 1848, a British manufacturer set up the first modern factory in what was or became the major local industry. The spirit of innovation often persisted in the British-founded firm; the James Jackson company in Saint-Etienne introduced modern methods of producing steel in the 1820s, and it was a grandson, William Fitz Jackson, who installed the first Bessemer converter in France in 1861.

No single English family did more for European industrialisation than the Cockerill clan, and though their experience was by this very fact atypical, they illustrate, nevertheless, something of the role the English entrepreneur could play. William Cockerill brought modern textile machinery to Verviers, in Belgium, at the end of the eighteenth century, thus launching the transformation of Verviers into a centre of machine-produced woollens. Under Napoleon, who made William Cockerill a French citizen in 1810, the Cockerill enterprise spread widely. The centre of operations was now Liège, where the family's machine-building factory employed 2000 people by 1812. Cockerill sons were busy selling and installing machines in various parts of France and Germany. The years after 1815 saw the Cockerills set up a machine-building plant in Berlin, on the invitation of the Prussian government, the first factory there to be lit by gas; one of the younger Cockerills, James, moved to Guben, in Prussia, and began the development of the town's wool manufacturing. John Cockerill was now the head of the family, with a vast mining, metallurgical and machine-building operation at Seraing, near Liège, – the largest integrated factory in the world by the 1830s – where he boasted that 'he has all the new inventions over at Seraing ten days after they come out of England'. With the backing of the ruling House of Orange, John Cockerill set up the first coke blast furnace in Belgium, from which came, among many other things, the cast iron lion atop the hill at Waterloo. Cockerill-built steamboats, machinery, even whole factories spread widely in Europe. The firm was a major disseminator of technical information, both to other continental entrepreneurs and to local workers, which it quickly trained to take over from its skilled English operatives. In the 1830s John Cockerill took a lead in railway building, and at the end of his life he was discussing building a line for the tsar of Russia.

Though his accomplishments were more modest, the career of Isaac Holden illustrates the impact a British entrepreneur could have in a single industry even in the middle of the nineteenth century. Wool-combing had long resisted mechanisation until in 1845 an Alsatian, Heilmann, finally developed an appropriate technique, and his machines were built in substantial numbers by 1848 by the Schlumberger firm, near Mulhouse. But in 1850 the Mulhouse stock exchange recognised the firm of Samuel Lister and Isaac Holden as 'the first comber in Europe'. Using the combing machine that Lister developed almost simultaneously with Heilmann, using English managers (often relatives of one of the partners) and artisans from Yorkshire, the firm had factories in three French cities, under Holden's direction, both to comb wool and to produce combing equipment. By 1870 it had several thousand employees and was still more efficient than its French competitors. An English colony at Reims was associated with wool-combing during the First World War.

Isaac Holden established himself in France from a mixed set of motives not uncommon among British manufacturers abroad. He had not been a success in England. He had a small share in a Yorkshire factory in the early 1840s, but argued with his employers over the quality of the plant's production; and he wanted to be at least a partner. A venture on his own in Bradford in 1846 failed because of the slump. So, after he met Lister, he went to France. He encountered less competition there, and innovation brought quicker results. But Holden felt a sense of mission as well, which carried him though the difficult period after the 1848 Revolution: 'Providence, I believe, has called me to be here.' The Cockerill family similarly responded to the great opportunity and the feeling of achievement they could find abroad. They were able, in fact, to work for their country's sworn foe, Napoleon Bonaparte. William Cockerill left England in 1797, because of the economic depression of that year, vowing to seek his fortune elsewhere. He did not care where he tried, and went to Belgium only after a machine-building venture in Sweden failed. He made his fortune many times over; but this was not, perhaps, his only goal. Certainly his son John, like most manufacturers of the top rank in the period, claimed a higher purpose. A Belgian observer correctly noted that John Cockerill saw 'a mission to extend manufactures everywhere and to fill the whole world with machinery'. These men believed in the industrial order that Britain was creating. They saw challenge, perhaps a duty, as well as profit in spreading this order. Often they left England because of disappointment or failure at home, but they usually worked for what they thought to be the broader good of their adopted land. If nothing else, they could not endure leaving technical backwardness untouched. W. T. Mulvany, no failure at all, but a successful Irish civil engineer who played a leading role in developing the Ruhr coalfield in the 1850s, expressed a common reaction to a needlessly underdeveloped area. Looking at a geological map of the Ruhr and at the inadequate transportation facilities in the area, he said to himself, 'These people do not know their own wealth.' In this situation, personal profit and a desire to serve could go hand in hand.

The British manufacturer abroad, then, knew his superiority, yet did not try to keep his advantages to himself. Many foreign manufacturers, such as Scrive in France, tried jealously to guard their hard-won British secrets from other eyes. Not so most of the British producers, particularly, of course, if they were machine-builders, where spreading technology and selling one's goods were part of the same process. This is why a few hundred entrepreneurs, scattered widely over Europe, had such a great impact.

It is clear that British manufacturers contributed more than technology to Europe. They brought initiative and organisational ability as well and, if only by competitive pressure, they could teach some of these attributes to continental industrialists too. Isaac Holden did not bring an unknown technique to France, for the French had a slight lead in mechanical wool-combing. His main rival, Schlumberger, was one of the most vigorous entrepreneurs in France. But the wool industry as a whole was traditionalist, particularly in centres such as Reims, and it took a Holden as well as a Schlumberger to move it forward. The point is not that the British had no peers on the Continent, for there were, quite early, European manufacturers of great ability. But particularly in countries such as France, where English initiative played an unusually great role, there were not enough dynamic industrialists; here a handful of British entrepreneurs filled a real need.

Continental manufacturers themselves recognised that British superiority was not simply or even primarily technological. French industrialists had a number of occasions to summarise their views of British advantages in the 1830s and 1840s, for they had to explain to a somewhat liberal government why they needed tariff protection. They pointed to some factors that they could not hope to duplicate, at least in the short run, but also to human and organisational elements that some of them did try to imitate. Their views, in turn, help illustrate how British example contributed to the general environment of European industrialisation.

The French were quite conscious of their inferiority in resources; they lacked the easy access to coal and metal that the British had, and textile fibres were harder to obtain too. They of course noted that their industry had 'only begun yesterday' in comparison with the British, and that the British lead in technology showed no sign of disappearing; so long as a French firm had to devote much of its attention to obtaining machines and technicians from Britain it could not hope to be more than a shadow of British industry. British capital was cheaper and more abundant, the French claimed, and the greater age of British industry had allowed many years of profits to be ploughed back into the firm for amortisation and expansion. All of these factors were inherent in Britain's resources and industrial leadership. All continental manufacturers felt inferior in these respects, for a considerable time at least, though the French may have been unusually fearful.

Many French industrialists claimed that their British counterparts had a distinctive spirit. They said that the British loved work more than the French did and that they had an 'adventurous genius' that could not be found elsewhere. Hence their early start in industry and their willingness to take risks, to speculate, to use credit and capital boldly. For some reason, and a Protestant manufacturer pointed to religion as a cause, the British had an ardour, a sense of compulsion in their industrial efforts that the French lacked. Most French businessmen had little desire to imitate this zeal; they felt that the more relaxed French way of life was superior and looked to tariff protection to carry them through. A minority, however, without necessarily seeing British manufacturers at work directly, tried to adopt something of the British spirit as well as British techniques. Some imitated only grudgingly, believing that imitation of Britain was 'one of those laws of force whose power one must recognise, while deploring its necessity'. Others were positively eager and looked forward to beating the British on their own ground. In sum, awareness of Britain's entrepreneurial vigour played some role in spurring a similar spirit elsewhere.

European manufacturers often pointed to the size of British companies as a key to Britain's industrial success. French businessmen noted that some British concerns were five or six times as big as the largest French firm in the same industry. This size allowed the British to spread general expenses, such as interest payments or the cost of office personnel, over a larger volume of production, and so achieve lower unit costs. It permitted a more detailed division of labour and an active, often world-wide sales force. French observers summed this up by saying that the British had a greater spirit of association than the individualistic French and, as some of them realised, 'association is as necessary to industry as the sun is to agriculture'.

Again, many French industrialists had no desire to imitate British business organisation. A rather vocal group claimed that bigness was an evil, creating undue dependence on uncertain exports and causing a huge gap between rich and poor. A certain element of conscious revulsion against the British model may have contributed, particularly in France, to the persistence of modest enterprise in many segments of the economy. To dynamic manufacturers, however, British example helped to inspire an explicit quest for big business units. Industrialists such as Eugène Schneider, of Le Creusot, who began building iron ships in the late 1830s from a professed desire to challenge Britain in this field, realised that the foundation of equality with Britain lay in the large size of the firm. Certainly one of the reasons that some sectors of French, and even more of German, industry developed giant companies earlier in their industrial revolutions than had been true in the British, was the example of mid-nineteenth-century Britain. The corporate form, so slowly applied to industry in Britain, could be taken over at an early stage of continental industrialisation. The same was true of industrial investment banking, the fruit of decades of industrial development in Britain, but applicable, as in central Europe, simultaneously in time, but at a far earlier phase of economic modernisation. Big business, big by nineteenth-century standards at least, had proved itself in England. Leading continental entrepreneurs had to imitate it, but in so doing they promoted a different, less liberal pattern of industrialisation than Britain had developed.

German businessmen were quicker than French to copy the organisational characteristics of British industry. They borrowed at least as many business methods as they did machine techniques. From the mid-nineteenth century onwards, Britain was flooded with German clerks; the London Chamber of Commerce rather fearfully estimated in the 1880s that a sixth of the clerks in big merchant and manufacturing firms were German. This sort of apprenticeship was one reason why German businessmen so quickly became capable of rivalling British merchandising and export techniques; it was one cause, among many, for the early size and sophistication of German industrial organisation. In at least one instance a Briton even more directly inspired a new departure in German economic organisation. Mulvany, the Irish colliery owner in the Ruhr, established the first Ruhr mineowners' group in 1858, largely to press the government to improve local transport facilities, but, to a degree, to regulate output in recessions as well. In 1871 he led an even larger number of mineowners, in Westphalia and the Rhineland, to combine to discuss factory laws, transportation problems and the like. Again, these rather loose groupings were copied from similar associations in Britain in the same period; but they occurred far earlier in Germany's industrial history and were, in the event, developed far beyond the British model.

British economic doctrine supplemented more direct industrial example in creating the environment for industrialisation elsewhere. The ideas of Adam Smith and his liberal descendants were quickly transmitted and translated both to the Continent and to the United States. What role did they play in setting the stage for economic modernisation? This is a difficult question, as it is for Britain herself.

Some industrialists in France, and many in the United States, mouthed liberal slogans, derived from British ideas, in defending their interests against the State. But they were not fully converted, as their simultaneous advocacy of tariff protection proves, and it is unlikely that most industrialists were particularly aware of liberal theory, much less inspired by it in their daily business. Many, as we have seen, felt that the lesson of British industry was actually opposed to undue individualism. British doctrine was far more important in its influence on statesmen, teaching them the legal reforms that were a precondition for industrial advance. The leading translators and advocates of Adam Smith in Germany in the late eighteenth century were the teachers of the early nineteenth-century German reformers in universities such as Halle and Königsberg. The work of men such as Baron Stein, in turn, helped force Germany from a largely manorial to a capitalistic and gradually industrial economy. In Italy a generation later, enthusiasm for English ideas infected moderate Italian liberals in the 1830s, and from their ranks came Cavour and others who built the framework for northern Italian industrialisation.

The industrial example of Britain caused revulsion as well as imitation. Industrialisation outside Britain, and to a degree the United States, occurred amidst considerable, pre-established hostility, based on truths and myths about what British industrial society was like. This, in addition to the less natural, more imitative basis of industrialisation on the Continent, helps explain why the industrial revolution caused more enduring social strains in Europe than it did in Britain. Most obviously, various kinds of socialist doctrines, drawing on the sufferings of English workers, moved on to the Continent along with or even before industrialisation itself. French and German labour did not in fact suffer as much in early industry as British workers had done, but they were soon greeted by social theories that explained their miseries and often told them that things were likely to get worse. Everyone seemed to know about the hardships of British industrial life in the first half of the nineteenth century, and this knowledge contributed greatly to the beginnings, however tentative, of most continental socialist movements, from France to Russia. Not only Karl Marx, but also Eugène Buret and Flora Tristan in France, Mazzini in Italy, Herzen from Russia studied or reported on British conditions. European workers were not immediately converted, of course. There was less unrest among industrial labour in Germany and France in the early stages of mechanisation than there had been in Britain. Revulsion against the horrors of early English factory life, however, helped cause a sweeping hostility to the

industrial order or at least the capitalist order that was partially absorbed.

Ironically, actual labour movements in Britain had a far less significant
influence. Early unrest, of the Luddites, the Owenites and the Chartists,
could not be imitated because no industrial system outside Britain was
well enough developed to echo it. Later British unionism, which for
skilled workers proved quite effective in a mature industrial society,
had many parallels in European and in American unionism, but these
arose largely from similar situations rather than from direct imitation.
French workers were stirred in the 1860s by the power of British unions,
as reported by visitors to British industrial expositions, but the growing
French labour movement followed quite distinctive lines. Later in the
nineteenth century individual union leaders often pointed to British
achievements. Belgian mining unions around 1900 worked to gain a link
between wages and coal prices comparable to that enjoyed by British
miners for several decades (a link which British miners were busily
trying to undo at that very time). But the gains of German and American
unions were cited far more often; and the tone of the British labour
movement as a whole was duplicated nowhere else.

The early concern about labour conditions in Britain prompted more
than socialism. Many economists hoped to avoid the worst excesses of
the factory system; even liberal theorists, as in France, could see that
some state intervention was necessary to limit abuse. They were more
alert to problems such as child labour in their own country because they
knew from British reports what might happen as industrialisation continued. Even manufacturers were influenced by this concern. Ruhr
industrialists brought back a social conscience, as well as machines,
from their visits to England in the 1830s and 1840s. Advocates of child
labour legislation in France, such as the Alsatian manufacturer Daniel
LeGrand, constantly referred to Britain. It was widely believed that
British labour conditions were worse than anywhere else. Some businessmen took comfort from this belief, and held that nothing more needed to
be done at home; others, however, sought preventive measures.
Furthermore, Britain by the 1830s provided examples of remedies as
well as lessons in misery. Most obviously, legislation on children could
be imitated. LeGrand and many others urged that the 1833 child labour
law be adopted and improved in France, and the French Act of 1841
was a rather faithful replica. Manufacturers with contacts in Britain
were sometimes aware of model factory experiments such as New
Lanark, and again some imitation resulted. More widely, alert entrepreneurs learned from their own skilled English workers that high pay

and good diets could improve performance on the job. A few, in fact, claimed that actual factory workers in England were better treated than on the Continent, and that this was why they did their jobs better. A number of firms, such as Le Creusot in France, tried to improve their labour policies accordingly.

To a degree, then, continental labour may have benefited from lessons their governments and employers derived from English example, both good and bad. The effect was limited, of course. Few manufacturers were influenced. Traditional activism by municipalities and central governments did far more than British example to inspire the early efforts at factory legislation. The Prussian child labour law of 1839, for instance, resulted primarily from the interests of military leaders in protecting the health of future generations of soldiers. More important, Britain early lost the lead in social measures. Even in the 1850s, obviously by the 1880s, with the social insurance laws, Germany provided the model for reforms in this field. On the whole the effects of revulsion against industrial conditions outlasted the interest in constructive British social policy in most European countries.

Problems of British industrial life were known to groups other than the various social reformers and their constituents. People who wanted to avoid industrialisation altogether were warned along with those who hoped to channel it in better directions. There were of course many in Britain who did not like early industrial society, but they could not be so sure as their continental analogues of the ultimate extent of the evils they suspected. Aristocrats in Germany did not have to criticise merely the greed and aggressiveness of a few small manufacturers at home; they could point to the whole of Britain in their efforts to protect a non-industrial economy. We have already seen that many small businessmen themselves, in France, quite consciously hoped to avoid the sort of economic structure they thought was developing in Britain. German master artisans were fairly consciously hostile to the principles of industrial economy by the 1840s; hence in 1848 they demanded restoration of the guilds. There were many reasons for this reactionary attitude, but among them was the fact that German craftsmen knew in advance what industrialisation would do to their traditional habits. They knew it from reports about British life, and they knew it from the competition of British machine-products, in cloth for example, that they experienced before the industrial revolution began in Germany itself. Certain groups, then, that in Britain made at least gradual and grudging accommodations to industrial life, on the Continent turned against it from the first. This contributed to the gulf between 'industrial' and 'non-industrial' segments of the population that lasted often into the present century.

Some intellectuals were affected in a similar way. It took four generations of industrial life in England to produce a Ruskin or a Morris. Aesthetic critics of industry, such as Richard Wagner in Germany, were active at the same time: that is, in the earliest stages of continental industrialisation. They did not necessarily talk of Britain directly, but, again, it was because of Britain that they knew what to expect.

British example, then, spurred not only industrialisation itself, but some of the reaction to it. Britain showed where the world was going. Manchester could be cited as perhaps New York or Chicago could be cited in the twentieth century, and with the same ambiguities. Forward-looking businessmen or statesmen could hope, did hope, to build new Manchesters, with perhaps a few improvements. To others Manchester meant all that was wrong or likely to be wrong with the modern world: grasping businessmen, misery, ugliness. In both of its guises, the image of Manchester influenced the spread of industrial society.

Britain's role in spreading the industrial revolution waned after 1850, though it did not disappear. Its influence was less in the mid-century revolutions of Germany and the United States than it had been of France and Belgium. The United States depended heavily on British industrial design for its first steps, but added inventions of its own, such as Eli Whitney's interchangeable machine-parts or Howe's sewing-machine, with surprising speed. It used British technicians and thousands of immigrant British artisans, and Britons were to be numbered among its industrial magnates, but its overall reliance on British managers and entrepreneurs was not great. Germany used British machines and designs more extensively at first; in 1850 its industry seemed almost entirely derivative, without any clear national character. This imitative quality soon disappeared, and within two decades it was Germany (along with the United States) that pioneered in new industries, notably chemicals and electrical equipment, as Britain had pioneered in cotton and iron.

In Austria, Italy and Russia, British example and influence remained powerful as industrialisation spread in the later nineteenth century. In these areas, however, Britain was increasingly merely one of several models. French, German and Belgian entrepreneurs, machines and skilled operatives were there as well, playing much the same role that the British had in their own countries earlier. There were other areas of British activity, and not only in the Empire. British companies multiplied in Spain after 1870, particularly in the mining of iron ore. Sixty-four British corporations were floated between 1871 and 1914 to mine Spanish ore. They encouraged a number of Spanish companies, not only in mining but in transportation and, occasionally, in metallurgy. Yet there was no clear Spanish industrial revolution at this point; indeed the most active industrial centre overall, Catalonia, was largely independent of British influence. British activities were not, of course, the main reason why Spain did not industrialise vigorously. It can be suggested, however, that the British entrepreneurs abroad, in Spain and elsewhere, were not playing the same generous role of their counterparts earlier. British efforts in Spain were largely supplementary to Britain's own industry; the point was to mine ore for British use. There was little effort to build a whole industrial complex in Spain, and perhaps some conscious desire to avoid yet another centre of competition. British entrepreneurs could no longer be so blithely conscious of their superiority; rising nationalism inhibited a sense of international industrial mission. The pioneering spirit seemed to have passed.

The slowing up of economic progress at home after 1870 was both cause and symptom of Britain's reduced role in industrialisation elsewhere. Increasingly it was the British who sought technical guidance from outside, even in her traditionally strong industries. Germany could teach superior methods of sinking mine shafts as well as of chemical production; Belgium could teach improved systems of mine ventilation; America had new automatic looms for cotton and new machines and speed-up methods in metallurgy. Even some key British developments were taken up more eagerly elsewhere than at home. The Gilchrist Thomas process for smelting iron ore heavy in phosphorus was basic to the German metallurgical boom of the 1870s; it had almost to be reimported to Britain, and began to be used only in the 1890s. It was sad but true. Britain had taught her lessons well, but her pupils had taken over. The transformation, satisfying to a true educator perhaps, had not been part of the planned curriculum.

Could Europe and the United States have industrialised without the many facets of British pressure and guidance? The question cannot be fully answered, of course, because in fact British inspiration was always present. The United States had the necessary entrepreneurial drive by the early nineteenth century, but perhaps not the population pressure and resultant markets that would have channelled this drive into new methods of manufacturing. Population pressure existed on the Continent and assured a continuation of the spread of domestic manufacturing already proceeding rapidly in the eighteenth century. But, without Britain, governments and businessmen alike might have been satisfied with largely traditional methods. One cannot be sure that the ingredients of inventiveness, of the sort present in England and Scotland, would have responded to the opportunities. The British artisan-tinkerer might have been hard to find amid the guild restrictions of the Continent. Entrepreneurs to exploit the inventions might have been hard to find among merchants eager above all to invest in real estate. Britain did not industrialise the western world singlehandedly. Alert manufacturers and workers and a sympathetic government were present in every country in which British influence took hold. The influence was a vital ingredient nevertheless.

British influence was not altruistic. British businessmen and workers made money abroad, British machine-builders made money as they sold their machines, and it was the highly profitable expansion of exports generally that provided the competitive spur that above all else spread industrialisation outside Britain. Yet the self-interest that motivated British manufacturers and workers was not necessarily narrow, certainly not narrowly national. Criticism of giving secrets to foreigners, never universal, waned rather fast. At the least, consciousness of British superiority prevented consistent efforts to monopolise the secrets of industry (at least outside the Empire, for Britain did directly reduce industry in India); at most there was a genuine desire to share the benefits of the new world Britain was building. Yet as she spread industry, Britain spread rivalry as well. Continental and American manufacturers almost invariably sought tariff protection against Britain, and everywhere by the late nineteenth century they had won out. Traditionalists resented British influence. The most dynamic businessmen, sympathetic to British ways, wanted to beat Britain at her own game, not just for their own sake, but for that of their nation. The defensive, nationalistic overtones of nineteenth-century industrialisation stemmed in large part from Britain's key role, even from British generosity, and they gradually forced a change in British attitudes as well.

Britain in 1800 was a peculiar nation, else she could not have taken the lead in such a momentous innovation as the industrial revolution. The commercial-mindedness of British aristocrats, the independence of British artisans, and the innovating spirit of British businessmen set Britain apart fully as much as the political structure did. A vast number of elements had to combine in order to produce the industrial revolution. The same dynamism quickly pushed industrialisation beyond Britain's borders. Sometimes intentionally, sometimes by simple contagion, Britain spread not just new economic forms, but a radically new society wherever people were open to its lessons.

SUGGESTIONS FOR FURTHER READING

The only extensive study of Britain's role in the spread of industrialisation, and it is a good one, is W. O. Henderson, *Britain and Industrial Europe, 1750–1870* (1954). E. F. Heckscher, *The Continental System* (1922) covers contacts between Britain and the Continent in a difficult period. Hrothgar J. Habakkuk, *American and British Technology in the Nineteenth Century* (1962) stresses comparisons more than mutual influences, but it is useful for the latter as well.

Historians of other national economies have often played down outside influence, in their focus on internal developments, but a few contribute both background and information on Britain's industrial impact. See J. H. Clapham, *The Economic Development of France and Germany* (1936); Arthur Dunham, *The Industrial Revolution in France, 1815–1848* (1955); K. R. Greenfield, *Economics and Liberalism in the Risorgimento*; R. Demoulin, *Guillaume Ier et la transformation économique des provinces belges* (1938); James Mavor, *An Economic History of Russia*, 2 vols (1925); Harold Faulkner, *American Economic History* (1960); and Caroline Ware, *The Early New England Cotton Manufacture* (1931). For the vitally important British background see J. H. Clapham, *An Economic History of Modern Britain*, 3 vols (1926–38).

2. Britain, the Financial Capital of the World

S. G. E. LYTHE

WHEN a now forgotten Restoration dramatist said that money speaks the language that all nations understand, the language must surely have been the Dutch of Amsterdam. In the nineteenth century it was, equally without doubt, the variously accented kinds of English spoken by the men whose activities centred on the City of London. London, in short, was a relative latecomer to the list of great financial capitals which stretches, both in time and space, across Europe via the Low Countries and France to South Germany and North Italy. By the eighteenth century London had acquired metropolitan status within the United Kingdom, but its domestic financial functions overshadowed its external. Nevertheless the acceptance of London as the pivot of the domestic financial system brought in its train habits and institutions of great significance and potentiality. The legal status and special relationship to government enjoyed by the Bank of England assured it a unique position, and, when it learned how to use it, a great power of leadership; the London private banks, offspring of the goldsmiths, scriveners and the like, served as the connecting link in the growing network of provincial 'country' banks; the handling of inland trade bills, the common instruments for the transmission of credits within the country, created in London a cluster of specialist bill-brokers in close association with the banks. As the clearing house of Britain, London was training to become – in Joseph Chamberlain's phrase – the clearing house of the world.

The external activities, though quantitatively smaller, were of no less significance as bases for expansion. London had long and deep experience of foreign trade and commodity markets, and foreign trading had its own financial apparatus. Apart from Consols the stock most familiar to the investing public for much of the eighteenth century was that of the overseas trading companies, notably the East India Company; trade required mechanisms for the provision of short-term capital; shippers required the kind of cover which marine insurance could supply, hence the rise of Lloyd's from a coffee-house to the world's greatest marine insurance organisation; the transfer of shares created an organised and regulated market which, in the Stock Exchange, had recognisable physical form by 1773.

While, in short, the North and Midlands were learning new techniques of industrial management and production, London was acquiring comparable skills in the handling of money, which, within a hundred years, were to bring her a dominance in the financial world even more penetrating than that of Lancashire in cotton. These two aspects of Britain's economic expansion, the industrial and the financial, must, however, be kept in close juxtaposition. In the final analysis the ability of London after 1815 to enter upon a century of vigorous overseas lending stemmed from the profit-making capacity of the British economy at large and the canalisation of much of the nation's surplus funds to London. It is true, as we shall see, that in some periods extensive lending was undertaken independently of London, notably by Scotsmen, but nevertheless the combination of technical industrial leadership in most major industries with the financial expertise and prestige of London provides the basic explanation of Britain's role as the great money-lender of the nineteenth century.

On the international political front, events moved in London's favour, especially with the dislocation of the Continent of Europe during the French and Napoleonic Wars. The wars put the seal on the decline of Amsterdam, which had at least been impending for decades. The wars retarded the progress of industry in any possible continental competitor to Britain. By proving that no continental capital was immune to hostile occupation, they weakened that confidence and sense of security which lie at the root of successful financial operations. London, by contrast, was a safe city. A Londoner in 1800 might have experienced domestic riots and might have heard from his father of the panic in 1745 when Charles Edward's Highlanders were only a five days' march away. But, unlike his contemporaries on the Continent, he had never heard enemy gunfire, for no enemy had approached London since the Dutch struck terror into the heart of Samuel Pepys by breaking the defensive 'Chane' at Chatham in 1667.

None came in anger, many came in peace, bringing with them a fund of skill and connections. Frenchmen fled from the shadow of the guillotine, and when the Revolutionary army invaded the Low Countries, Amsterdam financiers, notably Henry Hope, fled also to the safety of London. About 1800 Nathan Mayer, whose family had traded under the sign of the Red Shield (*Rothschild*) in Frankfurt am Main, arrived for a short spell in Manchester, and, moving to London five years later, established there a house of the world's greatest family financial network.[1] Others of rather earlier vintage, such as the Barings, were similarly of continental origin and had continental links, and as the nineteenth century went on the ranks were swelled by Huths, Doxats, Raphaels, Hambros, Goldschmidts, Göschens, Schroeders and a dozen others including, by the 1860s, a few Americans. Thus the 'Establishment' of the City of London – or at least that part of it which dealt in foreign loans – was, appropriately, the most cosmopolitan element in British society. Its wealth and culture wore down the reluctance of the British upper classes to accept even the upper echelons of the *Haute Juiverie*. Queen Victoria, as the pillar of convention, resisted Gladstone's proposal to nominate Lionel de Rothschild for a peerage: firstly 'she cannot consent to a Jew being made a Peer', and secondly, when Gladstone pressed the matter, 'she cannot think that one who owes his great wealth to contracts with Foreign Governments for Loans . . . can fairly claim a British peerage'.[2] But the tide of prejudice was on the ebb. The Prince of Wales revelled in the company of rich men and 'among them discovered a special affinity with Jews'. He cordially applauded the appointment of the first Lord Rothschild (a peer in 1885) as Lord-Lieutenant of Buckinghamshire;[3] certainly in his periodic financial embarrassments he could scarcely have chosen better confidential advisers than Anthony de Rothschild, Maurice de Hirsch and Ernest Cassel. In short the creation of London's capital market was not simply an economic happening: its social overtones could be detected across a wide spectrum from the self-indulgent urbanity of Ascot and the Opera at the one extreme to princely charity in the back streets at the other. It existed in London because, in the nineteenth century, no other spot on earth could provide comparable resources, facilities and freedom for the discharge of a global function.

The symbolism of Venus Anadyomene is inappropriate in economic history: nothing emerges whole and complete. The ancestry of nineteenth-century British overseas investment can be traced to the 'sheer magnitude of popular investment' which supported the overseas trading companies and colonisers in the days of Elizabeth I and the early Stuarts;[4] similarly the investment mania of 1824–5 might be regarded as an outbreak of an hereditary disease which had earlier broken surface in the South Sea Bubble. Nevertheless, though the exact balance remains a matter of academic debate, Britain's overseas credits in the eighteenth century were certainly heavily offset by foreign capital in Britain,[5] and it needed the combination of Industrial Revolution and Napoleon to tip the balance decisively in her favour. On any reading of the facts the nineteenth century differs from any of its predecessors in

the sheer amount of British capital invested abroad, representing a huge
geographical spread of purchasing power and a spearhead of economic
change. What is more questionable is whether the motivation was in
any sense novel. Put bluntly the question is whether, to use Sir William
Harcourt's language, Britain in the nineteenth century moved into a
phase of 'stock-jobbing imperialism'.

To what may be roughly classed as the Hobson–Lenin School the
answer was simple: 'it is not too much to say that the modern foreign
policy of Great Britain has been primarily a struggle for profitable
markets of investment'; the rentier class is 'the taproot of imperialism';
the need to export capital and make it politically secure has been 'the
prime mover for the modern imperialist powers'.[6] Others, grinding
lighter axes, have advanced the theory of 'informal empire', something
to be defined in terms of investment and trade rather than of political
status, and have argued that a crafty Britain garnered the fruits of
imperialism (for example in Argentina) without shouldering the
administrative and military burdens inherent in political acquisition.
The more radical of these views, the theory of capitalist imperialism,
appropriately developed most thoroughly by an Englishman, J. A. Hobson, was based on the commonly accepted nineteenth-century economic
proposition that the trend of profit rates in industrialised societies was
likely to be downwards over the long period. As a natural consequence
capital would seek more lucrative employment in fresh areas and would
tend to favour those where other factors of production (for example, land
or labour) were relatively abundant and cheap. From this it is an easy
step to the expectation that capitalist societies will protect their overseas
investments by political intervention. Against this it has been pointed
out that a simple correlation of the expansion of foreign lending and the
physical extension of British rule can lead to false deductions. The fact,
for example, that in 1911 £20 of British money was under local political
control in South America against each £1 under British rule in West
Africa gives point to Nurske's conclusion that 'British capital tended to
by-pass the primitive tropical economies',[7] and it is now widely accepted
that much of the expansion of the British political empire in the late
nineteenth century was determined by factors other than the needs of
British investors. Whether, as a major exception to this generalisation,
the South African War was simply a device to remove obstructive Boers
from the path of European high finance, or whether the British government was 'thinking not of goldfields but of the political supremacy of
Britain in South Africa', cannot be resolved in a sentence. Moderate
opinion might perhaps join with Professor Seton-Watson in ranking it

(along with the Russo-Japanese War) as 'coming closest to the simple Marxist pattern of imperialist war'.[8]

But decisions about the direction of investment were personal, or, at most, corporate, and it is not easy to see how they aggregated into a 'policy'. Equally it is hard to generalise about the extent to which decisions were influenced by current government policies, or how far investors themselves could shape these policies. The nineteenth-century attitude of the British Foreign Office to economic affairs generally was based on aristocratic aloofness justified if necessary by *laissez faire* philosophy. It can of course be argued that with the growing social acceptance of high financiers their private contacts with political families created a network of influence which involved neither memoranda nor public utterances, but against this influence there stood always the 'departmental view'. It is fair to argue that, in the 1850s, there was a 'Manchester interest' strong enough to exert pressure on Sir Charles Wood at the Board of Control, inducing him to infuse a dynamism into the economy of India by providing state guarantees of interest on private loans.[9] It is no less fair to Wood to say that he resisted any wholesale extension of this system of 'private enterprise at public risk'.[10] Nevertheless the creation of the Indian railway network, in substantial measure the outcome of this kind of arrangement, was mutually beneficial to Lancashire cotton magnates and the British investing public, and, indirectly, beneficial also to the Government of India. On the other hand, during much the same period when China was being brought into the sphere of informal empire, official British action there was confined to 'the creation of conditions in which investment in general might take place'. Individual projects were not officially supported, indeed in some instances the attitude of the Foreign Office towards Chinese railway concessions was positively chilling. It is possible to adduce a few instances in which the British Government underwrote a foreign loan, the Greek Loan of 1833 being a classic example, and it can be maintained that in chartering the Imperial Bank of Persia in 1889 it sought to create a 'chosen instrument' for British financial diplomacy in the Middle East, but these instances are few and far between.

In short, Disraeli's purchase of the Khedive's Suez Canal Shares in 1875, however consistent it may have been with Britain's policies in the eastern regions, is quite unrepresentative of normal British Government attitude towards foreign investment. It does not, in other words, seriously weaken the proposition that foreign lending cannot be regarded as an open instrument of British foreign policy in the sense that French capital was mobilised in Paris to bolster the Franco-Russian Alliance.

It has indeed been thought that finance and politics were so discreet that a flotation by an enemy power was possible in London, but recent studies of the classic case – the Russian loans of 1854–5 – show that dealing in London was in fact banned both by the Committee of the Stock Exchange and by a hastily drafted statute, though the substantial shift of credits from the Bank of England to some of the neutral continental money markets suggests that the loans were indirectly supported by British gold.[11]

The extent to which a sovereign power should intervene outside its frontiers in defence of the contractual rights of its subjects is a problem for political science. Most British statesmen in the nineteenth century would, in public anyhow, have accepted the Earl of Derby's view in 1876 that 'H.M. Government cannot depart from the policy of declining to intervene diplomatically in regard to foreign loans', though he added the rider that consular officers might act unofficially, as they had in fact acted for the previous generation. In the Commons' debate of 1847[12] Palmerston had left the question open to the discretion of the government of the day, and in his diplomatic circular of 1848, after making disparaging remarks about 'imprudent men' whose losses ought to be a salutary warning to others, he told foreign powers that there were limits to the tolerance of H.M. Government beyond which it might be necessary to resort to 'diplomatic negotiation'. Certainly Canning in the mid-1820s and Palmerston in 1831, in the face of great pressure, had both firmly adhered to non-intervention, and when Britain had acted in the River Plate in 1845–8, Buenos Aires bonds were at most a minor counter in the large game of diplomacy. Indeed it is not without significance that in each of the three classic cases of coincidence between default and open British intervention – Argentina, Mexico and Egypt – Anglo-French political relations were deeply involved. There are, it is true, some signs of a stiffening of British government attitude towards defaulters in the closing quarter of the nineteenth century, and Salisbury's statement in 1879 that he did not 'quite understand the principle of absolute abstinence' can be quoted as indication at least of doubts about traditional policy, though only two years later he was citing the 1848 *Circular* as holy writ. But outside the circle of official policy lay a broad periphery of semi-formal activity, and in the mind of a Peruvian or Mexican debtor the 'good offices' of a British consul cannot have been readily distinguishable from diplomatic negotiation. It is similarly likely that action for redress taken properly under international law must often have seemed to carry political overtones. Nevertheless, and with justice, the most recent student of the matter concludes that 'official intervention was denied to the bondholders unless their loans were under British government guarantee, or unless some incident had transformed their claims from the level of private debt-collecting to that of international obligation'. If, as Palmerston's circular had implied, investors chose to embark on speculative ventures of no obvious value to the nation, they must not expect H.M. Government to rescue their hot chestnuts. In fact plenty of fingers were burned, some the result of near-fraudulent promotions such as those of George McGregor, self-styled 'Cazique' of a vague Central American domain; some by mismanagement of funds by intermediaries such as the City of Glasgow Bank; many by the default of ostensibly reputable creditors among which foreign governments featured prominently. Bitter experience led bondholders to devise means of self-protection, notably through the establishment of their own council, a body proposed by Isidore Gerstenberg in 1866 and licensed by the Board of Trade in 1873.[13]

At most times, therefore, and in most senses, London could be regarded as a free capital market. But though its behaviour was rarely positively determined by political forces, there are major swings in the direction of investment in which, superficially at any rate, political sympathy seems to have been one determinant. In the light of these swings Feis concluded that 'the main course of foreign investment was in accord with the main national purposes. The feelings and decisions of the investors showed substantial identity with those of the government in power.' The behaviour of investors in the decade after Waterloo provides one such instance. When, in late 1816, the French found difficulty in keeping up their indemnity payments, Barings moved into action and secured at least the tacit approval of leading British statesmen for a loan which would bolster the credit of the restored Bourbons; the Greek loan of 1824, launched at a Guildhall banquet, was transmitted through a committee of which Byron was a member; the newly liberated (and ostensibly liberal) states of Latin America sounded a call in Britain which produced recruits for Bolívar and loans for almost any government which sought them. In these former Iberian colonies, mining prospects provided an additional material motivation so that 'the public, rejoicing at being able to serve its doctrines and its pocket at the same time, rushed for stock'.[14] One who rushed was the young Benjamin Disraeli.[15] Had his venture succeeded he might have become another Rothschild; instead he wrote *Vivian Grey*.

The boom and ensuing crash of 1824–6 is the first major landmark in the history of British overseas investment. Interest rates at home, as measured at least by the yield on Consols and by the conversion operations of the Treasury, had been moving downwards with the full return to a peace economy. Robert Stephenson's trip to Colombia and the emigration of Cornish miners to most South American countries illus-, trate the range of skills which Britain could provide to foreign borrowers. Company promotion achieved a vigour – and audacity – which the country had not experienced since 1719, and the suspension of payments by Colombia in the early weeks of 1826 pricked a bubble of scarcely less volume. It shook the confidence of investors in South America, but many solid marketable bonds remained, especially those of European governments, and despite defaults and sales it is likely that the yield on assets abroad was, in 1830, still adding some £4 million to the credit side of Britain's annual balance of payments.[16]

If Latin America was suspect, the other America, peopled largely by worthy Anglo-Saxon and Teutonic stock, seemed to offer more solid prospects. Notwithstanding memories of 1812 and the annoyances of the United States protective duties, commercial association was strong: Lancashire looked to the southern states for 80 per cent of its raw cotton; 16 per cent of Britain's exports were shipped to the United States; bills drawn by Americans on London financed their trade generally; the borrowers – state governments, banks and the like – had, at a range of 3000 miles, an air of reliability. So in the two decades before the crisis of 1837 much British capital went to build the infrastructure of the United States economy. Some of it was well employed, but the kind of success achieved by the Erie Canal (finished in 1826) triggered off a host of less judicious projects and, to give only one example, as early as 1829 the State of Philadelphia began a process of borrowing to meet dividend charges which ultimately more than doubled the original debt on her public works.

So again dividends were in default and, as Professor Jenks has said, it was highly embarrassing for an American to spend the winter of 1842–3 in London. As ever, economic lessons were learned the hard way. The American state governments had tried their hands as entrepreneurs and had been found wanting; henceforth the investor would look more favourably on private enterprise, and one by one the leading nations came to his aid with the appropriate instrument, the limited liability joint-stock company. The British limited liability company, founded on a series of enactments between 1844 and 1863, became the registry office where British capital could join in wedlock with foreign demand. In the same span of years this demand was sharpened by technological advance in communications, notably with the advent of the railway, the increase of steam in shipping, and the laying of the first long-distance ocean cables. Within Britain the promotion of railways, following the pattern established by canals, extended the shareholding habit to regions and social groups hitherto almost immune, and threw up a new species of contractors and promoters; beyond Britain more rapid communication further eroded the investor's reluctance to lose physical oversight of his capital. Nowhere, perhaps, was the process more evident than in Scotland, where, apart altogether from the great investment institutions of the late nineteenth century, lawyers became so involved that by the early eighties Edinburgh was said to be 'honeycombed with agencies for collecting money for use not only in Australia, but for India, Canada, South America – everywhere almost'.[17] A similar result from a different process can be observed in the dispersion of shareholding in some of the South American railways where the original issue was taken up by a core group of professional investors who acted in a sense as intermediaries between the public authorities of South America and the great mass of British subscribers. There, as in most lands old and new, the creation of public utilities called for skills and material resources which, in the early stages at least, Britain alone could provide. And in this phase, roughly the third quarter of the century, capital attained a mobility which accorded perfectly with the current concepts of free trade in goods and free migration of men. Partly because of this mobility, capital was cheap as never before. 'It is easy', wrote Clapham, 'to develop the world with capital at 2 per cent. The men of the fifties set about it.'[18]

So while Britain's capital investments had been important in the first half of the century in roles as different as building American turnpikes and bolstering financially embarrassed European thrones, the volume was slight as compared with what was to come. Imlah's estimates of annual earnings provide the milestones: in 1847 £10½ million, in 1861 nearly £20 million, in 1887 nearly £80 million, by 1900 over £100 million.[19] To an increasing extent continental Europe became able to meet its own capital requirements for industrial and transport development, and by the late fifties the French *Crédit Mobilier* and some of the Dutch and German finance houses could put up more than a superficial show of rivalry to London. Nevertheless the British promoters, notably Thomas Brassey, took a lot of beating at their own game, and to the end of the sixties European railway capital was still being raised in London. In general, however, the horizons had decisively widened, and British capital entered on a phase of world-wide employment which, with ups and downs, was to last until 1914.

The changing focus of attention reflects the emergence of fresh inducements and opportunities. Pressed, as we have seen, by British commercial interests, but seeking also a solution to a complex of internal economic and administrative problems, the Government of India offered concessions and guarantees to British investors with such success that by 1872 the quoted value of Indian railway stock alone was £90 million. Sponsored by such reputable names as Baring and Carr Glyn, the Grand Trunk Railway of Canada came onto the British market in 1853 and by the early sixties its book capital was £12 million. The enthusiasm over railway promotion in the United States in the period of reconstruction after the Civil War can be reduced to the cold terms of the London capital market issue figures: £6 million for 1871, £12 million for 1872 and over £14 million for each of 1873 and 1874. Impressive as such figures are – and they are simply samples – the totals subscribed for private undertakings were not more than one-third of the total in this hey-day of private enterprise. The fate of the £317 million which, between 1860 and 1875, went to foreign governments defies simple summary, for few areas have as yet been subject to the detailed study which Professor Ferns devoted to Argentina. The borrower whose name every schoolboy knows, Ismail Pasha, certainly pursued a colourful rake's progress, but he had some of the characteristics of a Western entrepreneur and his attempts to extend the cultivation of cotton and sugar must be set against the lavish vistas of Cairo and the grand staging of *Aida*. For Europe, where total government indebtedness roughly doubled in the ten years between Bismarck's rise to power and the establishment of the German Empire, the inference must be drawn that much of the borrowing was not, in the popular sense of the word, 'productive'. What the sum total of British investment had come to is equally uncertain. Hobson quoted Bowley's estimate of the total of British investment lying abroad in 1875 as £1400 million. Today's experts[20] put the figure somewhat lower, but certainly over £1000 million, and even that would make a fourfold increase in the previous twenty years.

In the days when economic history was less sophisticated (or perhaps less myopic) labels such as 'The Golden Age' and 'The Hey-day of Prosperity' were attached to the quarter-century ending in 1875. At first sight the magnitude of the capital investment abroad seems to recall such language and imply an heroic age in British capital export. In fact the effort – in terms of national abstinence – was less after 1850 than it had been before. As rough approximations we can assume that the sum involved was nominal in 1815, somewhere in the region of £200–230 million in the early fifties, and something over £1000 million in 1874. The growth in the second phase could have been accomplished by steady reinvestment and compounding at say 5 per cent. In the earlier phase, however (which suffered heavily anyhow from defaults), the growth cannot be explained by this process, and the remarkable feature is that this solid foundation was laid in a period when Britain was also adding immensely to her domestic stock of capital equipment in looms, blast furnaces, urban housing and the like. Nevertheless the mid-Victorians can claim credit (if it be a matter of pride) in having, as a race, ploughed back their overseas earnings in the form of fresh capital export. Perhaps this and the contemporary emigration of men provided them with the satisfaction which former and later generations derived from territorial expansion. It represented, on the national level, a confidence in the future and a willingness to defer consumption. The investors of the fifties and sixties created an immense hoard to hand on to the next generation, and in this sense the British economy in the later nineteenth century was cushioned by its inheritance.

In this field of study, as indeed in most branches of economic history, there is something sinister about the mid-seventies. With the Near East bankrupt, a trail of defaults swept over the financial world: even where the employment of capital had been ostensibly productive (as in U.S. railways) its disposition had sometimes been indiscriminate[21] and often in a pioneering role where a longish period of gestation was inevitable. In consequence the London foreign capital market ground almost to a halt and, from 1875 to 1880, the upward climb in earnings on British foreign investments was temporarily halted. In some important borrowing areas the latent hostility of the debtor to the money-lender surfaced as anti-British feeling. In Argentina, for example, as economic depression from 1874 to 1881 bred tension, British-owned banks and railways came under fire from the national Press with the usual charges of profiteering at the natives' expense, while the provincial government of Santa Fé went one stage further by closing the London and River Plate's banking office in Rosario. Though the British Foreign Office confined itself to indignant mumbling, the local chargé d'affaires summoned up a gunboat from Montevideo and the continued presence of H.M.S. *Beacon* no doubt reinforced his demands for restoration of the bank's facilities and gold.[22] Elsewhere in the world, financial crisis was a factor in political chaos. The Porte, in particular, faced catastrophe. By 1875, when his indebtedness had swelled to £200 million over the previous two decades, he was faced with the collection of revenue from dominions where disorder and rebellion were rampant, with the threat of war on his frontiers and with treason within his own palace gates. His financial solution, ominously suggested by the Russians and hardly encouraging to his Western creditors, was that for five years interest would be paid half in specie and half in fresh bonds. And even where political conditions were stable, a gloom descended on the economic horizon as the secular trend of prices turned downwards, increasing the real burden of payment for borrowers with fixed interest charges. In such conditions 'British investors became as cautious as they had been daring, and withdrew some of their capital from abroad, either by sale or by neglecting to reinvest on redemption'.

It can be argued that this aftermath – roughly the later seventies – is the real watershed in the history of British overseas investment between Waterloo and 1914. Jenks, whose brilliant study ends in 1875, justified his concluding date thus: 'In 1876 and 1877 Great Britain collected income from her foreign property for home consumption. She was at the end of an era ... The export of a capital surplus was over. Her further investments were to come for a generation from the accruing profits of those which had already been made 'and to such investments he applied the German economist's term 'the secondary export of capital'.

It is true that until 1906 no year quite rivalled the enormous investment of £83 million in 1873, though 1890 came very close, but when foreign investment had been resumed on a significant scale in 1881 the total mounted quickly. Bowley, writing almost as a contemporary and possibly over-estimating, believed that 'from 1881 to 1890 it seems not improbable that £600 million was added', and Hobson's figures for the last decade of the century would indicate another £360 million.[23] But when we put alongside the annual returns on income from abroad, mounting steadily until by 1900 they were of the order of £100 million a year, it is plain that all the yield was no longer being ploughed back. What in effect happened was that the yield simply entered the stream of income coming to Britain, and fresh investment, on average somewhat smaller in amount than the annual income, was made either by the recipients or by other people.[24] Nationally, therefore, Britain was taking a slice of her overseas earnings for home consumption.

As the total grew, its geographical distribution altered.[25] Whereas in the 1860s well below a half had lain with the political Empire and the 'informal' empire in Latin America, by the close of the century the fraction had risen to two-thirds. In part this reflected a withdrawal from Europe, and particularly from Russian loans which had appeared regularly on the London market down to 1872. Political friction in the Near East and over Afghanistan not only inhibited fresh Russian approaches to London, but also led to ostentatious selling of British-owned Russian bonds, especially to Germans and Frenchmen. A fore-warning of the ultimate triumph of the United States as the world's financial giant was sounded in the 1890s – especially after 1896 – in the repurchase by Americans of some of their railway bonds with such success that by 1905 British capital had been almost wholly displaced from a few companies. It was only a drop in a large bucket, but it illustrates the fluidity of British investment in the period.

The greater interest in imperial investment before 1900 had nothing of the selfconsciousness of the 'Money, Markets, Men' economic imperialism of the 1920s. A minimal element of official approval was conferred by the three Colonial Stock Acts of 1877, 1892 and 1900. These were in large measure the outcome of a campaign headed by Sir Julius Vogel, Prime Minister of New Zealand; but the first two, which created slightly preferential conditions for the transfer of colonial stock, fell far short of his ambitions, and it was not until 1900 that colonial stock was admitted to the trustee list. Even after that there is no strong evidence that the volume bought was materially affected by this official encouragement: before 1900 the effect of the Acts can have gone little beyond giving some publicity to the existence of colonial stock. The rising tide of imperial investment no doubt reflected, as the historian of one venture has put it, 'a positive desire to further colonial develop-ment and an interest in exploiting profitable opportunities', and in a general way it can be associated with the more keenly competitive economic conditions of the last quarter of the century from which capital investment could scarcely remain immune. In the economist's usage of the term, Britain probably continued to enjoy something near a 'monopoly' in the field, but rivalry was a growing reality, especially from France. There the *coup d'état* of 1851 had heralded a boom in finance hardly less spectacular than that in politics and metropolitan replanning so that, in 1856, *The Economist* could report that the *Crédit Mobilier* had 'partly taken Britain's place' as the principal promoter of foreign industrial enterprises. And though this boom ended with the collapse of the original *Crédit Mobilier* in 1867 and revival was delayed by the disasters of 1870–1, French external investment was resumed on such a scale in 1878 that by the eve of the First World War the grand total was of the order of 45 per cent of that of Britain. Even more challenging was the change in geographical distribution. Of French investment before 1881 all but 10 per cent was either in Europe or in the Ottoman Empire: of the much greater investment between then and 1914 the share of 'the rest of the World' was 44 per cent, of which about one half was in the Americas.[26]

Whatever the cause, it is plain that when active British overseas capital formation began again at the beginning of the eighties, Empire borrowers featured prominently. It has been estimated that Australian borrowing from 1881 to 1890 represented the equivalent of one-half of the entire value of her imports in those years. In part this was the response to positive government development policy, in part to the attractive array of enterprises ranging from banks to railways and freezing plants. In the Australian railway boom, which raised the mileage from 1600 in 1875 to 10,000 in 1891, lines 'were built to country race-courses that had hillbilly races twice a year, and to distant mining and pastoral towns'. The magnitude of British investment, something like £100 million between 1886 and 1890 alone, gives point to Blainey's recent summary that 'National Development was the slogan and British money lenders were willing to pay for it'.[27] Similar trends in New Zealand produced alarm in the minds of shrewd Scottish journalists: 'A midsummer madness seems in recent years to have possessed the Directors of some Colonial Companies . . . chiefly in New Zealand. That Colony since 1883 has been a paradise for adventurers and bank-rupts'.[28] In 1890-1, however, came the chilling effects of the Baring Crisis in London and of a fresh fall in the prices of primary goods almost everywhere. The Australasian madness subsided into a melancholy of financial gloom.

In the 1880s each major imperial territory had seemed similarly capable of providing its own glowing prospects. None outshone the gold and diamonds of South Africa, both now produced by capital-demanding techniques and both highly speculative. The 'Kaffir Circus' – that part of the London Stock Exchange which specialised in South African securities – revolved at exciting speed especially in 1889 and 1892, and then slowed down to cool its overheated bearings. Canada, developing from the firm political basis established in 1867, had lived down the poor financial reputation of her old provincial governments and the poor record of the Grand Trunk, her earliest major railway venture, and by the eighties offered in the Canadian Pacific and its associated prairie development a vast field for both men and money. Again there were thorns among the roses. In 1897, for example, when Canada appeared at the colonial pageant in London as 'the granary of the Empire, free homes for millions', there were days when Canadian Pacific shares changed hands at 46.

Nevertheless the political link which sustained the investor's faith in activities as widespread as Canadian wheat-growing, tea-planting in Assam or mining in the Rand could not, by the end of the century, be regarded as a certain assurance in South America, yet Brazil and Argentina were no less attractive than the official Empire. From 1875 to 1882 Argentina went through a rough cycle of economic depression and recovery, with parallel tension and relaxation in political life. By the end of the cycle, with the native Indian threat to stability finally removed, Roca established as President and the currency reformed, British capital began to move so that, in 1889, something between a third and a half of all new British overseas investment was in Argentinian securities. At the heart of the boom lay railway construction, and the holding of railway debentures rather than equities generated a sense of security which events were soon to demolish. As 1890 wore on, advices began to reach Britain from Buenos Aires and Montevideo of mounting monetary and political troubles, and by November the great house of Baring Brothers admitted its inability to meet liabilities on a mass of South American scrip which it had underwritten and still held unsold. Immediate bold action by the Bank of England kept the crisis within bounds and saved Barings, but the event nevertheless illustrates both the hazardous nature of a steep boom in foreign investment and the extent to which South America had become an integral part of the British financial empire.

One feature of the Argentinian investment boom had been the emergence of *cédulas*, land mortgage bonds, a local example of the trend in the period towards the greater employment of imported capital in land utilisation in one form or another. Whether it happened in Australia or Canada, the United States or Argentina, it was a logical second step from the initial foothold created by the railway promoters. An anonymous Dundee financial journalist (but who was likely to be better informed about this business ?) in his report for 1882 spoke of 'Investment, Mortgage, Land, Timber and Cattle Companies which within the last few years have grown so mightily both in numbers and in importance'.[29] The investment trust provided expertise in the selection and management of holdings coupled with the stability which might reasonably be expected from diversification of securities. Associated above all with Scottish investment in the American West, its origins can be clearly established in the early 1870s and its evolution equally clearly linked with the leadership of men such as W. J. Menzies, Robert Mackenzie and Robert Fleming. Exactly why Dundee became so heavily involved presents a challenge to its historians: the conventional explanation relies on the enthusiasm generated among its merchants by the yields on mortgages which they had accepted in the sixties in lieu of down payment for jute sacks. It has been estimated that in 1884, when the boom was temporarily halted, £20 million had been raised by Scottish investment and mortgage companies, and another £13 million for land, cattle or mining concerns. 'For a small country like Scotland to be able to spare, even for a time, tens of millions sterling, is one of the most striking paradoxes in the history of commerce. The Scotch, of all people in the world, are supposed to be best able to take care of themselves and their money . . . yet . . . they will face almost any risk for the sake of the difference between 4 per cent at home and 4½ per cent across the Atlantic.'[30] In fact there were plenty who never got their 4½ per cent, especially those who went into mining. The Scottish Pacific Coast Mining Company, established in 1881 and seeking gold in what the *Statist* called 'an expensive freak of geology', had a paid-up capital of nearly £95,000, yielded a grand total of £5541 in dividends, and eventually sold out for £613.[31] Not all ventures were so disastrous, even on the mining frontier, but most were confronted with the acute problems of remoteness of operations from the seat of 'top' management, and many incurred high costs from vexatious litigation.

As the tentacles of economic activity ranged farther and farther afield, so the resources of British capital were called on to provide the appropriate services in which, as yet, local experience was lacking. The credit facilities of the City of London throughout the nineteenth century supplied the lion's share of the instruments for the conduct of international trade. In banking the extension of British influence was a two-way process. In the one direction overseas depositors used the facilities of London: Bagehot in 1873 observed that in the last two or three years 'we have become to a much larger extent than ever before the Bankers of Europe';[32] in the other direction British capital and managerial skill went together to establish banks on the frontiers of the British commercial world. The process is well illustrated in China where, by the fifties and sixties, British-sponsored banks appeared to provide local services for western traders in the newly opened Treaty Ports.[33] British insurance companies provided a substantial part of the marine, fire and life cover not only in such obvious territories as India but also in the United States and Canada. Thus in 1879 23 per cent of all the life cover in Canada and 18 per cent of the fire cover in the United States depended on policies issued by British offices.[34] When the crunch came with the San Francisco fire of 1906 they paid out £10 million and not one failed to honour its obligations.

By and large the closing decade of Victoria's reign was a time of sombre reflection for the overseas investor. Reports on individual concerns tell their own stories of private misfortunes: cattle which existed on paper but not on the grasslands, calls on shareholders to   meet debenture charges, lodes petering out into useless rock and so on. More generally the Argentinian collapse of 1890 had seemed to spark off a trail of financial fires: a slump in South African mining shares, evidence of weakness in both Australian governments and banks, and, to aggravate matters, the protectionist policy of the United States and the slump in the value of silver with its repercussions on India. It is true that there were new or expanding opportunities: tea-planting in India, mining in Australia, the first bulk borrowing in the Far East, and after about 1896 the traditional borrowers began to recover their poise. But from the high level of £83 million in 1890 annual overseas investment fell to the order of £22 million in 1894 and 1895, then recovered somewhat in 1896 only to fall again to £17 million in 1898. In the eighties Britain had devoted nearly 5 per cent of her gross national product to foreign investment. In the middle and later nineties the corresponding fraction was little more than 2 per cent, and few contemporaries would have had the audacity to forecast that within their lifetime it could rocket again to the remarkable 8½ per cent of 1913.

Though they finished on this quiet note, the Victorians had wrought so monumental a work that by 1900 a figure of the order of £100 million appeared annually on the credit side of Britain's balance of payments as income from abroad. In other terms, it represented about 6½ per cent of the nation's income, a contribution roughly comparable to that made by agriculture, forestry and fishery.[35] The capital sum, on which this was the annual levy, had not been built up by any simple direct process. Throughout the nineteenth century the visible balance of trade had normally been unfavourable, but with the exception of three isolated years in the forties there was always a credit balance on the overall current account. The gap had been bridged by the earnings of British shipping, by banking and insurance revenue, by miscellaneous remittances and by the yield on capital on loan to outsiders. By 1875 the last item alone filled about one-half of the gap; in exceptional years, 1887, 1888 and 1890, it bridged it completely. Nevertheless in the earlier part of the century – the phase of 'primary' investment – the capital sum can have been created only, in Hobson's phrase, 'by stinting our imports'. In the later phase, certainly after 1875, the process was reversed when the income on existing investments was not only enough to cover all new investment, but also to pay for a substantial volume of imports not balanced by exports.

All capital creation involves abstinence from current consumption in the expectation of a fuller future. As, in this sense, there is no difference between domestic and overseas investment, the two can, within limits, be regarded as alternative outlets, and the pure economic man would determine the direction of his investment in the light of the respective returns in each market, tempered by considerations of security. He was confronted by very conflicting advice. In 1851 Porter had told him that while 'it is impossible to form a correct estimate of the profit and loss (in foreign investment) . . . the general impression is that hitherto the losses have much exceeded the gains';[36] but R. L. Nash in 1880, in spite of the troubles of the post-1875 depression, reached a diametrically opposite conclusion.[37] There were two sets of relationships: the one between the domestic and the overseas capital markets, the other between supply conditions in Britain and demand conditions in potential borrowing countries, and as economies tended with time to become more integrated, so the influences determining decisions became more subtle and marginal. Hence the old cliché about capital going abroad because it could find no profitable use at home is hard to substantiate as a valid generalisation; indeed, the converse argument, that capital stayed at home for lack of attractive external outlets, is perhaps easier to apply.

Throughout modern history, however, the belief has persisted that while the export of capital may be an instrument in the extension of national influence, it is in some sense socially harmful to the lending nation. It was argued at one time or another that it encouraged competition abroad and so, in the end, damaged British industry; that it 'starved' domestic industry; that it restricted social provision; that, by creating a rentier class, it was socially divisive; that, in the words of the Webbs, it led to 'patrolling the globe for the protection of profit-making enterprises' and hence, in the end, to war.[38] One instance may serve to illustrate the difficulty of striking a balance in economic terms alone. From his reading of the annual accounts of the Director of Indian Railways Jenks deduced that 'more than one-third of the capital invested in Indian railways down to the early eighties was spent in England for railway iron and the cost of transportation to the East'. In an average year, therefore, capital investment in India was creating in Britain a demand for iron and shipping services to the tune of £2 million. Without this kind of demand the growth of the British wrought iron (and later steel) industry might well have been retarded and the economies of large-scale production diminished, so that, in the end, all users of British iron and steel would have paid higher prices with consequences filtering down through the metal-using industries to the housewife's cooking pot. But this forced growth of the capital goods industries tended to distort the pattern of industry generally and certainly increased the sector notoriously subject to cyclical fluctuation and periodic unemployment. That part of the loans which did not go as goods represented a transfer of purchasing power out of the country, damping down the demand for the products of consumer goods industries and retarding their growth so that their competitive capacity in world markets was diminished.[39] Outside India the link between investment and capital goods is less easy to establish over any long period, and Professor Saul's argument that capital lending assisted exports not so much directly as by spreading purchasing power and thus financing multilateral payments is certainly more generally applicable.[40]

The distorting and damping effects, to some observers at least, produced their socially most harmful result on the provision of domestic housing in Britain. One examination of the trends in British capital exports and in house-building in London and twenty-nine American cities produced this conclusion: 'Long cycles of building in the U.S.A. and in London reveal a correlation with changes in the level of British capital exports – in the one case positive, in the other negative – sufficiently close to justify the supposition that the relationship is not merely a random one.'[41] In fact the volume of fixed capital in British residential housing was rising briskly to 1875 (notwithstanding huge capital exports to 1874), but fell from 1876–7 to 1880 when the capital export market was in the doldrums. The discovery that an industrial town the population of which had risen from 121,000 to 142,000 in the previous decade could, in 1881, have 3300 unoccupied houses[42] gives force to the belief that 'whatever happened elsewhere, building would have remained depressed for most of the eighties'.[43]

Some day the American school of 'New' economic history will produce a final balance sheet for British capital investment, based on a computer-aided calculation of what did accrue against what would have accrued had the money all been used at home. Until that day any answers to the question of whether foreign investment paid must lie in the category of more or less well-founded guesses.[44] Against the massive total of investment, defaults were relatively small and often were offset by high yields or good faith elsewhere. Thus in the tempestuous conditions of 1890 Chile maintained her high repute as a borrower, and continued even through and after civil warfare to honour her established debts.[45] And against the instances of poor or non-existent dividends must be set the performance of plenty of respectable British industrial concerns. In the winter of 1877, for example, a shareholder in enterprises such as the Wigan Coal and Iron Company would have had to tighten his belt every bit as much as his neighbour who held Near East government bonds.[46]

Suspicions of the socially harmful effects, to say nothing of the cynical view that nobody benefited except shippers, financiers and manufacturers, must similarly be weighed firstly against the proposition that capital export was a form of investment in the primary sector of the British economy. By providing the infrastructure – whether by irrigation works in India, grain stores and railways in North America or harbours in the Far East, British capital brought new resources of land and manpower within the reach of the British consumer. But for British investment it is hard to see how the British housewife in 1900 could have had her four-pound loaf for fivepence.

Secondly it was British investment which – to cite one instance only – created the beginnings of an industrial revolution in societies in South America hitherto based on the *peón* and the *patrón*.[47] Loans to governments, municipalities and private companies sustained the modernisation of town services, of transport and of power supplies, creating artisan and managerial groups whose skills and instruments were acquired from the more advanced nations. In such societies capital investment was the pace-setter of economic and social change. Down to 1914 Britain was able, more than any other nation, to provide the means. It was a likely consequence that, in the long run, the recipients would compete with Britain in the more elementary forms of industrial production: that Indian mills would eventually bite the hand that had fed them and that the tinplate of South Wales would not eternally roof the shacks of the American West. This, on the national level, was the risk in capital export. If in any genuine sense Britain starved her own development in the later nineteenth century it was in the neglect of the new industrial techniques by which she could, in the twentieth century, have met the more sophisticated world demands which her own capital had helped to generate. But this neglect was not so much a matter of money as of the attitude of mind of a people who had long – perhaps too long – been industrially pre-eminent.[48]

SUGGESTIONS FOR FURTHER READING

Experts in this field of study will recognise the extent to which this essay is drawn from a number of important secondary sources for which no specific footnote references have been given. The subject was virtually defined in C. K.

Hobson, *The Export of Capital* (1914) and elaborated in L. H. Jenks, *The Migration of British Capital to 1875* (1938). European aspects were brought together for the first time in H. Feis, *Europe, the World's Banker, 1870–1914* (latest edition 1964). The relationship between domestic and overseas investment is examined in A. K. Cairncross, *Home and Foreign Investment 1870–1913* (1953). Nobody so far has written a history of Scottish capital investment, but there is valuable material in W. T. Jackson, *The Enterprising Scot* (1968) and in J. C. Gilbert, *A History of Investment Trusts in Dundee*. A. R. Hall, *The Export of Capital from Britain 1870–1914* (1968) embodies a number of important articles.

For the relationship between imperialism and capital exports it is still essential to refer to the works of J. A. Hobson, especially his *Imperialism, a Study* (1902), but most of the relevant views are summarised in D. K. Fieldhouse, *The Theory of Capitalist Imperialism* (1967). D. C. M. Platt, *Finance, Trade and Politics in British Foreign Policy, 1815–1914* (1968) is essential reading in this context.

Studies of the volume and impact of British capital in particular areas increase annually. A useful selection would include H. S. Ferns, *Britain and Argentina in the Nineteenth Century* (1960); J. F. Rippy, *British Investment in Latin America 1822–1949* (1959); C. C. Spence, *British Investments and the American Mining Frontier, 1860–1901* (1958); D. S. Landes, *Bankers and Pashas. International Finance and Economic Imperialism in Egypt* (1958); J. D. Bailey, *A Hundred Years of Pastoral Banking: a history of the Australian Mercantile Land and Cattle Company, 1863–1963* (1966); N. G. Butlin, *Investment in Australian Economic Development 1861–1900* (1964); A. R. Hall, *The London Capital Market and Australia 1870–1914* (1963); W. M. Pearce, *The Matador Land and Cattle Company* (1964).

NOTES

1. Of the numerous books on the Rothschilds the most useful for the present purpose is B. Gille, *Histoire de la Maison Rothschild: i, Des Origines à 1848* (1965).
2. A. M. Hyamson, 'The First Jewish Peer', in *Transactions of the Jewish Historical Society of England*, xvii (1953), 287.
3. P. Magnus, *King Edward the Seventh* (1964), p. 215.
4. T. K. Rabb, 'Investment in English Overseas Enterprise, 1575–1630', in *Economic History Review*, xix (1966), 70.
5. C. Wilson and A. Carter, 'Dutch Investment in England', in *Economic History Review*, xii (1960), 434.
6. J. Strachey, *The End of Empire* (1959), p. 123.
7. R. Nurske, *Patterns of Trade and Development* (1959), p. 19.
8. H. Seton-Watson, *Neither War nor Peace* (1960), p. 310.
9. R. J. Moore, *Sir Charles Wood's Indian Policy, 1853–66* (1965), pp. 124–50.
10. D. Thorner, *Investment in Empire* (1950), p. 173.
11. O. Anderson, 'The Russian Loan of 1855', in *Economica*, xxvii (1960), p. 368.
12. *Hansard's Parl. Deb.* 3rd ser. xciii, 1285–1307.
13. A. Behr, 'Isidore Gerstenberg (1821–1876): founder of the Council of Foreign Bondholders', in *Transactions of the Jewish Historical Society of England*, xvii (1953), 207.

14. A. Maurois, *Disraeli* (1966), p. 31.

15. R. Blake, *Disraeli* (1966), pp. 24–6.

16. B. R. Mitchell and P. Deane, *Abstract of British Historical Statistics* (1962), p. 333.

17. J. D. Bailey, 'Australian Borrowing in Scotland in the Nineteenth Century', in *Economic History Review*, xii (1959), 272.

18. J. H. Clapham, *An Economic History of Modern Britain*, (1932), ii, 363.

19. A. H. Imlah, *Economic Elements of the Pax Britannica* (1958), pp. 70–5.

20. Notably Imlah, op. cit.

21. F. E. Hyde, 'British Capital and American Railway Enterprise in the North West', in *Economic History Review*, vi (1936), 202.

22. A. S. J. Baster, *The International Banks* (1935), pp. 131–7.

23. A. L. Bowley, *England's Foreign Trade in the Nineteenth Century* (1905), p. 75.

24. For a recent examination of the process of reinvestment see A. G. Ford, 'The Transfer of British Foreign Lending', in *Economic History Review*, xi (1958), 302.

25. M. Simon, 'The Pattern of New British Portfolio Investment, 1865–1914', in *Capital Movements and Economic Development*, ed. J. H. Adler (1967).

26. R. E. Cameron, *France and the Economic Development of Europe, 1800–1914* (1961), pp. 88 and 486.

27. G. Blainey, *The Tyranny of Distance* (1968), p. 254.

28. *Dundee Year Book* (1888), p. 147.

29. Ibid., p. 26.

30. 'Scottish Capital Abroad', in *Blackwood's Edinburgh Magazine*, cxxxvi (1884), 447.

31. J. C. Logan, unpublished dissertation (University of Strathclyde) based on Sessional Papers S19/C31 in Scottish Record Office, Edinburgh.

32. W. Bagehot, *Lombard Street* (1873), p. 17.

33. A. S. J. Baster, 'Origins of the British Exchange Banks in China', in *Economic History* (Supplement to *Economic Journal*), iii (1934), 145.

34. Article on 'Insurance' in *Encyclopaedia Britannica*, xiii (1881).

35. P. Deane and W. A. Cole, *British Economic Growth* (1962), p. 166.

36. G. R. Porter, *Progress of the Nation* (1851), p. 628.

37. R. L. Nash, *Short Enquiry into the Profitable Nature of our Investments* (1880).

38. S. and B. Webb, *The Decay of Capitalist Civilisation* (1923), p. 153.

39. A. G. Ford, 'Overseas Lending and Internal Fluctuations', in *Yorkshire Bulletin of Economic and Social Research*, xvii (1965), p. 19.

40. S. B. Saul, *Studies in British Overseas Trade, 1870–1914* (1960), p. 202.

41. E. W. Cooney, 'Capital Exports, and Investment in Britain and the U.S.A.', in *Economica*, xvi (1949), 351.

42. *Dundee Year Book* (1886), p. 163.

43. S. B. Saul, 'House Building in England, 1890–1914', in *Economic History Review*, xv (1962), 135. See also H. J. Habakkuk, 'Fluctuations in House-building in Britain and the United States', in *Journal of Economic History*, xxii, no. 2 (1962).

44. This language does less than justice to Sir Alec Cairncross's pioneer study in *Review of Economic Studies*, iii (1935).

45. F. W. Fetter, 'The Chilean Debt Payment of 1891', in *Economic History* (Supplement to *Economic Journal*), ii (1933), 609.

46. D. H. Turner, 'The Wigan Coal and Iron Company, 1865–1885' (unpublished dissertation, University of Strathclyde).

47. C. C. Griffin, in *New Cambridge Modern History*, xi (1962), ch. xix.

48. I am indebted to my colleague Dr J. T. Ward for many constructive comments. I regret that *The Export of Capital from Britain, 1870–1914*, ed. A. R. Hall (1968), appeared too late for its excellent contents to be fully used in the writing of this chapter.

3. The Great Migration

D. F. MACDONALD

THE century witnessed a mass movement of people from Europe which, by reason of its size, its character and its direction, transformed the world. The impulses behind it were many and must be recognised, since they determined its nature and its effects.

That the emigration should have attained such huge dimensions at the time requires some explanation. Its fundamental cause was twofold. First, there was an unprecedented growth of population at home, so rapid as to justify its being called an 'explosion'. The reasons for this have been the subject of much study and not a little dispute, but, put in its simplest terms, it was a case of population attaining a higher rate of survival, which in turn was accounted for by an expansion in the means of subsistence and an advance in living standards and medical knowledge. There was a glaring exception even to this elementary hypothesis within the British Isles; population in Ireland increased alongside a static or diminishing food supply; so it was that that country around the middle of the century underwent such physical privations as to force its people to emigrate in huge numbers as an alternative to starvation.

The growth began to assume substantial proportions in the eighteenth century; between 1750 and 1900 the population of Europe rose from 140 million to 401 million. It increased much faster than that of Asia or Africa, where, in the primitive state of the economies, nature exerted a decisive control. In 1750 Europe's share of world population was one-fifth, in 1900 one-quarter. The growth in Europe was exceeded only in those new lands which it did so much to populate, and which were stocked by people at Europe's expense and at the same time achieved a higher rate of reproduction, stimulated, no doubt, by the fact that there was so much room for expansion.

In this as in other spheres of activity Britain led Europe. In the same period her population increased fivefold, with a slowing-down in the latter part of the nineteenth century. Despite fluctuations and losses, her share of Europe's population nearly doubled, from 5·7 per cent to 9 per cent. It was no wonder that the British Isles should experience a greater exodus than any other country. Of a grand total of nearly 23 million estimated to have left Europe in the second half of the century, 10 million went from the British Isles, and this when, towards the end of the period, continental countries were pouring out emigrants in unprecedented numbers. For most of the century, statistics are either lacking or imprecise, and many from the Continent embarked from British ports. Even so, the figures reflect without undue distortion the overwhelming importance of Britain as a primary source.

There was the tremendous flurry in the forties and fifties, because of the abnormal volume from Ireland, but the phenomenon continued thoughout the whole of the century and reached a climax in the eighties. Its special intensity was perfectly logical, since it was directly related to the peculiarly drastic changes in the economy and in policies. There were revolutions in agriculture and in industry, which were by definition disruptive. A great many people were being compelled by the force of circumstances to move from their traditional habitats. Although new employments were being invented or extended, there was nevertheless a great deal of dislocation, especially on the land, but also in the towns, while population was increasing at a pace beyond the capacity or the inclination of the nation to absorb it.

The other of the twin causes was that, while these forces were working powerfully at home, new and comparatively empty territories overseas were beckoning, to a degree never known before. That this was so was due, not to the discovery of new countries, but again largely to the invention and extension of industries and services, not least transport, where Britain led the field. These both created a market in Britain for the primary products of the undeveloped countries and made it possible, by dint of capital and labour, to open up those countries in a way which had never previously been practicable, even if it had been desired. There were therefore basic dual forces at work, the repulsion of the old world and the attraction of the new.

The year 1815 is a convenient starting-point, since the French Wars had prevented any worthwhile movement overseas. Between then and 1840, when a new phase began, about 1 million people emigrated from the British Isles. Of this total almost exactly one-half went to British North America, rather fewer to the United States, over 58,000 to Australia and New Zealand and less than 10,000 to Cape Colony in South Africa. In the 'hungry forties' a great upsurge began, which the government made some effort to supervise and direct through its Colonial Lands and Emigration Commission, and by 1875 the total had risen to 7 million. In this second stage, however, the weighting of the emigration changed appreciably. The greatest pull was now being exerted by the United States, and this condition of affairs continued, with comparatively minor variations, until the end of the century. Thereafter a different orientation set in, with Canada, which had always topped the imperial league, replacing the United States in popularity; but clearly, up to this juncture, the British Empire was not regarded as a natural haven by British emigrants any more than by British capitalists seeking a place for investment.

There was no part of the world where the British did not penetrate, so that the scene is a veritable kaleidoscope of different settlements, each unique in its experience. Any brief study must therefore be highly selective, drawing on examples which illustrate, in broad outline, the ethos of emigration. One could perhaps for this purpose leave out India and the Far East, as regions where the British went, not as settlers in the normal sense, but as rulers and as entrepreneurs, to govern the native races and to exploit the native resources. There was no real attempt here to evolve a predominantly British kind of society, by merging with or by suppressing the native population; India remained Indian, with a small political and commercial clique superimposed, and as soon as independence could be declared – if it ever were – India could divest itself of British influence and even reject the English language, although clearly British influence and institutions would leave their impress on the country for a long time.

The situation becomes a little more complicated in certain other 'tropical' countries, but this does not invalidate this broad classification. In the West Indies the British had established their plantations, had imported slave labour from Africa to work them and had early in the nineteenth century abolished slavery, which was built into the whole economy of the plantations, at considerable financial sacrifice to themselves. Here one touches on another and intricate, not to say emotive, subject, the question of the nature of British imperialism, to which no historian has given a complete answer, perhaps because it is still too close in time for an objective judgement to be made. From the point of view of this essay it need only be remarked that a whole *mélange* of factors entered in, including commercial exploitation, international prestige (itself largely resting on trade) and foreign policy, together with (despite the cynics) a powerful infusion of genuine evangelism and the concept of trusteeship – that is the tutelage and protection of subject races and primitive economies by a nation well endowed, not merely with infinitely greater capital and industrial knowledge, but also with a superior civilisation.

This diversity is vividly brought out in Africa. For the greater part of the century Africa as a whole was not attractive to the British settler or investor, despite the blandishments of the home government and the speculator. It was a huge unknown continent, much of it inhabited by savage tribes; there were endemic diseases of man and beast; it was covered with well-nigh impenetrable jungle; and offered little in the way of inducement to the ordinary white settler. And most settlers were ordinary; pioneers there had to be everywhere, but the usual run of settler was a fairly pedestrian kind of person prompted by nothing more remarkable than the desire to make a decent living in decent surround-ings. The exception was South Africa. Here the British had established a firm foothold, essentially a strategic one, wrested from Holland as an admirably situated base for British naval power. The Dutch, however, were already strongly entrenched there, and their habits, their ambitions and their policies were markedly different from those of the British settlers, who in any case found the country of little appeal and had to be tempted by their government to settle there, as a counterpoise to Dutch ambitions, until they were more effectively lured by the gold and diamond discoveries in the latter part of the century. Certainly the British were transplanted there and took deep roots. Yet they do not present a typical case-study of the effects of British settlement, and are better looked at under imperialism rather than emigration, and not merely British imperialism. Despite the fact that the Dutch were physically pushed back into the interior, and that the friction between the two races finally ended in a war which Britain won, it was the Dutch conception of colonisation that was finally accepted by the generality of settlers as the standard.

One cannot, of course, simply write off the contribution made by British emigrants, whether in the short or in the long term, to the development of 'tropical' countries simply because the British settlers there were, in a sense, alien and transient. While the British government wielded the power, it imposed what even its critics would acknowledge to have been reasonably efficient and surprisingly honest rule, which might or might not survive a transfer of power to other hands. The settlers themselves brought with them an industrial expertise, an enterprising outlook and a supply of capital equipment which turned parts of Africa and other undeveloped countries into producers of vast wealth. They might have done more, in many of those regions, if they had not arrived so late in the century, when advances in medicine and transport and the revelation of new, latent mineral wealth made white settlements practical and profitable. Inevitably, however, in the circumstances, the annexation of those tropical territories by the British, with dubious exceptions, had in it from its very origins the ingredients of their own ultimate displacement from power.

It follows that, to make a quick assessment of emigration in its more orthodox connotation, one should concentrate on countries where there was a complete, or well-nigh complete, take-over by the British settlers. Even with this limitation, one can still identify two categories of emigration. There was the movement to a region already colonised, albeit only marginally (in more ways than one) by Europeans, many, if not most, of British stock. Here the impact of nineteenth-century emigration, while it might be very significant indeed, was relatively less severe, since it was cushioned by generations of well-established traditions. There was, on the other hand, the country so sparsely or weakly inhabited by an indigenous race that it was to all intents and purposes, in the context of European civilisation, virgin soil, on which the imprint of the white stranger was the first modern impression and, in the normal course of events, would never be erased. The obvious examples of those two disparate but associated types are America and Australia. They had one thing in common; in both the white incomers' supremacy was so overwhelmingly and so ruthlessly asserted that the native races were suppressed and came close to being exterminated.

One must now take a closer look at the origins of British emigration. The century witnessed the collapse of the doctrine of mercantilism, which had dominated governmental thinking in Britain as in other European countries for centuries. This doctrine applied not only to material things, where the criterion of success was the amassing of bullion, but also to population. The larger the population, the more powerful the nation. Military strength and industrial and agricultural viability were dependent on an adequate supply of people. It was also a part of this doctrine that special native skills should be conserved and denied to rivals. All this had a reasonable validity in earlier centuries, when population was relatively small and stagnant so far as growth was concerned. In the seventeenth century the famous Sir Josiah Child was echoing the sentiments of his age when he wrote of 'The Riches of a City, as of a Nation, consisting in the multitude of inhabitants'. With this went the official insistence that there was and must be enough employment for all at home – hence partly the tendency to dismiss poverty either as a dispensation of providence or as a moral failure on the individual's part.

The doctrine died slowly. Even in the early nineteenth century political economists were reluctant to discard the view that any outflow from the country was a tacit admission of weakness on the country's part and a source of strength to its competitors. As late as 1825 there was still on the statute-book a law forbidding the emigration of artisans, although it had never been really effective. What compelled the abandonment of restrictions of this sort was, first, that they were basically incompatible with the philosophy of *laissez faire* and free trade, and, more important, as an immediate catalyst, the stark fact that population was increasing at a rate which caused an imbalance between it and the means of subsistence. Malthus, with his *Essay on the Principle of Population* in 1798, brought this home brutally with his simple – his over-simple – prognosis that population was advancing at a rate which would lead to wholesale starvation unless the process were slowed down or mitigated in various ways. This was not a matter of economic theory; there was all too abundant evidence that much of the population of Britain was superfluous to its capacity to sustain it.

All this made officialdom receptive to new or refurbished doctrines which appeared to offer a solution of the dilemma. Wakefield and his disciples preached eloquently that the remedy lay in controlled emigration to new countries, preferably the British colonies. This was not a new gospel. Long before Wakefield the government had assisted impoverished people to go to the colonies, subsidising their passages and offering grants of land, and Canada in particular acquired most valuable settlements, which acted as 'growth-points', partly as a result of the aid given by government or by private philanthropy to emigrants. The achievement of Wakefield and his followers was to formulate a coherent system of controlled colonisation, as distinct from the spasmodic essays to find a place for paupers and convicts. They wished to have transported to the new countries small but complete communities, on the English model, ranging from the labourer to the capitalist entrepreneur, which would be more or less self-sufficient and would form the nucleus of larger settlements: what Wakefield called 'extensions of an old society'. The new countries would thus be developed in such a way that they became expanding markets for British exports and investment and, in the case of the colonies, kept predominantly British in their outlook, thus maintaining and strengthening a vigorous self-reliant empire. There was something for everybody in this policy: Britain would be relieved of the pauper, who would be given the opportunity to acquire independence and self-respect; the evangelist – with certain serious reservations – relished the thought that Christianity would be propagated throughout the world; the capitalist would profit from such ventures, since emigrants would take money along with them and, as the settlement progressed, would create a demand for more investment. John Stuart Mill asserted that overseas settlement was 'the best affair of business in which an old and wealthy country can engage', always provided it were properly supervised by the State.

The effectiveness or otherwise of the policies can best be observed in relation to particular cases. But even if there had been no policy at all, emigration would still have been on a massive scale, and its very size alone was of enormous importance. The sheer mass of people pouring into another country, even a country which already had a relationship of blood and culture with them, and which could therefore absorb them without undue strain into an existing mould of society, while it might not cause violent upheaval, was bound to create stresses and shifts, social, economic and political. The more primitive and unsophisticated the receiving society was, the less difficult was the process of settlement. In a country such as Australia there would be very little conflict, since opposition from the Aborigines was insignificant and easily disposed of by force. Even in the United States there were great tracts of land still waiting to be taken over, and there was never any doubt that the Red Indians would succumb. What was equally important – and in fact became of paramount importance as the West opened up and the availability of new territory proportionately diminished – was that the country was entering on a new stage of evolution, with the spread of industrialisation. At this stage people, skills and capital were even more essential than in the first white settlement, although the days of the pioneer were by no means over. Emigration from Britain was a very different proposition from the slave traffic. Apart from the transportation of convicts, which will be considered separately, emigration from Britain was wholly voluntary in character. Emigration was not – and rarely, if ever, has been – an exodus of people spontaneously electing to leave their homeland merely because of the superior attractions of another. Even the Israelites' Land of Promise was also a land of escape, and the same was true to a greater or lesser extent of the emigration from Britain. Considerable numbers of people who were already fairly comfortably off did freely choose to go abroad in search of glittering prizes; the gold rushes of the nineteenth century is the supreme example, involving thousands who wanted quick and easy money.

For the great majority, however, there were forces driving people away from their old habitat. Many of them merely abandoned the countryside for the town, but many more left the country itself. There was a variety of motives: they had been deprived of their land, or they had been denied the means of livelihood in other ways, or they suffered from social injustice. Even so, the fact remains that the emigrant elected to go, and this is of crucial significance in any assessment of the migration's character and effects. While individuals and families and even large groups were pressed by various means to move, those pressures were always indirect in nature. There was no actual compulsion and no direction by any central authority, such as there had been in other mass migrations, any more than there was, for Britain, in the flow of capital and commodity exports. *Laissez faire* operated here, as it did in the whole philosophy of Britain in the nineteenth century, though it exposed the individual to market forces and was, as in other fields of activity, conditioned in certain ways. For instance, there was a rough kind of selectivity where financial help was given to the emigrants, but mostly it boiled down to emphasis on youth and fitness, and it is mostly the young and fit who emigrate whatever the conditions. Indeed the government might positively dislike the preferences of emigrants, just as they might not favour the direction of the export of capital. Thus, in so far as the British government took any interest other than getting rid of surplus population, it would certainly have been unsympathetic to the draw of the United States and would have favoured the competing claims of the British colonies.

In practice, imperialist sentiment was lukewarm in official circles and the government therefore interfered to the minimum extent compatible with its financial involvement; this was never really on a large scale and was largely a matter of making appropriate gestures towards colonial demands. After all, there was constantly in the minds of the home government the consciousness that colonies would and should become independent and, so far as white settlements were concerned, the sooner the better. Certainly it would be preferable, even so, if they remained British in their new institutions and attitudes, not merely because British was best, which was taken for granted, but because foreign interlopers, with their strange ideas about monopolising trade and other things, should be kept out or at least kept in their place. So government throughout the period was never unduly concerned about where the emigrants went, so long as they went.

The superior attraction of the United States lay not just in its comparative geographical accessibility, greatly enhanced by cheap steamship travel, and the affinity already existing with Britain. In fact, national sentiment entered into the emigrants' consideration only to an insignificant extent, so far as the mass was concerned. It had played an outstanding part in the early settlement of Canada, when the Loyalists, many with little reason to be grateful to Britain, nevertheless fought on the British side in the American War of Independence and, having lost, deliberately crossed the border into Canada where they formed a vital element in what had been a predominantly French country, at a critical stage of the nation's evolution. Even in Canada, however, free trade and the final withdrawal of British preferences for Canadian wheat in 1846 imposed a severe strain on relations with the mother country, and there was a possibility that Canada might throw in its lot with the United States. Kinship certainly entered in, but not as an emotional thing; the practical consideration was that people from particular districts in Britain who had settled in particular districts overseas, whether in America, Australia, New Zealand or South Africa cajoled and subsidised friends and relations in the Old Country to join them, and the knowledge that there were friends awaiting them was of course a great inducement to the emigrants.

There were many cases where group emigration was the rule. There were settlements, such as Glengarry in Canada, which were dominated by people of one ethnic character – in this case Scottish Highlanders – and even by particular clans, who had had their traditional locale in Skye or Mull or some other self-contained area. They brought with them customs and traditions, including their own language, which, because of the comparative isolation of the new settlements and the people's nostalgic attachment to their old background, they built into their societies, which were reinforced from time to time by accessions from the same sources. This explains why Scottish settlements in Canada imbued Canada in its most formative period with a very strong Scottish character. Incidentally they also furnished models for the settlement of other countries, notably New Zealand. On the other hand, the American government, in contrast to the British and colonial governments, was opposed to the segregation of ethnic groups, despite strong pressure to give way, as from the Irish societies which would have liked to decant their impoverished compatriots into reserved areas. Congress decreed that this would be contrary to its principle of the integration of all immigrants into one composite multi-racial society. Immigrants were, therefore, not to have preferential treatment and in so far as a degree of separatism crept in, as it did in places, it was because of the gregariousness of the immigrants themselves. Here the different attitudes of the authorities were of fundamental importance for the future of America and the colonies.

Probably the chief reason for the popularity of the United States in the eyes of emigrants as a whole was that, so far from there being any attempt to restrict or regulate immigration, it was literally a free-for-all, with a bonus in the latter part of the century in the shape of a very liberal land policy. In 1862 the States gave positive proof both of its warmth of welcome and its material potential by giving free grants of land under the Homestead Act. Britain's policy towards its colonies, when it finally got to the point of having one, was in marked contrast. It was selective – and not necessarily any the worse for that – in that it put a premium on capital by making an economic charge for land grants, and at the same time left the comparatively destitute with little immediate prospect of breaking out of the old class setting.

Whatever the social repercussions – and of this more later – the economic results of British emigration to America were on the whole beneficial. The immediate problems raised by hordes of poverty-stricken, friendless and often sick people were very alarming, but those lacking money could quickly find employment of a sort. They might and did displace the colonial 'natives', especially before the American Civil War, when unemployment was not uncommon. On the other hand, those same 'natives', like their counterparts in England and Scotland, were inclined to have an aversion to the more menial tasks in industry and to the sweated atmosphere of factories. With the development of a more sophisticated society, too, succeeding generations tended to move upwards in industry (and the social scale) leaving vacancies beneath. At the worst, the 'natives' could move westwards.

The 'frontier' theory, which seeks to explain the pattern of westward movement in America is, therefore, that it was the old colonists who went pioneering in the first half of the century and the immigrant farmers who took over, and then, with plenty of land available, infiltrated westwards until by the seventies they had reached the prairies. To take over land, however cheap, the immigrants needed a financial 'grub-stake', and they either brought this with them, as many tenant farmers from England and Scotland did, or they worked as labourers on the land on the construction of canals, railways or other projects, and were then blown farther on their westward course by intermittent blasts of American depression. With the adoption of a free land policy in the sixties, it was easier for the immigrant to make right away for the frontier, and this he tended to do, whether he was of British or continental stock, always provided that he had enough money for fencing, stock and buildings. The immigrant, therefore, in the first place tended to take over and consolidate the gains already made from the wilderness and helped thereafter to create the wave-like irregular movement which opened up the North American continent.

The British immigrant merged more easily into the American land-scape than did any others; he spoke the language of the country, and economically he fitted fairly easily into his new environment. In industry he could at the lowest level provide unskilled labour, and in the higher reaches he could offer skills which America, from the beginning of the nineteenth century, sorely wanted but could not of itself at first produce. The Industrial Revolution, by now well under way in Britain, had bred a unique expertise among entrepreneurs, managers, operatives and even the navvying grades, as well as making available machinery and capital. As free trade in men and women, as in other elements of industrialism, became fashionable, there set in what was nothing short of a 'brain drain' from Britain to the Continent and to overseas territories. Previously the secrets and the skills of machine production might have to be smuggled out, as in the case of Samuel Slater, the superintendent from Lancashire, who, having memorised the plans of the new English spinning-frames, went to America in 1789, and became a cotton tycoon in Rhode Island and Massachusetts. Now there was a surplus of hand-loom weavers in the United Kingdom, and they swarmed into America to man the new cotton looms in Philadelphia. The exodus of cotton operatives was given fresh impetus by the interruption of raw material supplies caused by the American Civil War, while it was sustained thereafter by the boom in the United States economy, and employers in America took direct measures to attract workers.

The same process can be observed over the whole spectrum of the textile industries. In England there was a large shift in the location of the woollen industry from the south-west to Yorkshire, and many of the workers and employers, since they were in any event doomed to be uprooted, chose to go overseas. The first woollen mills in America were started by English businessmen. Kilmarnock carpet-weavers went *en masse* to Thompsonville in Connecticut in the late twenties, so that it became known as a 'Scottish town'. Free trade in the United Kingdom hit some of the more vulnerable industries very hard; for example, silk manufacture was given a deadly blow by the Cobden Treaty of 1860, whereas America was at the same time giving its infant industry high protection. The result was that after this date the English silk industry was virtually transferred to America; between 1870 and 1893, 1500 workers went from Macclesfield to Paterson, New Jersey. Often the promotion of manufactures in America was deliberately undertaken by British entrepreneurs – as it was in other parts of the world throughout the century – as part of the complex business of exporting capital goods and finding lucrative fields for overseas investment; the seduction of a well-protected market was obvious. Companies engaged in thread-making in Scotland and Northern Ireland set up operations in the United States and sent out supervisors and operators to run the mills. To quote Professor Berthoff: 'All together, as millowners, superinten-dents, overseers, carders, spinners or throwsters, weavers or knitters, dyers or printers, British immigrants formed the strong warp threads of the rising American textile industry.'

Naturally, as American manufacturers bedded down and generated their own expertise, as they did very quickly, the call for British skills became less acute, to a point where in some areas it could be dispensed with altogether. This tendency became more marked as manufacturing processes became more sophisticated and mass production increased. The call now was rather for cheap, unskilled labour and more and more it could be met by immigrants from the continent of Europe – although there was an intervening period when French Canadians took over from the Irish. British labour, although badly needed in the earlier stages, had always had its drawbacks in the eyes of many American employers. In some industries at least there was a positive dislike of it, and especially of English labour. It was efficient but troublesome, the workers being, it was said, 'great sticklers for high wages, small production, and strikes'. There was no doubt that the British immigrant workers were more accustomed to collective industrial action – indeed they might well have been sent out in the first place with the financial backing of their trade unions – and conversely they were less imbued than the native American with the philosophy of individualism. It was natural, there-fore, that they should seek, as they had done at home, to protect their livelihood by restrictive practices of various sorts. One or two of the British trade unions even set up branches in the United States and kept them in existence until well into the twentieth century; and it was to British trade unionism that the American unions looked for their models and for their leadership, not to continental Europe.

The resentment of British and even of European labour, as demon-strated by the unsuccessful experiment of importing Chinese labour, was not by any means entirely the fault of the immigrants. It was strong in the heavy industries, and the American employer in, for example, steel working embodied many of the capitalists' worst features – the merciless exploitation of labour, the suppression, by force if necessary, of trade unionism and so on. Even in this sector, however, British workers were essential. In the iron and steel industries the demand for British skills was more clamant than in most other trades; after all, Britain in the first half of the century was the power-house of technological knowledge. As late as 1890 some 15,000 British-born workers, or about one-tenth of the labour force, were engaged in iron and steel production.

Coal-mining relied heavily on miners from Britain, especially from Wales, for the two good reasons that, first, they were available – this was one of the industries where redundancy at home was countered by the trade unions subsidising emigration of their members – and, secondly, the kind of coal extracted in the United States until 1869 was mainly anthracite, of which Wales had a near-monopoly. Even ten years later it was said that the mining population of the United States was almost wholly 'foreign', and principally from England and Wales, although there were considerable pockets of Irish and German. As in textile manufacturing, they were increasingly replaced in the last quarter of the century by continental Europeans and were afterwards to be found more frequently among the supervisory and managerial grades.

The impact of immigration was, of course, not merely material. It could not be, since the impulses behind it were a blend of economic, social and political aspirations, together with the undefinable urge to go somewhere else. Not the least of the motives was the wish to break off the shackles of the Old World, which even in a comparatively progressive country like Britain were still strong and yielded slowly and at the expense of much endeavour and sacrifice, to the hammer blows of the reformers. It is therefore a little paradoxical that, when the emigrants went to Australia or to America, they rarely made their mark as revolutionaries. On the contrary, they usually wanted stable institutions, always provided there was freedom of opportunity. So they transferred in great numbers from Canada to the United States. Between 1870 and 1890 Canada took in 1½ million people and lost 2 million to the States. The flow was so marked that it spurred Canada into developing its own hinterland, especially by improving transportation – the Canadian Pacific Railway was completed in 1885 – and by adopting a much more generous land policy. As a result the Canadian prairies were being rapidly opened up at the end of the century and the beginning of the next.

British immigrants did not want an egalitarian society; they were the staunchest exponents of individual freedom, and competition – with all the inequalities this implied – was always the motif in America. An 'establishment' or ruling class evolved as a matter of course from those better endowed with worldly goods, which, even in the newest societies, imposed rigid inhibitions on social conduct. Even in religion, divergence from the norm was frowned on and a clerical hierarchy could be part of an immigrant community which was in its way as intolerant as any in the Old World. It was not unusual, therefore, to have clashes between rival creeds. There were of course many progressive thinkers in the ranks of the immigrants, especially the better educated, and some of the most radical experiments were directly imported, such as Robert Owen's socialistic communities, although the soil could, as in this instance, prove completely uncongenial. Nevertheless, in general, conformity was the rule, and was justified to some extent by the sheer necessity of maintaining solidarity in a strange land. This worked both ways. The immigrant, where (as in America) he broke into an established society, was in a sense alien, even coming from Britain, and might be resented by the old 'colonials'. The immigrant might, depending on his background, be rough and antisocial. He was prone to herd with his own kind, especially if he was of the labouring class, and might find difficulty in adjusting himself to his new circumstances, nor did he always try. The Irish in particular provoked considerable hostility. In mid-century there were far too many of them for easy absorption. Apart from their numerical bulk, they were usually poor; they got the reputation of being addicted to heavy drinking and violence; and they were mostly Catholic in a predominantly Protestant society. They were not alone in their idiosyncrasies, but, tending as they did to a kind of homogeneity, they evoked serious antagonism to the point of inspiring secret societies directed against them. This reaction also took the form of a counter-move towards strict social regulations, and the result was a revival in America, in mid-nineteenth century, of a kind of Puritanism, including a strong temperance drive. This gained ground rapidly after the Civil War and was undoubtedly sparked off by the colonials' response to immigration.

It remains broadly true that the characteristic mark of settlement was the insistence that the individual should be free to make the most of his own potential. Reaction against monopoly in land or business, which showed up in the later nineteenth century in America (as well as in Australia and New Zealand) was completely consistent with this policy. The slow growth of trade unionism in America was in part attributable to it, although the mass importation of cheap labour was a major cause. For the same reason, socialist doctrine, or state regulation, made little headway. Here America offers a contrast to Australia and New Zealand. In America the opportunities for individual enterprise were boundless; as the country was opened up, so it offered new riches, in the form of primary resources and secondary industries. The momentum of development was therefore maintained at increasing pace because of the wealth which was so obviously available, making the country the land of oppor-

tunity *par excellence* and inculcating attitudes – indeed, producing a kind
of civilisation – based on the plenitude of untapped material resources.

The precise manifestations of the social impact of immigrants are
impossible to quantify. It has been suggested that, out of 35 million
U.S. immigrants between 1815 and 1914, 20 million were British; but
this was really a matter of volume. It follows from what has already
been said of its nature that immigration would include a substantial
proportion of fairly well educated people, including professional men,
for the simple reason that education was more advanced in Britain, and
particularly in Scotland, than anywhere else. They imposed their own
inherited culture, or, in the case of America, confirmed it, since British
influence had been paramount there since its first settlement. This was
a factor of incalculable significance. The influence, although very
powerful and pervasive, was also comparatively unobtrusive, especially
where the English – as distinct from Scots, Irish or Welsh – were concerned. 'It is surprising', says Professor Hansen, 'that the English,
who have contributed the most to American culture, have been studied
the least by students of immigration. There is no English–American
historical society, no separate history of the English. Discussions of
English influence in America are invariably confined to the colonial
period and to the legal, economic and social institutions then planted.'
Perhaps it is a little less surprising than might appear; the English
naturally fitted easily into 'Old England' – the first U.S. census in 1790
revealed that 80 per cent of the white population was English and 92 per
cent British – and are by nature perhaps less prone to carry an assertive
nationalism with them than other British races. In any event, the
importance of the English influx can hardly be overestimated. It is an
intriguing thought that the United States, even in the nineteenth century,
might have taken on a different complexion had it not been for the
weight of English immigration – in the eighties alone it reached its peak
of nearly 645,000, and this was merely part of a long and continuous
process of reinforcement – since, especially in the latter part of the
period, there was also a very large influx of Germans, Scandinavians,
Slavs and Italians. But by the time these arrived in bulk, the United
States was so assuredly English that these other races could not, even
if they had wished to, impose their own kind of nationalism, except to a
minor degree. The Irish influx, much of it violently anti-English,
reached its zenith by the time of the Civil War, although it remained
very substantial thereafter; but between 1870 and 1890 the largest
single stream was the English, who outnumbered the Scandinavians and
even the Germans.

Australia offers a very different and very revealing example of the nature and effects of British immigration. Here was a faraway country of which at the start of the century little was known beyond the fact that it was of little apparent value except as an outpost of empire. It was a huge continent, as yet unexplored, and possessed (so far as was recognised at the time) of little or nothing in the way of useful material resources apart from pastoral land. Its situation was therefore analogous to that of the early American coastal settlements and, not surprisingly, the government had little interest in its development and no positive policy beyond the vague idea that the British foothold there should be maintained with the minimum of expense to the British exchequer. The remarkable thing was that the only incentive offered, the avail- ability of free land, should have attracted even a trickle of free colonists. The first group of these came to Sydney in 1793 and by 1830 there were still only 14,000 of them.

Yet, ironically enough, the government was almost wholly respon- sible for the early settlement of Australia. The reason was mainly self- interest, however much it might be dressed up. Convicts had been transported to America since Parliament first enacted the necessary legislation in 1714, but this dumping ground for undesirables had been closed with the declaration of American independence in 1783. The House of Commons accordingly resolved, with a nice mixture of expediency and piety, that 'The plan of establishing a colony of young convicts in some distant part of the globe ... where the climate is healthy and the means of support attainable, is equally agreeable to the dictates of humanity and sound policy, which might prove in the result advantageous both to navigation and commerce.' The first shipload of convicts was sent to Botany Bay in 1788 and in the next thirty years or so 22,000 men and nearly 4,000 women were sent, so that by the end of that period they constituted by far the greater proportion of the white population. Van Diemen's Land (later Tasmania) was used as well as New South Wales, and by 1876 75,000 had been transported to the latter and 28,000 to the former. Altogether between 1788 and 1867, when the system was ended, 137,000 were transported to Australia as a whole.

Transportation should not be condemned out of hand, either as a penal system or as a means of colonisation. In passing it might be noticed that it was never regarded as a grievance by the American colonists, even when they were listing their various grounds for breaking away from Britain. The penalty of transportation was often imposed for breaches of the law which would today be thought comparatively venial.

It has been suggested that perhaps 80 per cent of those transported fell into this category; there was also, however, a hard core of habitual and often violent criminals, and there is no doubt that the appeal of transportation to the British government lay in its convenience as an easy way of getting rid of rogues and other social rejects. Nevertheless, even allowing for its cruelties, including the dreadful rigours of the voyage and the harsh reception at the other end, transportation could, if only by default, represent a more humanitarian and imaginative approach to crime (however crime might be defined) than did incarceration in vile, overcrowded prisons, or execution. It was not on all fours with the slave traffic, which aimed to create a serf class in perpetuity; there were genuine chances to make a fresh start when 'emancipation' was granted, and in course of time a great many of those transported graduated to become respectable members of the community, while at least one became a rich shipowner, and an ex-forger achieved distinction as a lawful artist. It was not uncommon for them to become 'squatters'. Charles Darwin was probably not exaggerating when he said in 1836 that 'by converting vagabonds most useless in one country to useful citizens of another, and thus giving birth to a new and splendid country, it succeeded to a degree unparalleled in history'. Indeed Lord Bathurst thought this process was going too far and asserted in 1826 that transportation was losing its effectiveness as a deterrent.

Apart from those whom society dubbed criminals in the orthodox sense, there were many whose offence it had been to fall foul of the home government, through political or social agitation, which could all too easily be called rank sedition and dealt with as such. There were the Tolpuddle Martyrs or the less famous Scottish Martyrs and many more such from the ranks of the new proletariat. Ireland provided a host of political exiles and the Irish element was very strong in the first half of the century. As late as 1848 members of the Young Ireland Movement were sent to Tasmania and a group of Fenians to Western Australia in 1867. As transportees their gregariousness, which has already been remarked on, was intensified by their being segregated into separate camps because of their alleged special intractability, and certainly they appeared to have presented the governors with formidable problems. Up to the middle of the century the proportion of Irish in the population rose rapidly from one-tenth to one-sixth, of which perhaps one-half were 'assisted' immigrants from the multitudes of Irish paupers. From the forties on, the flow was towards America and of the total immigration to Australia, both assisted and unassisted, between 1860 and 1890, well over a half were English, one-third Irish and the rest Scots.

Transportation, by its size and the fact that it was imposed on an almost empty country, was much more important in Australia than it had been in America. Those transported were not likely to be quiescent in the face of authority, whether it was in Australia or in Britain. Often the challenge would be constructive, since the convicts might simply have been, like the Chartists, agitators against a repressive and unjust order of society. Transportation, however, had an immediate and very practical virtue, from the Australian point of view, in that it provided a source of vigorous labour, which could not be secured by other means, short of importing low-quality coloured labour, which was tried and quickly abandoned. The fact that it was forced labour and therefore to a certain extent wasteful, and that it presented serious difficulties in incorporating it into a comparatively rigid type of society, was more than compensated for in the opinion of the Australian authorities by the overriding advantage that it provided the muscle so desperately required in rough, unbroken territory.

Transportation, therefore, was not wholly bad from the point of view either of those transported, or of Britain, or of Australia. It was bound to be an interim sort of colonisation, but it is significant that the revulsion against it began in Britain. There had always been a pronounced and vocal moral animus to it at home, just as there had been from the outset a genuine distrust of colonisation as a form of exploitation and degradation of native peoples. As a system it was challenged by powerful figures such as Bentham, Romilly and Peel, on various grounds, especially that charity should begin at home and that the modernisation of Britain should embrace reform of the penal code and penal institutions. Their position was reinforced by the advent of colonial reformers who thought it incompatible with their theories of colonial settlement, and in 1834 the South Australia Act, establishing a Crown Colony there, prohibited it.

From then on it was on the way out. The newer colonies, such as Victoria, still demanded this source of labour supply, and the British government was reluctant to abandon the system altogether. As opposition in Australia built up, it looked for other repositories, and South Africa was decided on in 1842 as very suitable. In the event this proved a non-starter, mainly because there was already available an abundance of cheap coloured labour. Neither the British nor the Dutch in the Cape would tolerate it and only one shipload went out, in 1849, which was ultimately diverted to Van Diemen's Land.

Public opinion is moulded by facts as well as theories. The fact here was that free immigration was growing, that the colonies were becoming more viable and self-reliant, and that the onus of responsibility was shifting to the colonial governments, as independence was granted. After 1852 transportation was used only for Western Australia, which insisted on keeping it and which between 1850 and 1868 got close on 10,000 male transportees. It is more than a coincidence that this was also the last colony to be given self-government (1870). With the growth of independence the provinces became more averse to the dumping of Britain's rejects on their shores, and, while they continued to clamour for more immigrants from Britain, they also more and more assumed responsibility for their selection and transport, acting through the Emigration Commission and their own agents in the mother country.

The Wakefield school found in Australia and New Zealand the perfect setting for their methods. The *modus operandi* was the chartered land company and a beginning was made with the South Australia Company (1834). This settlement ran into the usual difficulties, not least the distrustfulness of the imperial government, but by 1840 it boasted a population of 15,000. The same policy was adopted for and gave a much needed injection of growth to New Zealand. Despite the misgivings of the government and the open antagonism of the Church Missionary Society, the New Zealand Land Company was launched and the first contingent arrived in 1840; Lord Durham was a member of the promoting syndicate and Wakefield's brother its leader. In its first year the New Zealand Land Company sent out 1350 people. There were other impulses at work, which were to adulterate the pure doctrine of Wakefield's thesis. In 1847, partly as a result of the Disruption controversy in Scotland, the predominantly Presbyterian settlement of Otago was established, with its own Free Church minister (T. Burns), who became the first Chancellor of Otago University. The fact that a university was so quickly created was an indication of the value placed by Scottish settlers on education, a legacy of their native upbringing, since Scotland at this time was in advance of any country in the world in regard to education. It had also shown itself in Canada – Dalhousie, McGill and Queen's universities – and the United States, although in the latter the first seventeenth-century prototype had been of English design. A similar settlement, with a similar bias, was set up in Canterbury, sponsored by the Church of England.

It was not only the new settlements which benefited from the Wakefield system. New South Wales received 30,000 British immigrants in 1831–40, of whom two-thirds had their passage paid, and in this decade the population of Australia as a whole rose from 70,000 to 190,000, but of this total the larger part consisted of transported persons.

The Aborigines in Australia were of little account in this respect; their numbers diminished with relentless regularity at an average rate of between 600 and 700 a year. It was of little avail that as early as 1837 an Aborigines Protection Society was set up, following a House of Commons' Committee Report which condemned their exploitation.

New Zealand presented a more intractable problem. For the native Maori race, the arrival of the white *pahekas* was nothing short of a disaster. There was trouble from the start, as there had been in America with the Red Indians, over the white encroachment on tribal lands, and this from time to time flared into vicious wars. The earliest casual callers, such as the whalers, brought disease, and the introduction of alcohol, the sale of firearms and the interaction of different and often inferior standards of behaviour were responsible for a grave physical and moral deterioration in the native population. The worst premonitions of the missionaries were in fact all too vividly fulfilled. As regards their lands, the Maoris proved more resistant than the Australian Aborigines or even the American Indians. The Treaty of Waitangi (1840) was an attempt to reassure them, by confirming the signatory chiefs in the possession of their ancestral domains, except for what had been bought up by the New Zealand Land Company, and by reserving to the imperial government the right of pre-emption. When self-government was afforded to the colony in 1852, the imperial government relinquished effective control over the waste lands, subject to minor qualifications, and the colonial legislature's Native Land Act ten years later opened the floodgates to the colonists' territorial ambitions. Land was disposed of with irresponsible haste, so that by 1892, when governmental right of pre-emption was reintroduced, the Maori race had lost the great bulk of its territory, except for some 4 million acres of inferior quality. 'Squattocracy' had taken over. Much of the great wealth of forests was also dissipated, for quick profits and through thoughtlessness.

The discovery of gold in Australia in 1851 and in New Zealand in the following decade introduced a new element into the colonial population, as it did in South Africa. There was a dramatic rise in the total. Up to 1850 it was only 400,000, and Australia seemed likely to remain a pastoral country. In the next ten years it shot up to 740,000. What was more, many of the immigrants were of a different type from their predecessors, possessed of a quite exceptional degree of dynamism. This drove them first to the goldfields and then, as the opportunities there faded, they left the country altogether or proceeded to create a more mixed kind of economy. The intake still remained almost exclusively British, as a matter of deliberate policy, and at the end of the century not less than 95 per cent were of British descent.

The settlement of tropical Australia by the British presents unusual features. It started with the discovery of gold, and, as other enterprises were introduced, *kanakas* were brought in to do the rough work, especially in the sugar plantations. As the diversification of the economy progressed, higher standards were demanded, the importation of *kanaka* labour was barred and the territory deliberately relied on self-reproduction of the white race, but still more on immigration; between 1870 and 1890 this accounted for almost 90 per cent of the total net increase in Queensland. This could not have been achieved without great advances in tropical medicine. The outcome was a kind of settlement which had no parallel elsewhere and has been described as 'the greatest tropical colony of white men in the world'.

With the development of the economy went a change in social and political attitudes. In Australia and New Zealand much of the land had been concentrated in comparatively few hands, with the result that, as the century wore on, the immigrants often found it difficult to get employment. Unlike the situation in America, the opportunities for self-advancement were limited because of the fewness of natural resources. The settlements, too, were isolated to a degree that Canada, bordering on a great country nurtured on *laissez faire*, was not. They were therefore both free and compelled to find their own solutions to their own problems. This took the form of a high degree of *étatisme*, state regulation, to an extent which would have been anathema to America, and which even in Britain was commanding acceptance more slowly. Socialism in the Marxist sense made little headway, but a powerful labour movement, political and industrial, grew up early in both Australia and New Zealand, with a close working relationship with the state in such matters as industrial relations. Protection in various forms made an appeal to various classes, including not only fiscal safeguards – at a time when the mother country was still committed to free trade – but strict control of immigration even from Britain.

It is obvious from this sketch that the consequences of emigration from Britain in the nineteenth century cannot be assessed in material terms. Indeed, they were so momentous and so many-sided that it would be absurd to attempt an assessment at all. The mass export of people, which meant the export of labour, skills and capital, was a pre-condition of the development of new countries, and Britain's share in this process was utterly out of proportion to its own insignificant size. Without it there would have been no British Empire or Commonwealth, and, while one can only speculate on what would have happened if Britain had not been in a position to provide the settlers in this period, certainly the development of Canada, Australia and New Zealand in particular would have taken much longer to achieve and their national characters would have taken a completely different form. But it was much more than a matter of empire. It is estimated that the total world population of British stock around the mid-twentieth century was about 140 million. Of this total more than half was in the United States, as compared with about one-third in the British Isles. The 'special relationship' between Britain and the United States has therefore a much deeper explanation than political expediency, having its roots in a common cultural tradition. The British 'take-over' in Canada, Australia and New Zealand created a new and permanent balance of forces. It has been said that British emigration was 'physically the most remarkable phenomenon in British history'. It was much more, for it radically altered the history of the world.

SUGGESTIONS FOR FURTHER READING

European emigration is put in its world context in chapter iii of W. Woodruff, *Impact of Western Man* (1966). Volume ii of the *Cambridge History of the British Empire* (1940) has a section on British emigration policies. There are standard works, notably W. A. Carrothers, *Emigration from the British Isles* (1965) and C. E. Carrington, *The British Overseas* (1968). There are also studies of special categories of emigration, especially that to America, including S. C. Johnson, *History of Emigration from the United Kingdom to North America, 1763–1912* (1913) and H. Cowan, *British Immigration to British North America* (1961). Brinley Thomas in his *Migration and Economic Growth* (1954) examines the economic implications of the cross-Atlantic movement and *The Economics of International Migration* (1958) edited by the same author has useful references. There is a detailed case-study of the interaction of emigration and investment in D. S. Macmillan, *Scotland and Australia, 1788–1850* (1967). For Australia and New Zealand the subject in general has not been so well served, although P. D. Phillips and G. L. Wood, *The Peopling of Australia* (1928) sketches the background and there is interesting material in the *Australian Encyclopaedia* (1965). Much information can, however, be obtained from the histories of development in these countries: for example, B. Fitzpatrick, *The British Empire in Australia* (1949) and J. B. Condliffe, *New Zealand in the Making* (1959), while V. D. Pike, *Paradise of Dissent* (1957) examines a formative stage in the growth of South Australia. The impact of the emigrant on the receiving country has received less attention than it deserves, but two outstanding works in this field are M. L. Hansen, *The Immigrant in American History* (1942) and R. T. Berthoff, *British Immigrants in Industrial America, 1790–1950* (1953).

4. The Rise and Fall of Free Trade

KENNETH FIELDEN

BY the later nineteenth century an overseas visitor could make a Free Trade pilgrimage round Manchester. He might begin with the Free Trade Hall, opened in its permanent form in 1856, replacing a building of 1843 which, together with an earlier wooden structure, had witnessed so many great Anti-Corn-Law League meetings, the patient arguments of Richard Cobden, the fulminations of John Bright. The Hall, a kind of monument to the League, had become the home of Manchester's music. Distinguished foreign musicians playing with Sir Charles Hallé's Orchestra might wonder at the strength of an economic principle which attached its name to a city's main concert hall. A few moments' walk away, in Albert Square, towered from 1877 Alfred Waterhouse's enormous neo-gothic Town Hall, symbolising the municipal pride of a city whose incorporation had formed a part of Richard Cobden's life work as well as Corn Law repeal. The square itself contained a monument to Prince Albert, 'architect' of the Exhibition of 1851, the confident emporium of the free-trading Workshop of the World, and eventually statues of Mr Gladstone, who completed the Free Trade edifice, and John Bright, the Rochdale cotton manufacturer whose name stood second only to Cobden's in the public memory of the Corn Law controversy. Cobden's own statue was a further short walk away in St Anne's Square, where rose, in time, the giant bulk of the final version of the Royal Exchange – the 'High Change' of the cotton merchants – on the site of Newall's Buildings, the League's Manchester offices.

The League proudly designated Manchester its Jerusalem, its Mecca. Following Corn Law repeal and Peel's budgets, when Britain seemed assuredly Free Trade, Richard Cobden confidently expected the whole world would speedily acknowledge the new shrine. In August 1846 he embarked on a missionary tour in Europe. He wrote:

> I am going on a private agitating tour. The other day I got an intimation from . . . a . . . confidant of the Emperor of Russia – that I should have great influence with him if I went to St Petersburg. Today I get a letter from the Mayor of Bordeaux, written at Paris after dining at Duchatel's the French Minister, conveying a sugges-

tion from the latter that I should . . . visit the King of the French. . . .
I have had similar hints respecting Madrid, Vienna and Berlin. Well,
I will . . . visit all the large states of Europe, see their potentates or
statesmen and endeavour to enforce those truths which have been
irresistible at home. . . . I am impelled to this step by an instinctive
emotion such as never deceived me.[1]

In France he met King Louis-Philippe and his first taste of disen-
chantment: 'I came away with the impression that the King did not
like the close discussion of the Free Trade question.' Cobden was
genuinely surprised: 'It is difficult, however, to conceive that a man of
his sagacity and knowledge can be blind to the importance of these
principles . . .' He visited Spain, the Italian states, Austria, Saxony,
Prussia, Russia, meeting welcoming banquets and speeches from Free
Traders. He buttonholed statesmen, Metternich in Vienna, Nesselrode
in Russia, even Pius IX, who professed sympathy with Free Trade, 'but
modestly added he could do but little'. A year later the naturally
optimistic Cobden returned home disillusioned, convinced there was
much ignorance of 'sound principles' in Europe, much uninterest
among statesmen, and no likelihood of immediate conversion to
Manchester's dogmas.[2]

Manchester's name was not synonymous with Free Trade for nothing.
It was the centre of the British cotton industry, the commercial centre
for the Lancashire mill towns. Cotton dramatised the forces pointing
Britain towards a liberal overseas trading policy. Cotton was increasingly and truly mechanised and industrialised even, though its machinery
was simple and its organisation uncomplex by later standards. Industrialised first in spinning, then weaving, by 1840 three-fourths of its
power was steam. Mechanisation, the rationalisation of production in
large factories, led to an enormous expansion and cheapening of the
product, the industry playing a central role in overseas trade. It imported
its raw material, some 450 million lb a year by 1840, and its production
far outstripped home demand, half being exported annually, a percentage
constantly growing. Between 1815 and the mid-forties cotton contributed
in the region of 45–50 per cent of British exports annually. With every
decade its manufacturers were more committed to overseas outlets,
beyond Europe and the United States, in Latin America and the Far
East; its army of workers focused the problem – not in mid-century
acute, but growing – of the relationship between the demand for food
and the capacities of home sources of supply, for a population rising by
over 2 million each decade.

Cotton illustrated a wider trend. Domestic exports contributed 10 per cent of national income after 1815, 22·5 per cent by the mid-seventies, large by other nations' standards, and they tended to grow more rapidly than national income as a whole. They were especially important to those industries leading early and mid-century industrialisation, iron and steel, for example, besides cotton. The stimulus of overseas markets was very significant in the process of continued industrialisation. Britain was too small for vast solitary industrialisation, too limited in demand, and in some types of material endowments. She needed markets, raw materials, prospectively food. As the century advanced she invested much capital abroad, especially in primary-producing lands, in general terms using her own wealth to provide for her needs and create demand for her products. Britain had to import, export and, since she increasingly imported in excess of exports in goods, to sell her services as shipper, insurer, broker, to provide a surplus. As trader and servant of others' trade her interests seemingly demanded, ever more, a well-lubricated and extensive flow of trade, as little as possible at the mercy of artificial disruption.

Cobden's initial confidence that Europe would adopt Free Trade was not simply ex-calico-printer's prejudice, but sprang from a strong, widely shared conviction that the teachings of contemporary, orthodox, British economists, including Free Trade, were scientifically exact, universally applicable and demanded assent. Yet Free Trade was a recent doctrine. Earlier centuries had not doubted the propriety of central authorities or corporate bodies, such as guilds, supervising production, quality, wages, training, or that governments should control external trade for fiscal purposes and to promote the general good as they understood it.

In the sixteenth and seventeenth centuries the emergent nation-states, Spain, Portugal, Holland, France, England, the former first, the latter following, extended their contacts with the non-European world, began trading with Asia and creating empires in the Far East and America. They desired to extend employment, develop trade and cease being purely agrarian. They believed colonies desirable for the production of commodities unavailable domestically, for home use or re-export. They wished to avoid adverse trading balances with other states that would drain away bullion, often regarded as the true source of wealth, to foreigners. All these factors, inextricably mingled, amid dynastic and religious wars and touchy national awareness, with considerations of warlike strength, led the States to create highly restrictive, state-supervised, colonial and commercial systems.

No two states acted alike, but there was similarity. The Iberian states' systems came first, the English and French in the later seventeenth century, reacting against Dutch commercial power. England's Navigation Laws (1651 and from 1660) came to require all imports into the colonies to travel in English or colonial vessels, largely native manned, irrespective of the goods' origin. 'Enumerated' colonial products – sugar, cotton, ginger, indigo, tobacco and others – could be sent only to England or other colonies, and all European goods had to go via England to her colonies. The aim was English dominance of colonial trade and the cornering of as much as possible of the valuable re-export trade in colonial goods. Systems gave preferences to colonial goods at home and bounties for producing especially desirable commodities. Some restricted colonial trade to given home ports. Privileged trading companies flourished. The shipping requirements most clearly linked the systems to power considerations: merchant fleets were nurseries of battle fleets. War was an instrument of commercial policy, for seizing rivals' trade and colonies. Few wars were wholly commercial, but few, say, of England's between 1660 and 1815 were devoid of commercial intent, against Holland, then France in the Caribbean, America, India. Spain and Portugal had theoretically the most rigid systems, by the eighteenth century dented by those powers' weakness. The Dutch eased theirs in the Caribbean in the same century, seeking to enrich their small islands by making them free ports. France was often stricter than England. Within Europe the states sought to feed themselves as much as possible and raised tariff barriers, partly for revenue – especially war revenue – reasons. Barriers tended to grow, even to prohibitive heights, in the eighteenth century as tender young manufactures were protected. Only bilateral commercial treaties eased the system in places. Within the systems western Europe prospered. British trade grew greatly by earlier standards, creating mercantile wealth, business organisation and expertise, while overseas, especially colonial, markets contributed, with many domestic factors, to the stimulation of industrial change.

The later eighteenth century questioned these systems. 'Mercantilist' thought was not static. As commerce grew complex, consideration was given to the nature of wealth, prices, money, trade, among other topics. European society was changing. In England, for example, the growing self-confidence of the middle-rank, landed and mercantile classes, their chafing at religious, economic, political systems imposed by Stuart monarchs, produced successful demands, focused on the struggle of King and Parliament, for greater individual, political, religious, economic freedom. Concurrently, philosophies developed concerned with the individual, his characteristics, rights, needs, his relationship to 'civil society', exemplified in England by Locke, and finding widespread acceptance in the eighteenth-century France of the *philosophes*. Such philosophies, backed by a belief in a 'natural order', a belief partly philosophical, partly derived by analogy with the 'natural order' revealed by physical science, in which the constituent elements of nature were found in their characteristics and functions not self-destructive, but tending to constitute the good of the whole, came to bear on economic thought. They suggested a belief that the best way to maximise economic good, economic development, was to allow each individual, seen as an 'economic being', a making, trading being, to pursue his own best economic path as dictated by enlightened self-interest, without artificial obstructions, since enlightened self-interest could not be self-defeating as it would be if it failed finally to produce the good of the whole of which the individual formed part. The 'invisible hand', latent in all natural order, whether providential or (in economics) the result of the mechanics of the market, of supply and demand, would ensure this. Labour, seen as the source of all value (a sign of the economic interests of a society turning slowly towards industry and less simply commercial), would become divided, since individuals (or states) if unrestricted intercourse were allowed, would concentrate on what their capacities and endowments indicated as most profitable, this being the most productive use of labour, resulting in a mutually beneficial interdependence based squarely on self-interest.

Such attitudes informed Adam Smith's *An Inquiry into the Wealth of Nations* (1776). Smith vigorously attacked Britain's own commercial system and by implication others'. 'Classical Economics' as the new 'science' was eventually named, was concerned with far more than economic policy alone, investigating all sides of economic activity, production, distribution, exchange, finance. Nor, conversely, did it totally deny the State a role in economic life – it might act where no individual could profit in doing so, in education, building roads, canals, harbours, besides justice and defence. But its effects on international commerce concern us, and although Smith admitted value (partly strategic) in the Navigation Laws, in this field their drift was clearly *laissez faire*.

Attacks on commercial restriction came from elsewhere. The French Physiocrats, notably François Quesnay (1694–1774), predating Smith, also believed in natural order, holding that only agriculture could produce surplus new wealth. They sought to free agriculture from restrictions, both 'feudal' tenurial obligations and restrictions on the free flow of produce within France, to encourage its expansion. Commerce and industry received the same freedom almost from indifference.

Spain also produced distinguished writers, partly derivative, and Italy. This current had its influence on some European governments, in the way of liberalising internal trade and industry and the opening of overseas trade to wider participation among their own subjects. Tuscany, Lombardy and Spain, where decrees of 1765 and 1778 opened trade to most of Spanish America, breaking the monopolies of Cadiz and Seville, and where some corporate restrictions on industry vanished – if tariffs were little affected – displayed this.

English restrictions on individual capitalist action in the internal economy had long been weakening piecemeal, attacked by 'improving' landlords and the mercantile and manufacturing classes. After the 1707 Scottish Union, Britain formed Europe's largest internal Free Trade area. Externally events questioned the old structures concurrently with the new thinking. Not only the American Revolution required the reconstruction of the Colonial System, but the early stages of the Industrial Revolution began to point towards future conditions. By 1803 cottons were already Britain's largest export. The demand for raw cotton, increasingly from America, and the West Indies' failure to provide raw cotton on a large scale, the wide acceptance of the manufactured product in Europe, America, eventually South America and farther afield, the lack of a real European competitor, the growing self-confidence, the certainty of expanding trade, produced a developing irritation at restrictional structures. After 1815 it was only a question of time before the other industries in which Britain excelled began to metamorphose their views as well.

Smith's ideas rapidly gained respectability. Pitt the Younger and Shelburne called themselves his disciples, and freer overseas trade had a false British dawn when Pitt, pursuing wider fiscal reforms, tentatively liberalised the trading structure, notably in the 1786 French Commercial Treaty. Yet Pitt's discipleship was limited and, within six years of the Treaty's operation, hostilities ended it, bringing both economic warfare and higher tariffs still to meet wartime revenue needs. The British tariff of 1815 was harsher than the eighteenth century's. In that year, too, the final great Corn Law excluded foreign wheat until home prices reached 80 shillings per quarter.

Smith's successors, the Classical Economists, David Ricardo (*On the Principles of Political Economy*, 1817) being the most distinguished, and including James Mill, T. R. Malthus, R. Torrens, Nassau Senior, J. R. McCulloch, were not doctrinally unanimous. Disagreements could be severe. Yet on free enterprise and anti-mercantilism they concurred. By 1820 these views were increasingly normative among businessmen and manufacturers, and in political circles, in the Whig Party, middle-class radicalism, among Benthamites, and even 'liberal' Tories. Frederick Robinson piloting the 1815 Corn Law through the Commons had misgivings on its validity. But theory could vanish before interest and fear. The Corn Law passed easily. It was in the next twenty years that the practical application of the new science to trade approached orthodoxy.

Britain liberalised her overseas trade by degrees. The confident trading of the early twenties allowed Robinson and William Huskisson to reduce duties in 1824-5, costing the Exchequer £4·1 million a year, to reshape the colonial system to one of imperial preference, abolishing many prohibitions, to alter the Corn Laws to a sliding scale, and to negotiate Reciprocity Treaties with some nine European and many South American states. In 1830, however, the tariff remained high, and the thirties concentrating on political and social reform and experiencing Whig financial ineptitude formed a hiatus in change. The acute depression of the late thirties, poor harvests, the unrest highlighted by Chartists and Anti-Corn-Law Leaguers, the 1840 Report (doctored by economist Board of Trade officials towards Free Trade) of the Select Committee on Import Duties, the growing fear of foreign retaliation, the belief that a majority of manufacturers now demanded change, his own desire to rationalise, administratively, fiscal policy and the tariff, all helped Peel, in his 1841 Ministry, to essay reforms. He began comparatively cautiously in the 1842 budget, then more energetically, especially in 1845 when 450 duties vanished and others were lowered, culminating, faced with the imperatives of Irish famine, in Corn Law repeal in 1846. Gradually imperial preferences were whittled down. In 1849 the Whigs repealed the Navigation Laws, in 1854 even opening British coastal trade. Gladstone's budgets of the 1850s, more especially 1860, in conjunction with the Cobden Treaty left little to be done later in the 1860s. In 1848 Britain had 1146 dutiable articles; by 1860 she had forty-eight, all but twelve being revenue duties on luxuries or semi-luxuries. Once the most complex in Europe, the British tariff could now be printed 'on half a page of Whitaker's Almanack'.

Yet the home of Classical Economics adopted Free Trade painfully slowly: eighty-four years from *The Wealth of Nations* to Gladstone's 1860 budget; thirty-one from Waterloo to the ritual victory of 1846.

Some difficulties were technical. Tariffs were central in national finance, in 1830 supplying over 40 per cent of revenue. Until Peel in 1842 regrasped the Income Tax nettle dropped in 1816, how to replace high tariffs as a money-spinner, at least until a rationalised revenue tariff could prove its fiscal effectiveness, was always a question. This factor was world-wide. The ubiquitous unwillingness to shoulder Income Taxes frequently inhibited tariff reductions.

Delay chiefly came, however, from the intertwining of commercial policy with the painful readjustments of an industrialising society and the consequent conflicts of class, interest, opinion. The 1815 Corn Law – passed to protect in peacetime an agriculture accustomed to war prices and inflated acreage – spotlighted this. For although in 1815 it contributed but a third of national income and employment, as food supplier and source of the rents of gentry and aristocracy, agriculture was socially crucial. No other group, not even the West Indian sugar planters, with an interest in preferences or protection, could match it. Free Trade would not only seemingly 'demote' agriculture, by implying ultimate reliance on foreign food, it would constitute, many asserted, a direct threat to the economic basis and so to the social and political ascendancy of the traditionally dominant classes. Cobden and Bright gloried in this, and although some great landowners had diverse economic concerns, here was why the Corn Law battle turned apocalyptic. Manufacturers wishing to end duties on raw materials, exporters in Britain's strongest industries – others were less keen – seemed set to gain most. But would working men gain anything? Some publicists seemed to imply that free markets would expand British trade not only by putting exchange into foreigners' hands, but also by lowering food prices and so wages and production costs. Many working-class radicals and Chartists came to see Free Trade as millowning rapacity, especially as it was inevitably linked intellectually to general domestic economic liberalism, not just in the final lifting of ancient state and corporate oversight of economic life, but the whole gamut of *laissez faire*: hostility to factory legislation, trade unions and state intervention in urban squalor, sympathy with the aims of the 1834 Poor Law. Even if Classical Economists were not rigid on these matters, and Cobden supported state education and the regulation of child employment, 'Manchester' businessmen were rarely associated in working-class minds with rural or religious paternalism, let alone Owenite socialism.

Abroad also, reorientation was imperative. Mercantilists linked wealth, commerce, empire, war. Should Britain now follow extreme Free Traders and adopt external policies relying on the beneficial action of free commerce to bind nations in 'peaceful fetters' of interdependence and abandon a 'balance of power' foreign policy? Should she, once the Old Colonial System vanished, logically free her settlement colonies politically, to become like the United States ideal trading partners on the basis of exchanging manufactures and primary produce, without defence and administrative costs? Should she rely exclusively on competitive capacity to secure markets and limit her influence to her trade's reach? Only extremists answered affirmatively without quali- fication. Virtually all allowed the government's right to extend the area of free commercial competition by peaceful persuasion and negotiation. The legitimacy of violence and the further annexation of territory was disputed. With no final decision, most men stood nearer Palmerston than Cobden. All this rethinking at home and, much more, abroad was hard to separate from British nationalism: 'Not a bale of merchandise leaves *our* shores, but it bears the seeds of intelligence and fruitful thought to the members of some less enlightened community; not a merchant visits *our* seats of manufacturing industry, but he returns to his own country the missionary of freedom . . .' So wrote the sincere internationalist Cobden, rejoicing to see, through free commerce, 'ameliorations bestowed by the hands of Britain upon her less instructed neighbours'.[3]

Similarly, nowhere was Free Trade propagated in laboratory condi- tions. It emanated from a Britain of great pre-eminence in industrialisa- tion, trade, finance. It was propagated into a Europe of existing states, national, supra-national, infra-national, of international rivalries, of gropings for national unity often thwarted, of conservatism and radi- calism in the afterglare of the French Revolution, of varied economic conditions and interests, of differing governmental traditions. A Europe where on the level of political decision commercial policies were conditioned not only by theory and strivings for prosperity and develop- ment but by internal and external political pressures, by a state's freedom of action or lack of it, and by varied responsiveness among governments to economic factors alone, few in the first half-century reaching the Manchester School's level of openly economically deter- mined politics.

Frenchmen, for example, smarted under recent defeats, still explored the implications of 1789, were deeply conscious of being French and sought prosperity in a land still heavily agrarian. Germans, split into thirty-nine states, recalled their 'national' war against France, were ruled by conservative dynasties looking twice at any disturbing influence, whether revolutionary students or machines. Most great powers eyed Britain and from 1830 France as dangerous in their comparative liberalism – a political liberality which clung around economic liberal- ism. In national terms Austrians ruled Italians, Magyars, assorted Slavs; Russians ruled Poles. Tariff policies could help forge a nation, defeat a political rival, soothe or irritate diplomacy. Above all, Free

Trade could rarely be disassociated from British pre-eminence and patronage. Free Traders, especially in the political sphere, necessarily kept one eye cocked at Britain. In the 1840s and 1850s, in Germany, political Free Trade even found a leader in a Prussianised English merchant resident in Berlin, John Prince Smith, an exponent of the full Cobdenite doctrine of Free Trade and world peace. Western European states wished to emulate Britain industrially; at least their middle classes did. Once Free Trading, Britain's prosperity still advanced: perhaps her policy should also be copied. British trade with Europe itself stimulated industrialisation, creating new demands, acting as a channel for disseminating British technology. Yet there was profound ambiguity both in the commercial strength and commercial policy of Britain. Both smacked of nationalism. Many saw in them a joint threat of British hegemony.

Cobden, before his 'missionary' travels, might usefully have considered some words from the German economic writer Friedrich List's *National System of Political Economy* of 1840:

> How vain do the efforts of those appear to us who have striven to found their universal dominion on military power compared with the attempt of England to raise her entire territory into one immense manufacturing, commercial and maritime city and to become among the countries and kingdoms of the earth that which a great city is in relation to its surrounding territory. . . . A world's metropolis which supplies all nations with manufactured goods and supplies herself in exchange from every nation with those raw materials and agricultural products . . . which each other nation is fitted to yield her – a treasure house of all great capital – a banking establishment for all nations. . . . The world has not been hindered in its progress but immeasurably aided in it by England. . . . But ought we on that account to wish that she may erect a universal dominion on the ruins of other nationalities? Nothing but unfathomable cosmopolitanism or shopkeeper's narrow mindedness can give an assenting answer. . . . At this time more than one nation is qualified to strive to attain to the highest degree of civilization, wealth, and power.

But not via Free Trade. Rather, List pointed to Britain's protective past: 'It is a very common clever device that when anyone has attained the summit of greatness, he kicks away the ladder . . .'[4]

Outside Europe List's apprehensions found relevance: 'The doctrine of Free Trade is not science but cant, and cant of that kind which is meant to fill the pockets of its originators at the expense of its dupes . . . Let us beware being bled to death . . . to fill the pockets of an oligarchy which treads down Englishmen as it does Irishmen when they stand in its way.' Thus the colonial journalism of David Syme in the Melbourne *Age* in 1860.[5]

Perhaps beyond Europe apprehensions might be magnified, for it was in peripheral areas, especially the newly developing or emerging areas, that the imperious pull of Britain's and, as she gradually industrialised, Western Europe's economy as a whole was most keenly felt. As European communications by road, canal and, by mid-century, rail improved, as sailing ships reached new heights of efficiency and even in peripheral lands communications advanced, the world's economies became gradually more interlocked. Even in the first half of the century, international trade payments were made increasingly on a complicated multilateral basis, less bilaterally or regionally, a development coming to fruition later in the century. Non-European tariffs were inevitably influenced as they became part of a Europe-centred economy of imbalanced strength. Yet local conditions, not all simply economic, mattered. The United States had to decide her place in the world economy, whether to industrialise seeking self-sufficiency, or to act as a feeder to Europe, but in so doing she faced fundamental questions on the nature of her society and Union, for Southern slavery was implicated. Commercial policy involved all this. Canadians had to decide whether they had an independent economy and, indivisible from this, whether they were one nation, two or none. Latin American states, freeing themselves from Spain, faced similar problems, finding themselves the objects of great British interest as markets. But unlike North America they were politically weak. It was debatable whether they would be allowed to decide their own policies. Even more doubtful were decaying Empires such as Turkey, or lands only just and unwillingly opening themselves to European traders, such as China and Japan, unindustrialised, with governments not thinking within Western conventions. Here, almost as much as within existing colonial empires, or areas without governments Europeans could fully recognise, as in much of Africa, the response to Free Trade might be determined by the decisions of Europeans, especially Britons, based on deliberations over the exact relationship of Free Trade and national interest. Could Free Trade be imposed?

Free Trade did have an independent life as part of an intellectual system. The Classical Economists had European followers, not least in France where J. B. Say (1767–1832), who regarded himself as Smith's interpreter (though dissenting on several topics), and later the populariser Frédéric Bastiat were among the best known. Many German universities opened their doors to Free Trade teachings. At Göttingen, Halle and

Königsberg *The Wealth of Nations* was expounded even before 1800, influencing many students later important in early-nineteenth-century Prussian administration. Ricardo, too, found his German disciples later. Everywhere, as in Britain, Classical Economic doctrines gained an audience from those seeking to remake economies on capitalist lines by their teaching an internal *laissez faire*: equally, encountering suspicion from conservatives, and, on the left, from early socialism.

In fact by 1870, generally, tariff levels had distinctly fallen. Some European states felt the pull of economic forces similar to those affecting Britain, especially Belgium, the only European state proportionately to its size keeping almost in step with Britain's own industrialisation. She repealed her Corn Laws in 1850. Other than Britain, the second and third trading powers, France and the United States were particularly significant in their tariff policies. France and a state-in-the-making, Germany, displayed well the variety of forces making for lower European tariffs by the sixties.

In Germany, with its strong tradition of state economic activity, economic policy was inseparable from nationalism, unification and the shape unification should take, whether a liberal Germany as middle-class nationalists desired or one forged by either of the major German states, Prussia and Austria, both conservative. A confederation of thirty-nine states, Germany, still heavily agricultural, was pitted with customs barriers and river tolls, possessed an agriculture still encumbered with 'feudal' obligations and restrictions and a commerce and industry with corporate sanctions. Development demanded change: 'Thirty-eight customs boundaries', ran a merchants' petition at Frankfurt am Main in 1819, 'cripple internal trade and produce much the same effect as ligatures which prevent the free circulation of the blood.'[6]

In the twenties, following the promulgation of Europe's most liberal tariff (aiming at balancing protection against Britain, together with revenue, against a minimum of smuggling), Prussia emerged as leader of moves towards economic unity. The slow creation, from 1819, of the Prussian Customs Union (Zollverein), watched nervously from Vienna, produced counter-unions of varying duration among southern and middle German states, motivated both by political apprehensions and economic differences. When fully effective in 1834 the Zollverein already contained eighteen states and 23·5 million people. Some states stayed out because overseas trading traditions made fiscal independence and low tariffs valuable, as the Hanse Towns; some, like the north-east German states, as grain exporters thinking of the reactions of their customers, including Britain. By the 1840s, partly through protectionist pressure, Zollverein tariffs rose. Within Germany Free Trade pressure came from agriculture, still exporting, especially in the east, from merchants and overseas traders. Protectionism attracted the newer industries of the Prussian Rhineland, Silesia and the southern states, especially cotton, iron and steel, though not unanimously. Protection gained intellectual defences. 'Romantic' economists, such as Adam Müller (1779–1829), upholding an organic state, condemned Classical Economics as disintegrating society. Idealising the Middle Ages they had misgivings on industry and capitalism. List did not. Advocating both national economic unity and capitalist organisation, he travelled far with Classical Economics. Yet he upheld nations as *the* economic units, and though accepting Free Trade in situations of equality believed states newly essaying industrialisation had the right to protect 'infant industries' in the interests of national wealth. This became the stock popularising argument of contemporary economic nationalism.

After 1850 Austria and Prussia fought it out for economic mastery in Germany. Austria made more than one attempt to form wider customs unions including herself and the Zollverein. But she was still economically backward, ultra-conservative, protectionist. She made fiscal concessions, but Prussia's aim, following her political humiliations in the wake of the 1848 Revolutions, and despite Austria's attractions as a market for manufactures, was Austria's exclusion. The entry of some Free Trading states into the Zollverein (Hanover, for example), the generally low tariff leanings of agriculture, perhaps the need for British equipment in the final burst of industrialisation, genuine Free Traders in Prussia's administration, Bismarck's willingness after his accession to power to placate the Prussian National Liberals whose support he needed and who included Free Traders, all this tended to lower tariffs: but Prussia's gaze was on Austria. In 1862 – following the Cobden Treaty – a liberal commercial treaty was negotiated with France, Bismarck making its acceptance by all members a condition of renewing the Zollverein in 1865. Finally, despite much dissent in the south for economic reasons, the members yielded, definitively excluding Austria, an exclusion the Seven Weeks' War ratified politically. Once established, the Zollverein tariff's downward trend continued and was maintained after 1870. Iron and steel duties were reduced in 1870, and in 1873 it was proposed to end almost all iron and steel duties by January 1877. The German Empire began its course well on the Free Trade road.

If two states' rivalry helped indicate low Zollverein tariffs, the appraisement of international relations assisted a parallel movement in France. Restoration France, reduced to her own frontiers, weary, supremely distrustful of British material power and ambitions, under-estimated her potential and maintained high protection, indeed pro-hibition, both at home and colonially. Cereal producers, cattle and sheep breeders, iron masters, textile manufacturers, all, for varying reasons, demanded high protection, obtained in 1816–18, and suffered only mild tamperings, however much academic economists and some industrialists criticised, before the fifties. Economic development, slowish by British standards, there was, but politically opinion was rigid. When Napoleon III, formerly resident in England, eager to promote economic develop-ment and social advance, not uninfluenced by Free Traders in his administration, sought to reduce duties (he actually managed small reductions on iron and steel, wool, some foodstuffs, by decree), he met insurmountable opposition in his legislature, especially in 1856 in seeking to remove prohibitions generally, and again in 1859.

Surmounting this obstacle initiated the century's biggest burst of tariff reductions. Diverse strands wove the 'Cobden' Treaty. By the 1852 Constitution the Emperor could negotiate commercial treaties having legal force without legislative agreement. In late 1859 Anglo-French relations were strained. Old British distrust of Napoleon, high-lighted by his Italian activities, and a scare that France was stealing a march in ironclad warships, contributed to this, yet neither sought total rupture. Against this background a private sounding of Napoleon on a Commercial Treaty by Cobden, following suggestions by the French Free Trader Michel Chevalier, was transformed into an official negotia-tion. Pacification was Cobden's aim, even more than trade. In London, Gladstone at the Exchequer, seeking to use a chance surplus further to reduce duties, assented. Palmerston and Russell, like Napoleon, had mixed motives. Napoleon mixed a desire for tariff liberalisation (out-flanking his legislature) with a hope that Britain would be compliant in Italy. The treaty (January 1860) removed French prohibitions on British goods and lowered other duties. Britain admitted most French manufactures free and made great concessions on wines and spirits. Britain generalised her reductions to the world. France did not, but a most-favoured-nation clause required each to extend to the other any new reductions made to a third party.

Cobden's internationalism seemed catching, for though Anglo-French relations were not ultimately better in Italy, or over Poland and Schleswig-Holstein later, the treaty became the first of a series. Britain had achieved Free Trade, France was now but moderately protective. These changes generated an inevitable influence, but the hope of paci-fication was present in many of the most-favoured-nation treaties which multiplied after 1860. Prussia led the way, wishing to share Britain's privileges in France – and for reasons already outlined. The Zollverein's treaty with France was followed by some nine others, each reducing duties, including Belgium, Italy, Switzerland, Spain, Sweden. All were most-favoured-nation. France became the pivot of a low tariff area. Britain contributed several more treaties, including Belgium, the Zollverein, Austria and Italy. Even the most protection-wedded states, the reactionary and backward east European empires, lowered barriers in some degree: Austria and, although not joining the treaty system, even Russia. By 1870 a remarkable transformation was achieved.

The United States (with 8 per cent of the world's exports and imports in 1840 the third trading power) also experienced tariff falls between 1846 and 1860. Internally the biggest single Free Trade area, her society was rampantly individualistic and capitalist. Before the war of 1812 with Britain, her tariffs were primarily for revenue, although Alexander Hamilton had argued for protection in the 1790s. The first truly protective tariff appeared in 1816 at the close of the war, when anti-British, anti-European nationalism pressed the danger of relying on European manufactures – a supply economic diplomacy and war had recently stifled. The war and earlier embargoes had stimulated the beginnings of industry in New England, the middle states, even, to an extent, in the South. The 1816 Tariff received wide southern support.

Later tariffs were less unanimous. Not all sections saw America's future identically. The South, staple producing, especially cotton and tobacco, industrially unsuccessful, valued America's Atlantic links, the supply of primary products to Europe and low tariffs. Schemes like the Kentuckian Henry Clay's 'American System', which foresaw a self-sufficing America with a Northern industrial potential providing a market for Western and Southern food and agricultural raw materials, with less European dependence, the whole based on a large dose of 'internal improvements' (highways, canals, etc.) binding America together, and tariffs, failed to inspire Southerners. Clay and writers such as Matthew Carey and the editor Hezekiah Niles used the 'infant industries' argument in urging protection.

By 1830 America divided on tariffs sectionally. Middle and Western states, New York, New Jersey, Pennsylvania, Ohio, Kentucky, sought home markets for agricultural surpluses – Europe still feeling fairly distant. Pennsylvania and New York had growing industry, while in New England traditionally Free Trading mercantile and maritime interests slowly yielded to manufacturing concern for domestic outlets. These espoused protection. American tariffs reached a contemporary apogee in the 1828 'Tariff of Abominations'. The 1832 Act, although somewhat lower, proved the flash point. South Carolina, believing her economic interests disregarded, her Negro slavery ever more execrated by Yankee abolitionists, fearing the growing population and prosperity of the Northern and Western 'free' states would upset the scales of the Union, 'nullified' the 1828 and 1832 Acts within her borders, issuing a clear states-rights challenge to Federal authority. The whole American social, economic and political structure was involved. Eventually compromise emerged, involving a new 1833 tariff with progressively falling duties, reaching 20 per cent generally by 1842. Except briefly (in 1842), Southern influence sufficed to maintain moderate tariffs until 1860, especially from the 1846 Walker Tariff (mildly protective, but winning British plaudits), which President Buchanan's Southern-influenced administration further reduced in 1857.

Beyond her borders Britain did little to propagate Free Trade officially. It was strongly held that converts should be won by example alone. There was prejudice against commercial treaties, memories of restrictive eighteenth-century examples surviving. Cobden faced stern criticism in 1860, and the readoption of orthodoxy on this point by Gladstone's 1868 ministry weakened its will to uphold the survival of the low tariff bloc. There were individual activities: Cobden's journeys, correspondence with foreign Free Traders, participation in an International Congress in 1847. The Anti-Corn-Law League was accused of meddling in American politics – with some justice. In the 1830s and 1840s British administrations pressed low tariff German states to avoid the Zollverein.

Yet the government's right to extend the markets open to free competition was widely admitted – if means were disputed. Although rarely, in her confidence, seeking exclusive advantages, Britain did sometimes act to secure her position in peripheral areas in a way limiting those areas' commercial freedom. In the 1820s she negotiated most-favoured-nation treaties – some perpetual – with her important Latin American markets, which, although with one exception not limiting tariff levels, denied those states the power to discriminate against Britain. She went further. The 1838 Convention of Balta Liman with Turkey – always needing British support – bound Turkey to 3 per cent import duties. Of the treaties opening the Far East, the Japanese of 1858 (made concurrently with other powers) bound her to low duties. Free Trade had imperialist aspects. The non-self-governing British dependencies were kept firmly in line, most flagrantly India, where the element of calculation seemed greatest. Though willing to breach *laissez faire* in internal Indian development, she consistently prohibited high protective duties for Indian manufactures, cotton outstandingly, which were competing with British. From the Mutiny small revenue duties, including cottons, were maintained, gradually reduced, duties being lowest in the eighties. The set-piece came as late as 1894, when Britain insisted that a new 5 per cent revenue duty on cottons be countervailed by a 5 per cent excise on qualities of Indian yarn competing with Lancashire. In 1896 both were reduced to $3\frac{1}{2}$ per cent. The hand of Manchester seemed all too clear.

Thus by 1870 the major trading states led the world to lower tariffs. World trade in the basically prosperous mid-century rocketed, by 40 per cent in the 1840s, 80 per cent in the 1850s, 50 per cent in the 1860s, passing £2000 million annually by 1870. Railway building in Europe and beyond – America was crossed by 1869 – the first telegraphs, the steamship's encroachment on short hauls, the sailing ship's speed on longer, gradual industrialisation in Western Europe suggesting a future of more states seeking overseas outlets, the advancing complexity of international payments needing free credit flows, all seemed to indicate liberalisation, following British economic doctrines, as not unnatural. Other agreements were negotiated, on telegraphs, posts, rivers, seaways, money, of commercial value. Yet motivation was complex. The balance of forces permitting states to visualise their economic and political policies in liberal terms could easily shift. In America all depended on Southern political ascendancy; in France on Napoleon III; in Germany on hostility to Austria, agricultural interest in Free Trade, the political position of German Liberals, on Bismarck; internationally on mid-Victorian optimism permitting a tenuous Cobdenism, on Europeans' power to impose their will overseas, on Britain, needed yet feared, her example repellent yet attractive.

The world was a more nervous place in the 1870s. Politically, after the Second Empire collapsed in the Prussian War of 1870 and the new Bismarckian German Empire appeared (including Alsace and Lorraine), France eyed her neighbour balefully. Germany sought security, yet good relations with Russia were hard to maintain; Austria-Hungary's and Russia's Balkan interests clashed. Britain, following the collapse of Palmerstonian diplomacy in bluster over Denmark, felt, as Disraeli stressed, unacceptably excluded from inner European counsels.

Economically things also seemed harsher to decision-makers. From 1873 complaints of depressed conditions multiplied. The 'depression' was basically one of world prices and profits. Not affecting all industries, the world output of heavy manufactures had temporarily outpaced demand, while the growing production of foodstuffs and raw materials in peripheral nations (for example, the Americas and British settlement colonies) in which Britons and other Europeans had placed capital, depressed prices on that front. Europe was prosperous before 1873, railway construction drawing capital and industries expanding to meet that and other demands. In 1873 the boom collapsed, and for a quarter-century prices and profits tended to be low, although there were fluctuations, and by the century's end both picked up. Nor did complaints of depression necessarily imply a static economy or world trade. Absolutely the latter grew enormously, its gold value doubling in thirty years, its volume perhaps trebling. France was the only major state whose exports fell absolutely. Germany entered her great period of industrial growth, in iron and steel (she out-exported Britain by the 1890s), machinery and, from the eighties especially, in the new chemical and electrical industries, aided by advanced technical education, research and management. Few European states escaped some industrialisation. The U.S.A. took her place as a major manufacturing power. In years when the disparity between 'advanced' and 'backward' states became acute, the 'division of labour' between manufacturers and primary producers (Canada, Southern United States, Latin America, Australasia, India, Russia, etc.) more palpable, when Germany and France besides Britain needed some imported raw materials, international trade began to bulk almost as importantly in other states' economies as it long had in Britain's, though Germans and Americans had bigger home markets than Britons. These were the years of the real Victorian transportation revolution, Suez, steamships, refrigeration. Telegraphs made world commodity prices possible, and payments became truly multilateral and world-wide, based on London's financial power.

Many winds were cool, however. Competition among European states was greater, their reliance on Britain less. British businessmen of 1880 were almost obsessed with domestic and foreign German competition. The world was more integrated but more cloistered, more easily encompassed and enclosed. Businessmen and statesmen turned again to the state's protective arm – and this in a decade when American grain followed by other foodstuffs from overseas began to pose severe problems for European agriculture. Industrialisation too brought Europe social problems long familiar in Britain, of urbanisation, of large urban working classes, of urban poverty, cyclical unemployment, factory conditions, housing, sanitation. Socialist protest at capitalist society grew louder as Marx loomed larger than Adam Smith in the days of the International, the Paris Commune, the German Social

Democratic Party. Conservative governments had to face these problems even at the cost of sacrificing individualistic theories.

Although not the first to raise tariffs, Germany, who experienced her biggest industrialising burst in the early seventies, well displays the pressures operating. In 1864 the Zollverein produced 847,650 tons of pig iron; the (larger) German Empire of 1872 produced 1,927,064 tons. After 1873 these investments were less rewarding. In 1873-9 the iron trades turned to exports, but with falling prices and fairly high production costs, difficulties remained. Some exported at a loss. The industry lost its remaining protection in 1877. Cotton, linen, paper, coal, among others, also faced difficulties. 1876-7 saw the first large-scale grain imports – from Russia and the Danubian area more than America initially – turning formerly exporting east German landowners into seekers after protection and guaranteed home prices: a demand steadily more insistent. Wool growers joined in. Not all farmers found it easy to diversify their products. In 1876 the protectionist Central Alliance of German Industrialists for the Promotion and Preservation of German Labour was formed.

Bismarck saw fiscal policy, as everything, as bound up with Imperial security, strength, unity: internally, with the balance of the German states and the Empire, Federal executive and legislature, the state of parties in the Reichstag. The Empire could not impose direct taxes, but depended on the states' contributions: excises and high tariffs could obviate this dependence. Bismarck was concurrently shifting his support in the Reichstag away from the National Liberals towards the Catholic *centrum* and the conservative groups among whom protectionist industrialists and converted eastern landowners counted. Germany had her social problems. The Social Democratic vote was rising, and in 1879 the Bismarckian social insurance legislation was only four years away, beginning with sickness, passing on to accidents and old age pensions, paid for by workers' and employers' contributions with state help where needed, and designed in part to deflect the socialist challenge. Liberals accused Bismarck of 'state socialism'; but it was classical liberalism which was a declining German force. State direction appeared more often, while industry added trading agreements, larger organisations, cartels, to fiscal protection in its defensive armoury. British merchants deplored the 'ungentlemanly pushing' of German exports by German consuls abroad.

Intellectually 'Historical' Economists, such as Gustav Schmoller, demanding a more historical approach to economics and insisting that all theory was relative to time, place and institutions, argued that

Germany's situation demanded state action in pursuit of power and wealth. Such notions coloured the background of Germany's colonial flirtation of the 1880s and her new end-of-the-century navy. The protectionist reaction, beginning moderately in 1879, rising up to 1900 (especially on the agricultural side), was determined by all these strands, broadly similar ones acting with varieties of emphasis throughout Europe. Governments of 1880 were more economically conscious, open to direct economic pressures than in 1815. The great economic spectacles were now America and Germany – both protectionist – not Britain.

Most of Europe toed the protectionist line. France, acutely conscious of Germany, transforming her economy with difficulty, experiencing export problems and declining farm prices, gradually denounced her liberal treaties and raised home (and colonial) tariffs from the eighties, culminating in the highly protective 1892 Méline Tariff. Italy, Spain, Austria, Russia above all, reversed liberalisation. Tariff wars flared (Germany and Russia 1893–4, France and Italy 1889–98), but there were mitigations. The low tariff bloc of the sixties vanished, but numerous most-favoured-nation treaties were negotiated, doing much to prevent discrimination against participating states, while some developed dual or multi-level tariffs, reciprocating states receiving lower rates. Tariffs were rarely prohibitive.

Across the Atlantic the 1861 Constitution of the Southern Confederacy outlawed protective tariffs, but, Southern influence gone, the Morill Tariff also of 1861 reversed previous trends of Federal tariffs. Finance largely motivated subsequent wartime increases, internal excises often countervailing them. However, peace failed decisively to end (for a time it lowered) tariffs, though the excises vanished. Although by 1880 large-scale foodstuff exports were joining cotton and tobacco, the war had raised industry's weight in the American scale. By 1886 she passed Britain as the world's major steel maker. Until the century's close industry, mainly interested in home markets, was accustomed to protection, and neither political party ever adopted a platform Britons would have considered Free Trading, though from 1887 the Democrats stood for reduction. Yet the tariff remained high, in the 1890 McKinley Act reaching 49·5 per cent on average and in the Dingley Act, 1897, 57 per cent – a height Europe rarely equalled.

To the north, Canada followed America's protective path, although, like all British settlement colonies, far less industrialised. In the later 1840s Canadians faced the (not unconnected) novelties of self-government and British Free Trade. 'Canada' to be was still several economically diverse provinces. Problems of provincial relations, of tensions between French and British Canadians, of future economic development crowded together. Traditionally the St Lawrence colonies competed with eastern American ports for trade in the produce of the whole west, both sides of the border, despite disadvantages of climate, distance and costs. Prosperity developed in a continental trade involving a certain dependence on America, on Britain also for privileges for Canadian timber, grains, etc., in imperial markets. Now America was increasingly nationalist – even annexationist. Britain was bent on what Montreal merchants thought an outrageously nationalistic Free Trade policy. In future, was reciprocity possible with America with a share in her cornucopia for Canadian products and in American exports ? Or was a more nationalistic policy essential, which, while developing Canada's role as a primary exporter, would seek diversification through industrialisation, stress inter-provincial trade, forward railway construction, ultimately transcontinental, and build up Canada's west, drawing immigrants through an attractive land-settlement policy ? This would be costly and revenue depended on customs, indicating higher tariffs for cash as well as 'infant' industrial protection. Such a policy would parallel closer political unity and proclaim Canadian nationality before America, Britain and provincial or racial separatism. There were always those, from the 1854 Reciprocity Treaty to the negotiations of 1911, to argue the former policy, but broadly the latter took hold even before Confederation in 1867, being from that point particularly associated with Sir John Macdonald's Conservative ministries, yet in fact often maintained by his Liberal opponents. Already in 1859 the Province of Canada's tariff changed from pure revenue to 'incidental' protection – Britain's acquiescence marking a stage in the commercial independence of self-governing colonies. Tariffs became really significant from 1879, when Canada felt some of the world's problems, slowing economic growth. Like all primary producers Canada felt the variations of the world market peculiarly keenly. Canadian foodstuffs sold on a low-priced market. Industry, too, in Ontario and elsewhere, felt the pinch, yet the absence of American reciprocity plus low prices for primary produce suggested further industrialisation. Canada's trade fell in value, affecting revenue, at the height of the 'national' policy. Tariffs accordingly rose in 1879, remaining high, but in a world of tariffs and restrictions, the old impulse to wider assured markets displayed itself in American flirtations and, more, in longings for imperial trading privileges. In 1898 Canada explicitly granted British goods a 25 per cent reduction on her general tariff, hoping Britain would adopt Imperial Preference in return.

By the early 1900s New Zealand, Australia, increasingly South

Africa, followed, for not ultimately dissimilar reasons, Canada's lead, Victoria beginning back in the sixties. One feature boldly displayed in Australasia was the relationship of tariffs and social policies. New Zealand from the eighties and then the Commonwealth of Australia linked tariffs and 'state socialist' schemes, most blatantly in the Australian policy of 'New Protection' in the 1900s, when attempts, not always successful, were made to deny to companies not maintaining minimum working standards the benefits of protective tariffs and other subsidies. Emerging Australian nationalism envisaged not only a balanced economic structure, but crude minima beneath which citizens should not fall, even if both required the flouting of traditional views on state functions and commercial legislation.

In South America protection also appeared, especially where industrial interests outweighed pastoral. Chile and Brazil, for example, raised tariffs. In Asia, Japan, though not actually putting up tariffs, sought to end the treaties limiting her freedom. Few states with independence kept low tariffs. In Europe, Denmark defended her agriculture not by protection, but by developing its dairying side, seeking a large slice of the British market and retaining low tariffs. Holland, strongly commercial, and Belgium, still most closely paralleling Britain, remained liberal, but Britain herself remained the glaring exception from protective economic nationalism.

British Free Trade was inevitably harder to shift, being seemingly underpinned both by experience and emotion. Popular memory indissolubly linked Free Trade and the mid-Victorian boom, however much other factors contributed. Individualism ran deep in the business community and government circles concerned with trade: consuls found emulating their German colleagues distasteful. Socially the application of collectivist solutions to urban problems, though advancing, was slow: in social insurance Germany passed Britain. 'Self-Help' died hard. An early tariff-reformer entitled a protectionist book *The Policy of Self-Help* unconsciously displaying his difficulties. Gladstonian Liberalism was hardier than German, and whereas socially workers might query *laissez faire*, in an age of cheap American wheat and the first Australasian frozen meat, protectionists needed acute arguments to convert them. The Victorian schoolgirl who reputedly believed John Bright had invented bread highlighted both an emotional reading of the past and a potent – and not unjustified – belief about the present.

Certainly after 1873 Britain shared the world's difficulties: none more. By 1900, though still the major trading power, her exports had grown more slowly. She was but one industrial power among several and had not for a quarter-century displayed the dynamism of Germany or America. Exporters had found many traditional markets for traditional exports, textiles, iron, steel, machines, tougher as Europe and the United States industrialised, supplied themselves and competed abroad, while tariffs rose. Britain basically responded conservatively, tending to continue to export traditional wares in more distant markets, Asia, the Empire old and new, where capital for development had been and was increasingly, invested. This paralleled much conservatism domestically. There was adaptation, a broadening of economic activity into newer industries, into distributive and consumer trades. Yet managements were often conservative, limited in horizons, tied to existing investments and obsolescent industrial organisation, sometimes failing to take advantage of even British-developed techniques, suffering in newer, science-based industries for want of advanced scientific education.

Britain had always needed the world for industrialisation. She was still deeply committed. Her home market remained comparatively small, and, although living standards were rising, its purchasing power was less than it might have been. The continued dominance of industries traditionally more committed to foreign than home markets strengthened Free Trade, for protection acted at home and was doubtfully useful abroad. Imports still outpaced exports, more so with food importation, and Britain relied ever more not only on her services, in shipping (she still carried half the world's trade), banking, insurance, but on the income from overseas investments (£4000 million in total by 1914) to make ends meet. The City of London, at the peak of its power as the centre of world finance, the clearing house of the world's multilateral payments, remained committed to Free Trade. Probably, in keeping her great trade wide and free, by assisting free flows of goods and credit, Britain did the world economy a great service of lubrication.

Concern there was over the economy: official and unofficial enquiries investigated it – including commercial policy. Economic science had advanced far since 1815 but most English economists (such as Alfred Marshall), if not always using earlier arguments, came down on the Free Trade side, though there were protectionists such as Sir William Ashley who were influenced by Schmoller's ways of thought. Tariff Reform as a political cry began in the seventies among manufacturers considering themselves hit by foreign tariffs. In the eighties they gained agricultural support from grain producers hit by overseas imports, not all of whom could diversify into livestock, dairying or market gardening. Moderate duties were sought on competing foreign manufactures and on foreign, but not empire, foodstuffs.

In a tariff-ridden world it was argued politically that Britain had two alternatives. To go on as ever, or build safe lodgings at home and in the empire. Undoubtedly the need of markets, investors' hopes, together with disquiet about Britain's power status and the security of her trade, assisted the rebirth of stronger, active interest in the empire, self-governing and dependent, especially from 1880, and a willingness, at least when pushed by other powers feeling similar pressures, to extend more rapidly areas under her influence or direct control. Tariff Reform early crossed the empire's path and Imperial Federationists' hopes for a more economically, politically, militarily unified empire. But here there were great difficulties. Self-governing colonies with nationalist tariffs might, in the economic climate, urge Imperial Preference; but the same nationalism made them cautious on political or defensive unity. For Britain, preference arguably meant risking foreign retaliation and losses on her non-imperial trade, still, although empire markets were significant, most important. Joseph Chamberlain argued the case most cogently from 1903 uniting Imperial Preference, political unity and strategic power together. He won wide Conservative support. Yet that party split, while Liberals and many in the new Labour party held traditionalist views on trade policy. In the Britain of pro-Boers and J. A. Hobson, as well as of Chamberlain and Milner, no interest group was strongly enough committed or powerful enough to compel change in a nation politically divided on a self-image as the centre of an imperial economic-political-military bloc over against (above all) Germany. It was still possible for Balfour, Prime Minister to 1905, to treat the question as one of political expediency, not one demanding any drastic, imperative changes. The Liberal victory of 1906 settled the issue for the time being. Free Trade was safe until the First World War and the rethinking and reshaping the inter-war years demanded brought to it a challenge far beyond that posed by events since 1873.

SUGGESTIONS FOR FURTHER READING

Beyond national economic histories certain old standard works yield much factual information on tariffs, for example: Percy Ashley, *Modern Tariff History* (1904 and later); C. J. Fuchs, *The Trade Policy of Great Britain and her Colonies since 1860* (1905). W. O. Henderson, *The Genesis of the Common Market* (1962), discusses the 1786 Anglo-French Treaty, the 1860s and customs unions. For British tariffs see Sir John Clapham, *An Economic History of Modern Britain*, 3 vols (1926–38). On Free Trade and politics John Morley's *The Life of Richard Cobden*, 2 vols (1879) is still revealing; see also Benjamin H. Brown, *The Tariff*

Reform Movement in Great Britain, 1881–96 (1943), and Alfred Gollin, *Balfour's Burden* (1965). For the relation of tariff policies to the growth of trade see A. H. Imlah, *Economic Elements of the Pax Britannica* (1958) and S. B. Saul, *Studies in British Overseas Trade, 1870–1914* (1960).

On Germany: W. O. Henderson, *The Zollverein* (1937); Theodore S. Hamerow, *Restoration, Revolution, Reaction: economics and politics in Germany, 1815–71* (1958); Ivo N. Lambi, *Free Trade and Protection in Germany, 1868–79* (1963). On the Cobden Treaty: A. L. Dunham, *The Anglo-French Treaty of Commerce of 1860* (1930). On America: F. W. Taussig, *The Tariff History of the United States*, 8th edn. (1931). On Canada: O. J. McDiarmid, *Commercial Policy in the Canadian Economy* (1946); Donald Creighton, *John A. Macdonald, the Old Chieftain* (1956). On Australia: two works by J. A. La Nauze, *Political Economy in Australia* (1949) and *Arthur Deakin, a Biography*, 2 vols (1965).

D. C. M. Platt, *Finance, Trade and Politics in British Foreign Policy, 1815–1914* (1968), is valuable. On economic theory: Eric Roll, *A History of Economic Thought* (1938); and the earlier sections of T. W. Hutchison, *A Review of Economic Doctrines, 1870–1929* (1953).

NOTES

1. John, Lord Morley, *The Life of Richard Cobden* (one vol. edn. of 1903), pp. 408–9.

2. Morley, op. cit. ch. xviii.

3. Richard Cobden, *The Political Writings of Richard Cobden* (1867) i, 45, 333; my italics.

4. Friedrich List, *The National System of Political Economy*, trans. by S. Lloyd (1916), pp. 293–5.

5. Quoted in J. A. La Nauze, *Political Economy in Australia* (1949), p. 123.

6. W. O. Henderson, *The Genesis of the Common Market* (1962), p. 94.

5. The British Parliamentary System and the Growth of Constitutional Government in Western Europe

D. R. WATSON

We are proud of our country: and there are many things in it, as far as men may rightly be proud, we may be proud of. We may be proud of this, that England is the ancient country of Parliament . . . England is the mother of Parliaments.[1]

Thus spoke John Bright in Birmingham Town Hall on 18 January 1865, in the course of a speech demanding reform of the franchise. Although as part of his case he compared the limited British franchise of 1832 unfavourably with the more democratic franchises of the United States of America, of the self-governing British colonies and even (not very accurately) with European countries, the tone of his speech was that of the quotation above. It was the expression of immense pride in the British system of government, of complete certainty that wherever liberty and representative government were to be found, they must be guaranteed by institutions modelled on these evolved by the mother of Parliaments.

Of course it could not be expected that foreigners would at once be able to operate the subtle Westminster system, but they would learn in time. Already many states (Belgium, Holland, the Scandinavian countries) seemed to be close to the British model. Even France, which had diverged from the parliamentary path on more than one occasion in the past, seemed with the consolidation of the Third Republic after 1875 to be on the way to operating something like the Westminster system. It was only in the twentieth century that observers began to point out that parliamentary government in European countries, instead of becoming more like the British system as time went on, developed in each country traditions and methods of its own which diverged from the original model. We now realise that it is futile to talk of one ideal parliamentary system (be it British or that of any other country) which the others approach in greater or lesser degree; it is now accepted that on the basic juridical framework, imitated from the British constitution, other countries have developed their own, differing, but equally valid, systems of parliamentary government. The very flexibility of the model has allowed these very different systems to be developed from a roughly similar institutional basis. But this does not alter the fact that in the nineteenth century it was the British Parliament at Westminster which provided the institutional model for the introduction of constitutional monarchy in western Europe, and thus we can still agree with Bright that England is 'the mother of Parliaments'.

Virtually all observers from Bright's day to ours have agreed with this view.[2] It is true that the conservatively inclined German school of constitutional lawyers stemming from Gneist developed a theory by which the ideal parliamentary system was that operated in the German Reich, while the British, since their two Reform Acts of 1832 and 1867, had debased their constitution by allowing too great an influx of democracy. But even this group did not deny that it was from the unreformed British constitution of before 1832 that their ideal type of parliamentary government was derived. Even in the twentieth century, when the prestige of Britain and of the parliamentary system have both declined, the same viewpoint is upheld by such British and foreign political scientists as Sir Denis Brogan and Maurice Duverger.[3] The purpose of this essay, then, is to attempt to examine, in so far as it is possible to be precise about such a concept as the influence of one political system on another, the truth of the idea summed up in Bright's metaphor. It is limited to the influence of the British parliamentary system in western Europe and to the period between 1789 and 1880. For once a country had established some form of parliamentary government it was much less likely to be influenced from outside; rather it would develop according to its own political culture and traditions, barring some revolutionary upheaval, such as that which swept away the German monarchy in 1918. It was in the eighteenth century and the first half of the nineteenth century that the influence of the British system was greatest. When the states of central Europe came to set up parliamentary forms of government at the end of the First World War the British example was not important: by that time a quite distinct form of European parliamentarism had developed, of which the French Third Republic provided the extreme example, and it was this, rather than the British system, which was influential.

Constitutional government in the modern world can be divided between parliamentary systems and presidential systems; the only exception is the Swiss regime, which is *sui generis* and will not be further considered in this essay. In so far as it has been influenced from outside, it is derived from the late-Revolutionary French 'Directorial' type of constitution. With this exception the parliamentary system is practised at the present day by all European countries that enjoy constitutional government, and in the course of the nineteenth century there were relatively few European attempts to depart from the parliamentary system, always unsuccessful. Across the Atlantic, on the other hand, the presidential system, with a more complete separation of powers and a balance of power between the executive and legislative branches, has been the most common form of constitutional government since the setting up of the United States: the presidential system is operated not only in the U.S.A., but also in those Latin American countries which are not dictatorships. France, of course, since 1958, has been in an ambiguous position between the parliamentary and presidential systems. It might even be added that, in real terms, the flexibility of the British constitution has produced a situation here in which the enhancement of the power of the prime minister is such that classical parliamentary government has given way to a system with some presidential elements. In the nineteenth century, however, there was a clear distinction between parliamentary and presidential types of government. The parliamentary types were more obviously derived from the contemporary British system, but the presidential type also finds its origin in theories of constitutional government developed in England during and after the Civil Wars of the seventeenth century, theories which remained in the field in Britain itself until 1832. Presidential types of constitution stem from the American constitution of 1787 which transformed into a democratic republican form the ideals of Whig limited monarchy evolved in Britain in the previous century. At the same time Britain herself was passing from limited monarchy to a fully parliamentary regime, in which the independence of legislative and executive was no longer desirable. It was this form of British parliamentary government that influenced the Europeans in the nineteenth century, but it is important to remember that the presidential type of constitutional government was derived from an earlier form of the British constitution. It was only with the passing of the first Reform Act that the Separation of Powers ceased to be the ideal of radical critics of British government. To some extent the debates in the French Constituent Assembly of 1789–91, between the advocates of a complete separation of powers, and the defenders of a balanced or mixed monarchy, were between adherents of rival versions of what the British constitution was, or ought to be.

In the nineteenth century advocates of a presidential system were the more complete democrats. For their ideal involved placing the legislative power in the hands of the representatives of the people, without any check, and often the election of the head of the executive by the people as well. It was, of course, impossible to combine a presidential system with the preservation of monarchy. This alone would be enough to explain the absence of presidential systems of constitutional government in nineteenth-century Europe. Parliamentary government, on the other hand, offered a much less extreme programme. A parliamentary constitution can be at any point on a scale which goes from 99 per cent monarchial power, a system under which (as in Tudor England) the existence of a representative assembly hardly checked royal power at all, down to, say 1 per cent, in which the head of state, who may no longer be an hereditary monarch, is a mere figurehead. Classical nineteenth-century parliamentary government was somewhere around the middle of the scale. It is impossible to be more precise, for the characteristic of parliamentary constitutions is that the balance of power between monarch and Parliament is not set by institutional checks, but depends on the actual political situation, the pressure of real forces, and the personalities of individuals at decisive moments.

It follows that it is impossible to give a precise date for the introduction of full parliamentary government in any country, as opposed to that early form of mixed government in which royal power is only slightly checked by the existence of a representative assembly. Dates are given, such as the crisis of 1782–4 for Britain, the revolution of 1830 for France, 1848 for the Netherlands, 1867 for Sweden, 1876 for Italy, 1884 for Norway; such markers are not without value as long as it is remembered that they have as much, and as little, value as the date of 1784 in British constitutional history. In most cases they are not the occasion of a sudden change from one type of regime to another, but merely important turning-points in a gradual evolutionary process.

Before we begin to discuss the question of British influence it is necessary to have a picture of the introduction of parliamentary government in western Europe. The process took place between 1789 and 1875, and in most cases during the sixty years between 1815 and 1875. In the decade of the 1780s Britain was the only European state of any size to have effective representative institutions. Neither the Netherlands, nor the Swiss cantons, nor the remaining local provincial assemblies in the absolute monarchies amount to exceptions to this statement. In the absolute monarchies, provincial estates might be an obstacle which the central government had to deal with; in no sense did they themselves form a part of the active governmental machine. In the

Netherlands and even more in Switzerland the powers of the central government were nominal, and representative institutions were effective only at the local level. *A fortiori* Poland before its reformed constitution of 1791 was not so much a state with a liberal constitution as a union of virtually independent landed aristocrats. It was not surprising that Rousseau thought that democracy was possible only in small states. Absolute government was the rule in all the major powers except Britain, although in some cases the suppression of medieval representative institutions was recent. Although important in preparing the way for modern parliamentary government, medieval and early modern representative assemblies were certainly not the same as modern parliaments: they had not been the same in England, and in the countries of continental Europe where these institutions survived down to the seventeenth and eighteenth centuries they were static or declining in importance: only in England was the evolution towards modern parliamentary government taking place.

France began the movement to set up constitutional government, although the constitution of 1791 departed radically from the British model, which was deliberately rejected as leaving too much power in the hands of the monarch. This constitution was operated for only a brief period, and legally abolished on 21 September 1792, when the Convention abolished the monarchy and proclaimed the Republic. The constitution for the new French Republic was drawn up in June 1793, but at once suspended. Neither this Jacobin constitution nor the various other constitutional arrangements with which the French experimented between that date and 1814 are of much relevance; they were all far removed from the British parliamentary pattern, and none of them provided a workable system of free self-government. So that we may say that, after the false start of 1791, it is really with Louis XVIII's Charter of 1814 that French constitutionalism had its origin. From that time onwards, except for the authoritarian period of the Second Empire between 1851 and 1860, French rulers always had to cope with some form of parliamentary limitation.

Apart from the French experiment of 1791 there are no significant examples of attempts to imitate British parliamentary institutions before the end of the Napoleonic Wars. For completeness' sake one must mention the Polish constitution of 1791, that of Sweden established in 1809 and the Spanish and Sicilian constitutions of 1812: but for different reasons they do not interest us in this essay. The two which were modelled on the British system (the Polish and the Sicilian) were ephemeral and vanished virtually without trace, the Polish one because of the final extinction until 1918 of Polish independence at the hands of her neighbouring absolute monarchs, and the Sicilian one with the alteration in the military situation which had called it into being under the aegis of the Royal Navy.[4] The other three were not at all closely related to the British system; Sweden drew on her own native traditions and re-established the Four Estates system, which had lasted down to 1772, while the Norwegian and Spanish constitutions were both modelled on the French constitution of 1791. The contrast between the successful stability of the Norwegian constitution (which in its main lines remains in force today) with the total failure of the Spanish ever to make their 1812 constitution the framework of a viable system of government is a good example of the obvious truth that social structure and political culture are of more importance than institutional devices in establishing constitutional government.

It was in the period of reconstruction at the end of the Napoleonic Wars that the influence of Britain on the political institutions of continental Europe reached its high point. Britain had immense prestige, having been the linchpin of the coalition that had defeated Napoleon. A complete restoration of the *ancien régime* and absolutism seemed impossible in many states, while extreme 'Jacobin' democratic constitutions were totally discredited. Only the British middle road remained. In any case some version of the parliamentary system seemed at the time to be the only way of reconciling hereditary monarchy with a constitutional form of government.

In spite of some contrary assertions it is obvious that the British parliamentary system was copied in France, both in the system advocated by Napoleon in his hypocritical *Acte Additionel*, issued after his return from Elba, and in the system of government set up by the Charter issued by Louis XVIII.[5] The British example was also followed in the kingdom of the Netherlands, which abandoned its native traditions: the Estates system of the seventeenth and eighteenth centuries had been completely different from the centralised parliamentary monarchy set up in 1815. Constitutional government was still confined to the area of north-western Europe. Apart from Britain, France, the kingdom of the Netherlands and the Scandinavian countries, only some of the small states of southern Germany enjoyed constitutional government in the years immediately after the end of the Napoleonic Wars. The liberal programme was to campaign for the introduction of constitutions in states where absolutism remained entire, and to attempt to swing the balance away from 'throne and altar' and towards 'the people' in those states where some form of limitation on royal absolutism already existed. In this period Britain, in spite of the limited representative nature of the unreformed franchise, stood out as being the state in which royal power was effectively limited in a way that it was not, even in the other parliamentary monarchies, in all of which the King still retained a much greater degree of initiative than did the son of George III.

Throughout the period between 1815 and 1848 the liberals were to have little success. Although there were several revolutions in Spain and Italy, they did not lead to the setting up of a viable form of constitutional government. Progress made in the German states was minimal, and did not affect the two important states, Prussia and Austria. Portugal and the newly independent Greece set up parliamentary governments of a sort, but the political life of these small Mediterranean countries was far removed from what was known at Westminster. The only important developments were in the states of western Europe that already had limited monarchy in 1815; the 1830 revolutions which established a fully parliamentary regime in France after the ambiguities of the 1815–30 period, and led to the new state of Belgium. Belgium, indeed, was to be the model of parliamentary monarchy under its 1831 constitution which spelled out in clear juridical language the rules of parliamentarism which could be only dimly discerned in British institutions and conventions.

It was 1848, the year of revolutions, which marked the first widespread liberal successes. Although national aspirations were uniformly defeated, there were few states in western and central Europe which did not have some form of constitutional government when the dust had settled. Denmark went at one step from complete absolutism to a constitutional system which has functioned ever since. Prussia established its own weak form of parliamentary monarchy, which might well have led on to genuine parliamentary government but for the genius of Bismarck. Piedmont did just this: the *Statuto* of 1849 provided the framework on which a parliamentary form of government developed and was eventually extended to the whole of Italy. In the Habsburg Empire, although absolutism was temporarily restored in 1850, it was on the basis of the experiments of 1848–50 that parliamentary forms were established after the Ausgleich of 1867, especially in the Hungarian half of the empire. Of the states that already had constitutional government before 1848, the Netherlands moved some way towards a more powerful Parliament under the impact of the events of 1848, while France attempted, for the first time in Europe, to combine constitutional government with democracy, by establishing universal male suffrage. This led to the temporary collapse of parliamentary government, but outside France the lesson of 1848 was that, although extreme revolutionary solutions of all sorts had failed, the steady evolution of parliamentary government had been given considerable impulse. Countries such as Prussia, Denmark and Piedmont now had parliaments for the first time: in other countries monarchs had lost ground to parliaments. By the mid 1860s, when Bright coined his famous phrase, the general trend was clear enough. Ten years later, with parliamentary government established in Spain, France and Austria-Hungary, and in the newly created German Reich (however limited the powers of some of these parliaments), the triumph of the British model of constitutionalism was complete. We can agree with Bright that at least in the main lines of their institutions all major European countries were influenced by the British system. They were nearly all monarchies: they all had two legislative chambers in some way reminiscent of the Houses of Lords and Commons at Westminster. They all operated a cabinet type of executive, which sought support for its actions from a majority of the popular house of the Legislature. It is hard to imagine that such a system could have evolved without reference to the British constitution. Certainly the way in which these institutions operated was very different from one country to another, and was nowhere an exact replica of the British system, largely because of the completely different evolution of the party system, itself a reflection of social and economic structures, and of political and cultural traditions which differed fundamentally from one country to another.

Having outlined the evolution of parliamentary government in western Europe, we can now attempt our assessment of the extent of British influence. In the space available it would be impossible to attempt a chronological treatment for each country, especially when crosscurrents and indirect influences have to be borne in mind. I have, therefore, chosen five keypoints for investigation, which seem to me to be those at which the British example was the most important. They are France between 1789 and 1791; the period of reconstruction at the end of the Napoleonic Wars; the 1830 revolutions in France and Belgium; the question of British influence in the revolutionary year of 1848; and, finally, the period 1866 to 1875, which saw the adoption of parliamentary forms of government in such major states as France, Austria-Hungary and the German Empire. Spain also established in 1874 a constitutional monarchy deliberately modelled on that of Britain, while Sweden in 1867 replaced her traditional Estates system by the normal parliamentary type. I wish to deal first with the influence of the British constitution on

French liberal thought in the eighteenth century, and then on the constitutional debates of 1789–91. In some ways this was the most important period of any, although the immediate practical results were minimal. But it was in this period that the main lines of the liberal scheme of government were developed by European writers, largely under the influence of the British example, and it was in this period also that Britain stood out, and was admired, as the one major state that was not ruled by an absolute monarch. Thus the growth of liberal political thought in Europe, and especially in France, was dominated by the example of the British constitutional monarchy. In a general sense, no doubt, it is true that liberal ideas can be traced back to ancient Greece and Rome, and another stream of influence flows from medieval ideas and feudal institutions. History is a seamless web, and everything interconnects. Nevertheless some circuits are more highly charged than others. Although nineteenth-century European liberalism rested on a foundation of centuries-old respect for the rights and privileges of individuals, groups and communities of all types, a respect which was never completely overriden by the claims of absolute monarchs, it was only in England that the political crisis of the seventeenth century produced an effective form of limited monarchy. Modern ideas of constitutional government first appear in the political pamphlets of the English Civil War, and in the various constitutional proposals of the Interregnum period. The institutions which emerged in England in 1689 came to be seen as a new and, to many people, desirable form of government. It was in France that most interest was taken in developments across the Channel: in the first half of the eighteenth century the volume of translation of English political writing, and of French comments on English history had already reached considerable proportions. It was on this basis that Montesquieu was able to introduce his analysis of the British constitution into his *De l'esprit des lois*, by far the most important single book for the spreading of ideas about the British system of government through Europe. Only a relatively small section of the book is devoted to Britain, and it is very far from giving a detailed and accurate account of British institutions. But to dismiss Montesquieu because of this would be completely mistaken. He was well aware that he was not describing the actual working of British institutions, but using them to create his own ideal type of political life. His famous insistence on the separation of powers was by no means as misguided as has sometimes been claimed. With the development of cabinet government and the atrophy of royal power in the nineteenth century it became silly to talk of the separation of the executive and legislative power in Britain, but this was by no means the situation when Montesquieu wrote. At that time the King was still in a real sense the head of the executive, and it was precisely because a separate legislative body existed in the Houses of Parliament that the British monarchy differed from continental absolutism. The problem of political management in eighteenth-century Britain was to ensure that the independent powers of executive and legislature were kept in step. It is not so much in Montesquieu as in his disciple de Lolme that the application of the doctrine of separation of powers to British government became a caricature. De Lolme abandoned Montesquieu's subtle nuances and produced a rigid mechanical scheme which bore little relation to British political practice in 1771 when he wrote it, and none whatsoever in later years. The frequent reprinting of de Lolme's treatise, both in English and in French, down to the middle of the nineteenth century is a strange phenomenon. The development of cabinet government, and the decline in the independent royal power made his description of the British constitution almost totally false. It is clear that, in practice, few of those who had knowledge of British politics took any notice of de Lolme's ideas; yet his book remained virtually the only account of the British constitution, at least for continental readers, and one of the most widely read even in Britain.

From the time of the publication of *De l'esprit des lois* in 1748 down to the outbreak of the Revolution in 1789 there was an increasing volume of discussion of the problem of restraining arbitrary royal power in France: the British constitution was at the centre of this discussion, whether it was being eulogised or attacked. Both Anglomania and Anglophobia have been studied in French writings of this period, but the conclusion is that admiration for the British system was the stronger current.[6] Outbreak of war between the two countries tended to produce waves of Anglophobia except among those intellectuals who were completely opposed to their own government, but the return of peace usually produced a reaction to more favourable attitudes. It is true that after 1770 a critical note was struck more frequently: but even so much of the literature was favourable except during the period of the American war (1776–83), and it is also clear that the French critics of the British contribution were echoing native British radicalism in their condemnation of aristocratic influence, royal power and corruption. The ideal constitution envisaged by the French liberals was based on the British radical view of how their own government should be organised if its principles were obeyed. It was this radical view of the British constitution that the American colonists were thought to have established as their system of government when they proclaimed their independence. Thus the advocates in revolutionary France of a constitution modelled on that of the United States of America were defending an idealised version of the British constitution. The clearest indication of the influence of British politics upon French political thought at the end of the eighteenth century is to be found not in the adoption of specific theories of political organisation, but in the extent of the adoption of Anglo-Saxon words into the French language in this period. Linguistic studies have shown that the framework of the French language of the nineteenth century for political theory and institutions was almost completely reconstructed by borrowings from English in this period – in many cases by the return of words which had an original French root but which had developed quite new meanings in the Anglo-Saxon context.[7]

It was the people in the middle of the road who were the chief advocates of British institutions: adherents of absolute monarchial power condemned them; so did the radicals, who took over from British radicals the view that the British constitution had been perverted by parliamentary corruption, so that a complete separation of legislature and executive was required in a truly free state. When in the summer of 1789 the Estates General turned itself into the Constituent Assembly and began to draw up a constitution for France, there were two models to copy, both derived from similar seventeenth-century sources, but now quite different from each other, the American system of presidential government and the British parliamentary system. For all the frequency of assertions that the French need not copy anyone in giving themselves a constitution, the debates of 1789–90 were to a large extent about the relative merits of a British and an American type of constitution. It was the American example that was followed, with the great difference that the head of the executive in France was an hereditary monarch, and not an elected president. The arguments were not merely an abstract discussion of the relative merits of these rival institutional patterns, but were bound up with the position of the speakers in the whole spectrum of revolutionary politics. The advocates of a British type of system were known as the 'monarchiens' as opposed to the 'patriots', and the real question was the degree of trust that could be placed in the King.

In fact two versions of the British system were presented to the Constituent Assembly, and both were rejected. The group known as the 'monarchiens', or 'Anglophiles', had a majority on the first committee on the constitution. The scheme which Lally-Tollendal presented on behalf of the first committee in September 1789 was based on Montesquieu's idea of the British constitution, and left the King in control of a largely independent executive power, with a power of veto over legislation, but without the link between executive and legislature provided by the presence in Parliament of the royal ministers.

It was Mirabeau and Thouret who in the course of the debate pointed out this essential feature of the British system of government, and showed that it should not be regarded (as it was by the radicals in Britain and in France) as a means by which the Crown 'corrupted' and subjected the legislature, but as an essential means for keeping the two parts of the government in step, and a means which in fact allowed Parliament to control the King's ministers, rather than the other way round. Mirabeau's presence in London at the end of the political crisis of 1782–4 had allowed him insight into the actual working of the British constitution denied to those who relied on the accounts of Montesquieu or de Lolme, and equally to the radicals like Sieyès who rejected de Lolme as a 'liar', but who saw only corruption and royal tyranny in those practices of English politics which Mirabeau correctly analysed along the lines of nineteenth-century theories of parliamentary government.[8]

But the Constituent Assembly was in no mood to listen either to Lally-Tollendal or to Mirabeau: ignoring Mirabeau's remark that an exact analysis of the theory of the separation of powers would show 'the ease with which the human mind confuses formulae with arguments', the Assembly wrote into the Declaration of the Rights of Man the dogma of complete separation of powers. It then rejected both Mirabeau's idea that ministers should sit in the legislature and the constitutional committee's advocacy of a royal veto. This led to the resignation of the 'monarchiens' from the committee and the appointment of a new committee dominated by Sieyès. The constitution which was eventually adopted reflected Sieyès's idea of a rigid, mechanical separation of powers, although the King was allowed a suspensive veto. The question which dominated men's minds was that of complete separation of personnel. Members of the Assembly not only could not be ministers, but were not to accept any office from the King during their period of membership of the Assembly or for two years afterwards. Any development of the parliamentary system would have been impossible under the constitution of 1791: in fact, in the political circumstances the constitution was completely unworkable. From the first the Assembly had shown in practice that it wished to control the royal activities, and was quite unwilling to allow the King the freedom of action which the constitution prescribed to him as head of the executive. From the first weeks of the new Assembly elected in 1791 committees of the Assembly were appointed to supervise the day-to-day doings of the executive power, and the ministers, who had been so carefully excluded from the Assembly because of fear of their power to dominate and corrupt its members, became complete ciphers. Duguit pointed out in his magisterial article on the separation of powers and the National Assembly of 1789 how the Assembly refused to admit in practice the separation which was in theory the touchstone of a free constitution; Sieyès's rigid institutional devices led to a more complete concentration of power in the hands of those who dominated the various revolutionary assemblies than the monarchy of the *ancien régime* had known. The revolutionary contribution to the inventory of governmental systems turned out to be not a system of Separated Powers, but the system of *Régime d'Assemblée*, something quite different from a parliamentary government.[9]

We need not, therefore, pursue French constitutional developments through the revolutionary period. With the outbreak of war all things British were officially condemned in much stronger terms than even at the height of earlier periods of hostilities: serious and informed appreciation of the British system was far removed from the diatribes which were produced when the Club des Jacobins, at Robespierre's instigation, discussed the vices of the British constitution. The various constitutional schemes which followed the collapse of the Jacobins were mostly influenced by Sieyès's ideas, and were all very different from the British system: in practice the elaborate balancing of separate powers led to the institution of the *coup d'état* as a normal method of government until Bonaparte established his own dictatorial authority.

In conclusion, then, the British example was advocated by the moderates in the Constituent Assembly, a group who were soon completely swept away. As the Revolution led to more and more extreme solutions, partly because of the political breakdown produced by the unworkable constitution of 1791, the moderates were ground between the two millstones of left and right. As Britain became the centre of the anti-French coalition, advocates of a British system of government were forced to keep quiet. Which is not to say that they did not exist. It is likely that they were in fact a majority of the educated political classes, but their time was not to come until 1814. This brings us to the second period we have to discuss – the period of reconstruction at the end of the Napoleonic Wars. If the British constitution was most influential in theoretical terms during the eighteenth century, it was at this time that viable parliamentary monarchies first appeared on the continent of Europe, in France and the kingdom of the Netherlands, both inspired by the English example.

It is true that the advisers of Louis XVIII who drew up the *Charte* of 1814 did not envisage it as producing a blueprint for the introduction of a British type of parliamentary system into France. They rather saw it as providing for a return of the consultative bodies of the old French monarchy: but in fact the *Charte* provided the constitutional framework for developments parallel to those in England at an earlier period. Strangely enough it was the Ultras (the extreme right-wing royalists who wished to put the clock back to before 1789) who pressed, in the years immediately after Waterloo, for the evolution of a full parliamentary system. For they had a strong position in the Parliament, and felt that the King and his ministers were making too many concessions to the liberals and moderates. Thus it was the royalist Chateaubriand, who in his pamphlet *La Monarchie selon la Charte*, gave wide publicity to Constant's ideas about parliamentary monarchy. The studies of Barthélemy and Michon give many contemporary references to the British parliamentary system. Barthélemy writes: 'It would be difficult to quote any speech, article or pamphlet on constitutional questions which does not mention, either to recommend or to attack it, the British example, and especially on the question of the control of the cabinet by the House of Commons.'[10]

Madame de Staël and the most important French theorist of parliamentary government, Benjamin Constant, advocated the British system; Constant analysed the working of cabinet government in far clearer terms than any British writer of the time. Even those who opposed the copying of British institutions in France, because, they said, the effect would be quite different in a society where the aristocracy had lost the immense prestige it retained in Britain, still adopted many of the elements of British constitutional ideas; Royer-Collard and Guizot come into this category. But it was only gradually that the conventions of parliamentary government were adopted. At first many ministers were not deputies, and did not even attend the Chambers to defend their actions: but the normal rules of ministerial responsibility and frequent contact between the Cabinet and the Chamber of Deputies gradually evolved. Barthélemy argues that the formation of the Martignac government in 1827, imposed on the King by the majority of the Chambers, was the first example of the working of proper parliamentary government in France. The Polignac ministry saw Charles X attempt to revert to personal rule, but the 1830 Revolution opened the way for the definitive establishment of the rules of parliamentary government along British lines. Barthélemy's conclusion is that the British example was important, but not decisive: the establishment of parliamentary government in France resulted from the compromise political settlement of 1815. The political nation accepted the return of the Bourbons, but not unconditionally: those who had formed part of the Napoleonic establishment, and who had not compromised themselves during the Hundred Days, demanded limited monarchy, so as to secure their own position. Louis XVIII's long exile in Britain did not convince him that the British constitution was ideal even there, and certainly not in France: but his knowledge of British institutions helped to resign him to the introduction of a similar system in France, when circumstances made some yielding of royal authority unavoidable. Barthélemy, in fact, like other French authors, goes too far in denying the importance of the British example in 1815. Granted that political circumstances made a compromise between the forces of the old France and those that had emerged since 1789 inevitable, there is no doubt that the institutional form in which that compromise was expressed was directly derived from the example of British parliamentary monarchy, both in the juridical basis provided in the *Charte* and the way in which political life developed in the years after 1815. For example, Chateaubriand's pamphlet was based on British political practice when he laid down as essential features of parliamentary government that the ministry must be taken out of the majority of the Chamber, and that the Chamber's right to control the actions of the ministry should be expressed by the system of questions from deputies which ministers must answer.

It was in the work of Benjamin Constant that the classical nineteenth-century theory of constitutional monarchy emerged.[11] His theory was based primarily on British experience, which he analysed in a far more realistic and sophisticated manner than any writer since Montesquieu in either English or French. Indeed it could well be argued that his analysis was a more accurate and subtle account of the working of the British nineteenth-century parliamentary system (allowing for the fact that at the time he wrote some features were still only incipient) than any other, including Bagehot's famous book, which had a much cruder and in some ways misleading analysis. Constant saw the limited independence of the executive as an essential feature of parliamentary government, and was not led, as was Bagehot, to argue that the separation of powers was completely irrelevant to British practice or that the ministry was a mere committee of the legislature.

The only other European state which established parliamentary government in 1815 was the kingdom of the Netherlands: again the British example is important. The system set up was quite different from the pre-revolutionary system of Estates, under which local particularism had been of far more importance than the central body. French revolutionary armies had swept away the power of local groups and provinces and accustomed the inhabitants of the Low Countries to a strong centralised government. But in 1815 it was the British example that was followed with the setting up of a parliamentary monarchy, in which, at first, the King retained very considerable powers, but which, after 1848, rapidly evolved into a constitutional system under which the royal power was very limited.

A crucial stage in the introduction of constitutional government in Europe came with the 1830 revolutions in France and Belgium. There is less direct evidence of British influence in France in 1830 than there had been in 1814 and the years immediately following: for by now the French had their own knowledge of the working of parliamentary institutions, and had their own precedents to refer to. But it is clear that the French liberals were influenced also by their knowledge of the effective working of limited monarchy across the Channel, and in so far as their ideas about constitutional government were derived from the writings of Benjamin Constant, they were taken from Britain. This was the period when, as J. S. Mill put it in a letter to Alexis de Tocqueville, 'English ideas seldom make much way in the world until France has recast them in her own mould, and interpreted them to the rest of Europe.'[12]

An even better example of this process than the French parliamentarism of the July Monarchy was the Belgian constitution of 1831. When the Belgian National Congress came to draw up the constitution of the newly independent state, they did not explicitly look back to the institutions of the area as they had been under Spanish and Austrian rule before 1789, although the traditions of self-government which went back to those times were no doubt important in the smooth working of the parliamentary system in Belgium. The most obvious sources for the Belgian constitution of 1831 were the two French charters of 1814 and 1830: a third of all the clauses of the Belgian constitution were copied word for word from the French charter of 1830. But, as we have already pointed out, these French documents were themselves based on the British system, and the debates of 1831 show that the Belgians were themselves well aware of the nature of British government. The Belgian constitution-makers, with all the advantages of *tabula rasa*, drawing up a system of government for a new state, and not having to deal with established institutions, were able to formulate the ideal type of nineteenth-century liberal, bourgeois, parliamentary monarchy. As Professor Hawgood has put it:

> The Belgian constitution of 1831 completed the formalization of monarchy, and by reducing the sphere of the King to functions prescribed by the Constitution and performed through ministers responsible to a popularly elected legislature, succeeded in reconciling in a satisfactory and logical way the continued existence of monarchial institutions with the full recognition of the sovereignty of the people. The British constitution was felt rather than known to have bridged the same gulf, but in 1831 nobody, even in England, could quite explain how: the revised Charter of 1830 in France was capable of being interpreted in the same direction, but it was also capable of interpretation in quite different directions.... It was Belgium, and not Britain, France, Sweden or Norway, that became the pattern and prototype for constitutional monarchies everywhere during the century following 1831.[13]

Certainly, as far as direct copying of documents is concerned, it is the Belgian constitution that is to be found in the constitutions of such states as Rumania, Bulgaria, Greece and Serbia, and, in a less obvious way, mingled with other borrowings (notably from the French charters) in the Piedmontese constitution of 1849. But it is perverse to argue from this as does Professor Mirkine-Guetzévitch[14] that the Belgian example was more important than the British and to state that even if England had practised quite a different political system, parliamentarism would have inevitably evolved in Europe. For it is clear that the Belgian and French parliamentary systems, which were so widely imitated in Europe, were themselves derived from the English example. The general influence of Britain on French and German liberal political thought, and on the institutions of major countries such as France, Germany and Italy, is of more importance than the textual borrowings from the Belgian constitution on the part of minor Mediterranean and east European states.

We come now to the question of British influence on the development of constitutional government under the impact of the revolutionary year of 1848. It is clear at the outset that direct British influence is already less in evidence than it was at any of the three earlier periods discussed. France had by this time developed her own form of parliamentary government and French liberals no longer needed to take their arguments from British practice. It is true that the prestige of the British system remained great; especially after the attempt to set up a quite different system in the Second Republic led to Louis-Napoleon's *coup d'état*. Moderate liberals were again to be found extolling the virtues of British constitutional monarchy. But in 1848 itself, during the drawing up of the constitution for the Second Republic, in spite of the presence on the drafting committee of such an Anglophile as de Tocqueville, the British example was dismissed as irrelevant for a country determined on the establishment of a fully democratic system. Similarly at the Frankfurt Parliament and among Italian revolutionaries, the British constitution offered no inspiration to the men of 1848. For the radicals it left far too much power in the hands of the monarchy and aristocracy; while, on the other side, even the moderate liberals thought that, removed from its own social context, it would place too much power in the hands of the people. In any case, in Italy, Austria and Germany the great problem was that of redrawing frontiers to allow for national self-determination, and on this point the British constitution was irrelevant. The constitution drawn up by the Frankfurt Parliament and adopted on 28 March 1849 was influenced more by the constitution of the United States of America than by the British constitution, except for the fact that the head of state was to be an hereditary monarch. Both because of the federal nature of the proposed German State, and because of the desire for a fuller democracy, the American example seemed more appropriate than the British. The various Italian constitutions of the revolutionary year were derived either from the Spanish constitution of 1812 (and thus indirectly from the French of 1791) or from the French charters of 1814 and 1830; this was particularly the case for the Piedmontese *Statuto* of 1849, the only Italian constitution to survive.

British influence in 1848 is to be sought not in the countries which had revolutionary upheavals, which in no case led to the introduction of the sort of democratic constitutional government aimed at by the revolutionaries, but in the smaller countries which, although they themselves saw no revolutions, were impelled by the revolutionary spirit of the year to move towards parliamentary government. This applies particularly to Denmark, which went in one step with the constitution of 5 June 1849 from the absolutism which had reigned there since the seventeenth century to a parliamentary monarchy along British lines, which functioned smoothly, and with little legal change down to 1953 when a new constitution was drawn up. The King retained considerable powers after 1848, as did the Upper House of Parliament, while the franchise was a limited one: but the transition to a fully democratic parliamentary system came smoothly enough in the succeeding half-century without upsetting the basic institutional framework set up in 1849. Similarly in 1848 the kingdom of the Netherlands escaped revolutionary activity, but, under the impact of events across its borders, moved several steps along the road from the limited monarchy set up in 1814 to a full parliamentary system with a responsible ministry.

There is not much evidence of direct British influence on the evolution of constitutional government in the major European countries in 1848. Already European liberalism was very different from the British variety, and the problems facing European liberals were such that the British example was not directly relevant. Dr Olive Anderson has stated that the confused situation of British politics between 1846 and 1867, together with native criticism of administrative inefficiency during the Crimean War, meant that 'on the continent the prestige of British political institutions remained very low'.[15] Dr Zeldin has also argued that in this period European liberals no longer looked to Britain for inspiration.[16] These views would seem, however, to be somewhat overstated. It can be granted that both extremes of political opinion on the Continent, at this time, as earlier, rejected the British example. On the Left, the radicals and democrats were well aware of the strong oligarchic and aristocratic tone of British political life: this had been their continuing critical view of British politics from the eighteenth century onwards, and it was not until 1867 that Britain proved that her institutions, nevertheless, were capable of taking further steps in the direction of democracy. While on the Right there was a similar continuity in the view that only Britain, because of what Bagehot dubbed the built-in deference and docility of the mass of the population, could combine her aristocratic social structure with institutions which placed such great power in an elected house of representatives; especially in view of the fact that, even before the franchise reform of 1867, the British House of Commons represented a far wider section of the populace than that of any European constitutional monarchy, with the exception of the short-lived democratic parliaments of 1848. No other country had an aristocracy and an established Church that combined wealth, prestige and popularity without serious challenge. Elsewhere, British institutions would, it was argued, lead only to social anarchy or to a repetition of Jacobin tyranny.

But in between these two extremes the moderate liberals, advocates of a bourgeois constitutional monarchy, still found inspiration in the British parliamentary system. It was in this period that this middle ground expanded until it became the dominant current among the politically conscious middle class in most European countries. The defeat of more radical plans in 1848, the re-establishment of absolutism throughout the Austrian sphere of influence, and still more the immense shock (for such it was to liberal opinion) of the destruction of the French Second Republic by Louis-Napoleon, in the long run greatly increased the prestige of the British constitution. In the 1850s Britain stood out once more, as she had not done since 1815, as the only one of the Great Powers which had been able to preserve a constitutional system of government. The decade of the 1860s was marked by the coming together of many different strands of opinion on the Continent (especially in France, and Italy, to a lesser extent in Germany) in favour of a moderate constitutional monarchy with many of the features of the British constitution.

We cannot examine this process in detail, but a glance at the constitutional developments in all the major European countries will confirm it. In 1859 Britain alone of the five European Great Powers had a constitutional government: elsewhere parliamentary monarchy was well established in the small states of north-western Europe, Belgium, the Netherlands, Norway, Sweden and Denmark, while regimes that can best be called pseudo-parliamentary were to be found in the small countries of the Mediterranean and the Balkans, Portugal, Spain, Greece. Piedmont, Prussia and most of the small German states had representative institutions limiting the power of the ruler to some extent, but which were in most cases a long way from fully responsible government.

By 1875 we find a very different picture. Now only Russia among the Great Powers is an absolute monarchy. Piedmont has become the nucleus of a newly united Italian state retaining its constitution as laid down by the *Statuto* of 1849, but rapidly evolving towards a parliamentary monarchy in which the royal power was severely limited. Prussia, which also retained the main features of its constitution of 1850, has made itself the master of the new German Reich. The German constitution of 1871 was essentially that drawn up in 1866 for the North German Confederation by Bismarck from a draft by the historian Max Duncker.[17] It was complicated by the fact that the German Reich was a federal state and its democratic façade meant little because Prussia with its oligarchic regime and only slightly mitigated absolutism, dominated the whole, but in principle the German constitution of 1871 was very similar to documents such as the French *Charte* of 1814 or the Italian *Statuto* of 1849 from which parliamentary monarchies had evolved. France had begun to follow the same pattern of evolution towards constitutional monarchy with the creation of the liberal empire and the constitution of 1870: the process was interrupted by the Franco-Prussian War. The resulting confused political situation seemed for a time to give a chance to both extremist groups in turn, first to the radical republicans, and then to the Legitimist monarchists. But with the voting of the constitutional laws of 1875, the end result was not very different: as de Broglie pointed out, the choice was between a parliamentary republic verging on a constitutional monarchy and a constitutional monarchy verging on a republic. The Third Republic was a compromise in which the Orleanists accepted the absence of the hereditary principle (both for the head of state and in the Upper House), while the republicans gave up almost all the other elements of their programme, so that the resultant regime was virtually a constitutional monarchy without a king. Bagehot's interpretation of the British constitution was important in bringing the republican leaders Ferry and Gambetta to accept a parliamentary type of constitution for the Third Republic, with features alien to the French republican tradition such as a two-chamber legislature.

Austria, too, by the Ausgleich of 1867 turned itself into two parliamentary monarchies, a genuine one on the Hungarian side, but only for the Magyars who dominated their subject races, and a sham one on the Austrian side, where the Emperor retained a very large degree of initiative because of the political confusion resulting from the conflict of different national groups.

Finally, among the second-rank states, Sweden had in 1867 replaced her traditional Four Estates system by a modern parliamentary monarchy, while after 1874 Spain, under the guidance of Cánovas, a great admirer of the British parliamentary system, for the first time in the nineteenth century achieved some measure of genuine constitutional government.

What conclusion, then, do we arrive at, at the end of this examination of the influence of the British parliamentary system on the introduction of constitutional government in western Europe ? Professor Brogan has written that 'it can be said of the nineteenth century that its favourite political export was a variation of English parliamentary government' and that 'We all know that the English House of Commons is the mother of Parliaments,* and we all know how children can grow up and change so much that even their mothers cannot recognise them.'[18] The second half of this *bon mot* is as important as the first, for it is obvious that parliamentary government is far from being a precise thing, producing an identical form of political life in all states which have adopted it.

* What Bright actually said was that England was the mother of Parliaments, the House of Commons being presumably her eldest child.

Indeed it was its very flexibility which accounted for its widespread success, when adopted by European countries with very different forms of social structure, political traditions and intellectual developments. A recent French survey of European parliamentary regimes decided that 'Parliamentarism is one of those traditional juridical concepts whose content is as imprecise as their utilization is widespread', and its authors abandoned their attempt to find an exact definition that would cover all the regimes they wished quite rightly, and according to general usage, to discuss.[19]

Thus it is clear that the mother of Parliaments found that her European children were ugly ducklings or perhaps swans, but at any rate quite different from their elder sister at Westminster. The reasons for this can be grouped under three main headings. In the first place there is the question of the social, political, legal and religious background. In all these respects no country was much like Britain: although some turned out to provide a soil in which parliamentary government could take root and thrive, it was still in a form quite different from that of Britain. In particular no continental country has yet produced a two-party system of the Anglo-Saxon type. It was also the case that many states could look back to ancient representative institutions of their own. Nowhere was there complete continuity back to the Middle Ages, but it is important to remember that the British Parliament had its origin in a medieval body with parallels all over Europe. Sweden is the best example of the importance of native traditions, and Swedish historians are agreed that their 1809 constitution owed everything to their own constitutional history and nothing to the British example, although in 1867 Sweden moved over to the common European pattern influenced from Britain.[20]

In the second place no continental country set out to adopt the British system *en bloc*. At certain periods and in certain countries the idea of copying the main lines of the British parliamentary system gained ground, but it was always modified in a thousand details, and in many major matters. In particular, the crucial role of the House of Lords could not be copied in societies where the nobility was an estate, and therefore much more numerous, but on the average much less wealthy and influential, than the British aristocracy: Europe had no Whigs. In any case the British constitution was not to be found codified and easily assimilable – those who wished to copy British institutions had first of all the difficult task of finding out what they were. One difficulty was that the British form of government changed radically in the course of the period over which it was most imitated, and in many cases continental liberals were quite misinformed about the actual working of the British constitution. The influence of the Swiss journalist de Lolme is important in this. His book on the British constitution, first published in 1771, went through innumerable editions, and as the cabinet system of government developed out of eighteenth-century limited monarchy, it became more and more remote from anything that went on at Westminster. It is true that far more accurate accounts of the British system were provided by Benjamin Constant and Guizot, but at least for the first half of the nineteenth century de Lolme's book was far more widely read.

In the third place the very fact that European countries were introducing new institutions meant that their constitutions differed fundamentally from the British, as Emile Boutmy observed in 1888.[21] They were all written constitutions as opposed to the 'unwritten' (perhaps Bryce's terms of 'flexible' and 'rigid' would be better) British constitution: they lacked the prestige and authority which the British constitution derived simply from its age-old appearance. Although Britain made constitutional changes, and in fact her constitution was completely altered between 1782 and 1884, at any one time the one legislative innovation that was recent appeared small, even the biggest of them, besides the rest of the structure which remained intact. Some of the most important changes required no legislative sanction at all. All this was quite different in the written constitution of European countries. Thus it is not surprising that the great models for the other constitution-makers of Europe were the French *Chartes* of 1814 and 1830, and the Belgian constitution of 1831, not the inchoate mass of British statute law, common law and convention with its contradictory interpretations.

It would be too flattering to British pride to see the spread of parliamentary government in Europe as the simple copying of Westminster by dazzled admirers. Europeans took up parliamentary government because it seemed the best solution to their own political problems at a particular time and place, and as the century wore on there was less and less specifically British about the idea of parliamentary government. From the first the presence of common factors in the political situation of Britain and of continental countries is at least as important as imitation in the explanation of the growth of parliamentary government. In the last resort it was the existence of broad similarities of social structure and of intellectual development (in spite of myriads of differences from one area to another at a less elevated level of generality) that made for the growth of parliamentary government in Britain and on the Continent.

Where these similarities did not exist, as in Russia and in the twentieth-century attempt to transplant parliamentary systems to former British colonies in tropical Africa, parliamentarism never took root. It is also important that all parts of Europe where parliamentary regimes developed in the nineteenth century had known some form of representative institutions at an earlier period in their history. However tenuous the connection, they were to some extent building on native tradition.

It is not surprising, then, that instead of European countries developing political systems that became more and more like the British the longer they were established, it would be nearer the truth to say that the opposite happened. The British example was most important at the beginning, and countries which had successful parliamentary systems became more distinctive as they grew older in parliamentary ways, until quite distinct forms of government appeared, each equally entitled to the title, in different countries. Sometimes these forms of parliamentarism were not very successful; this has often been said about the French type, distinguished by the weakness of the executive, but it may be pointed out that the Third Republic did provide a country which is notoriously difficult to govern with several generations of political stability. There could be no denying that the Netherlands and the Scandinavian countries have developed a form of parliamentary government which is at least as successful in terms of providing for political stability and social cohesion as that of Britain, and yet quite different from the British form. It would be the height of insularity to regard our own form of parliamentary government as the ideal type from which all others are deviants. Indeed, continental constitutional lawyers are finding it more and more difficult to fit the British system into their definitions of a parliamentary regime. It would also be as well to remember that British parliamentary practice has been to some extent influenced by other forms of parliamentary government. When in 1882 the House of Commons had to tighten up its rules of procedure to deal with Irish obstruction, the new device for putting an end to debate was called *clôture*, in evidence of its French origin. As one member protested: 'I am sorry and indignant that England, the mother of Parliaments, the country from which all others have derived their lessons of parliamentary procedure, should condescend to borrow this undesirable system from such mushroom imitators.'[22]

But when all is said there remains truth in the idea that the British constitution was important in the spread of parliamentary government in Europe. It is not easy to agree with Professor Mirkine-Guetzévitch, who states that parliamentary government would have developed in exactly the same way in Europe if Britain had never known it. First of all Britain provided a continuing example of political stability, escaping the revolutions which at one time or another rocked nearly all European states. Britain was a perpetual illustration of the possibility of combining representation of the people with an aristocratic social structure, the preservation of hereditary monarchy in all its traditional splendour, and with the maintenance of Great Power status. It also seemed to many people that her phenomenal economic growth was also connected with her political institutions. In all these ways Britain's success was pointed to by European liberals as an example which confounded those on their right and on their left, who decried for different reasons this particular compromise as betraying the principles of legitimist conservatism or republican democracy. In a more precise way the British constitution offered the example of a particular institutional pattern which allowed the combination of liberal and democratic ideas with traditional and hereditary principles. It was not very easy to disentangle the mechanics of the British parliamentary system, but it was possible. From whatever source he derived his ideas Mirabeau already revealed a clear understanding of them in the debates in the Constituent Assembly, and Benjamin Constant worked them out in his elaborate treatises. From Constant's work they were absorbed into the stream of European liberal thought, to be used by those who drew up successful parliamentary constitutions such as those of Belgium and Piedmont. One reason for the success of these European parliamentary systems was the great flexibility of parliamentarism, in contrast to rigid constitutional schemes based on complete separation of powers. Statesmen in different countries, and at different times, could combine the constituent elements of parliamentary government in various mixtures: at one extreme the powers of the monarch were only limited in a very small degree: at the other the head of state was no more than a ceremonial figurehead. The German tradition, as expressed both in the ideas of the German school of constitutional lawyers, and in the realities of political life under the Second Reich and in the Austrian half of the Austro-Hungarian monarchy, always involved a weak Parliament and a strong monarch, while the French after 1875 went to the other extreme, with a very weak executive, a form of government which met with criticism by most French constitutional lawyers as departing from the true principles of the parliamentary regime.

This very flexibility of the parliamentary system makes it impossible to measure in any precise way the degree of British influence over any one European country, but this cursory review of the evidence has left me with the belief that, although less vital than might be thought, the impact of the British form of government on the constitutional evolution of continental Europe in the nineteenth century was real enough.

SUGGESTIONS FOR FURTHER READING

General works on the subject of this essay include J. A. Hawgood, *Modern Constitutions since 1787* (1939); M. J. C. Vile, *Constitutionalism and the Separation of Powers* (1967); and A. L. Lowell, *Governments and Parties in Continental Europe* (1896).

For books on individual countries see R. Fusilier, *Les Monarchies parlementaires* (1960) (it covers the Scandinavian countries, Belgium and Holland); J. Gilissen, *Le Régime représentatif en Belgique depuis 1790* (1958); M. C. L. Deslandres, *Histoire constitutionnelle de la France*, 3 vols (1932–7); J. Barthélemy, *Les Institutions politiques de l'Allemagne contemporaine* (1915); and F. Hartung, *Deutsche Verfassungsgeschichte*, 8th edn. (1950).

Monographs include J. Dedieu, *Montesquieu et la tradition politique anglaise en France* (1902); G. Bonno, *La Constitution britannique devant l'opinion française de Montesquieu à Bonaparte* (1931); R. K. Gooch, *Parliamentary Government in France, revolutionary origins, 1789–91* (1960); J. Barthélemy, *L'Introduction du régime parlementaire en France* (1904); L. Michon, *Le Gouvernment parlementaire sous la restauration* (1905); Th. Wilhelm, *Die Englische Verfassung und der vormärzische deutsche Liberalismus* (1928); R. J. Lamer, *Der Englische Parlamentarismus in der deutschen politisches Theorie im Zeitalter Bismarcks* (1963); and F. Eyck, *The Frankfurt Parliament* (1968).

NOTES

1. J. E. Thorold Rogers, *Speeches on Questions of Policy by John Bright* (1868), ii, 112.

2. For example, A. F. Pollard, *The Evolution of Parliament* (1926), p. 3, and H. Sidgwick, *The Development of European Policy* (1903), p. 420.

3. Sir Denis Brogan in *Parliament: a survey*, ed. Lord Campion (1952), p. 72. M. Duverger, *Institutions politiques et droit constitutionnel* (1960), p. 239.

4. D. Mack Smith, *A History of Sicily* (1968), ii, 343–51. H. M. Lackland, 'The Failure of the Constitutional Experiment in Sicily 1813–14', in *English Historical Review*, xli (1946), pp. 210–36. R. Carr, *Spain, 1808–1939* (1966), pp. 92–105. J. A. Hawgood, *Modern Constitutions since 1787* (1939).

5. P. Bastid, *Les Institutions politiques de la monarchie parlementaire française, 1814–48* (1954).

6. G. Bonno, *La Constitution britannique devant l'opinion française de Montesquieu à Bonaparte* (1931). F. Acomb, *Anglophobia in France, 1763–89* (1950).

7. F. Brunot, *Histoire de la langue française*, ix (1927). G. von Proschwitz, *Introduction à l'étude du vocabulaire de Beaumarchais* (1956). F. Mackenzie, *Les Relations de l'Angleterre et de la France d'après le vocabulaire* (1939).

8. R. K. Gooch, *Parliamentary Government in France, revolutionary origins, 1789–91* (1960).

9. L. Duguit, 'La Séparation des pouvoirs et l'Assemblée Nationale de *1789*', in *Revue d'Economie Politique*, vii (1893).

10. J. Barthélemy, *L'Introduction du régime parlementaire en France* (1904). L. Michon, *Le Gouvernment parlementaire sous la restauration* (1905).

11. P. Bastid, *Benjamin Constant et sa doctrine* (1960).

12. A. de Tocqueville, *Œuvres complètes*, ed. J. P. Mayer (vi), *Correspondance anglaise*, p. 332.

13. J. A. Hawgood, *Modern Constitutions since 1787* (1939), p. 145.

14. B. Mirkine-Guetzévitch, *Les Constitutions européennes* (1951), i, 24–5.

15. O. Anderson, *A Liberal State at War* (1967), pp. 92–3.

16. T. Zeldin, 'English Ideals in French Politics during the nineteenth century', in *Historical Journal*, ii (1959), 46.

17. F. Hartung, *Deutsche Verfassungsgeschichte* (1950), pp. 267–75.

18. Sir Denis Brogan, 'The Possibilities of the Presidential System', in *Parliament as an Export*, ed. A. Burns (1966), and in *Parliament: a survey*.

19. P. Lalumière and A. Demichel, *Les Régimes parlementaires européens* (1966), p. 2.

20. D. V. Verney, *Parliamentary Reform in Sweden, 1866–1921* (1957).

21. E. G. Boutmy, 'La nature de l'acte constituant en France, en Angleterre, et aux Etats Unis', in *Etudes de droit constitutionnel* (1888).

22. A. Todd, *Parliamentary Government in England*, abridged edn. (1892), ii, 74.

6. The Humanitarian Impact

OLIVER FURLEY

SENATOR FULBRIGHT wrote recently that America in the twentieth century has adopted the same attitude that Britain had in the nineteenth – when the possession of wealth and power inclined the British to develop a sense of universal responsibility. Americans now pursue a form of welfare imperialism; the same could be said about the 'arrogance of power' wielded by Britain a century ago; and the people who sought to mould British policy overseas along welfare lines, on the assumption that Britain was the trustee for the moral and material welfare of the races of the earth, were the humanitarians. Some politicians, wealthy merchants, colonial administrators and missionaries may be labelled as humanitarians, but one should use this label with caution. Although there were certain threads of continuity in the attitudes of these classes, their principles and methods varied greatly according to the circumstances of empire, the activities of foreign powers, the progress of reform in Britain and so on. Similarly, although Wilberforce could command a great following in Parliament at one stage, and Buxton at another, and missionaries such as John Philip could sway policy in South Africa, yet there were other times when humanitarian influence was slight, in government circles or in the field. If the humanitarian movement is to be an object of study, then close regard must be paid to the time-scale. Furthermore it would be a mistake to confuse it with some of the other movements which may so easily be lumped together; missionary zeal, for instance, was not necessarily the same as humanitarian zeal. If humanitarianism means a concern for material welfare, social and economic betterment, happiness, the enjoyment of reasonable civil rights and the protection of civilised laws, then the missionaries often showed comparative unconcern for these things, and in some cases ignored them. Among the agents of expanding trade and empire who called in humanitarianism to dress their actions in acceptable attire, ulterior motives could often be perceived, showing the dress to be pretty threadbare.

The Englishman was never at a loss for an effective moral attitude, Bernard Shaw complained. Often this attitude was focused sharply on the plight of peoples with whom the British came into contact overseas; strong pressure was exerted in some areas by the humanitarians, even to the extent of influencing other powers.

The fight against the transatlantic slave trade is the most prominent example where Britain set herself up as leader in a cause and sought to make others follow. Attacks had been made on the iniquities of the slave trade in the seventeenth and eighteenth centuries, in Britain, Europe and America, but it was only when the British Abolition Committee enrolled William Wilberforce and Henry Thornton to engender parliamentary support that there was a prospect of action. The 'Clapham Sect' was a powerful, wealthy pressure-group inspired with evangelical zeal, and their methods set the pattern for most humanitarian campaigns thereafter: a flow of books and pamphlets, numerous public meetings, societies with branches all over the country, addresses and petitions to Parliament all became regular features, and the influence of the pulpit, especially in nonconformist churches, was perhaps the greatest power of all.

Wilberforce, Sharp, Thornton and Grant, prominent abolitionists, were also connected with the Sierra Leone Company, which received its charter in 1791, and the Sierra Leone experiment was a vital source of inspiration to the abolitionist movement for it provided something positive to add to the negative cause of abolition. Britain had set free the surprisingly large number of slaves in the country, and Sharp linked the idea of abolition and emancipation with colonisation – the provision of a colony in West Africa for slaves freed in the course of the abolition campaign, the colony to be under a benevolent, paternal British administration which would foster Christianity, education, agriculture and trade, and even lead to eventual self-government under a representative system. Many of the special aims of British humanitarianism in Africa were thus already taking root in Sierra Leone, and those who would abolish the slave trade always harboured further ambitions of emancipation and regeneration in Africa. The African Institution was founded to maintain these general aims in Sierra Leone and other parts of Africa, with the abolition of the slave trade by foreign powers as its first aim.

In the meantime Britain had declared the slave trade illegal for British subjects in 1807. The first great aim of the Clapham Sect was achieved, and it had been anticipated only by Denmark, a comparatively minor slave-trading power. There followed some remarkable efforts by the British navy to enforce the Act by intercepting slave ships off the coast of West Africa, freeing the slaves and bringing the crews to justice. Not many ships could be spared during the Napoleonic Wars, but after it the African Squadron represented a great effort and much sacrifice. At its height in the 1840s it constituted one-sixth of the navy, cost three-quarters of a million pounds per year and suffered a high proportion of casualties. One has only to read some of the accounts of the naval commanders to realise that humanitarian zeal played a definite part in their actions, even though it was a glorious time for 'showing the flag' and asserting naval supremacy in the area, while the prize money was also a consideration. British slavers were soon driven out of business, and during the Napoleonic Wars British warships had intercepted foreign 'enemy' slavers too – French, Dutch and Spanish – which was the first indication that Britain hoped to stop the entire transatlantic slave trade in the ships of any power whatever. In the peace negotiations of 1814–15 Britain insisted that an anti-slave-trade clause be inserted into the treaty signed by the powers, with a condemnation of the trade as contrary to the principles of civilisation and human rights. Indeed the European powers were incredulous that Britain should press so hard, and suspected that there were motives other than humanitarianism. British commercial interests were of course involved.

In any case foreign powers were most unwilling to allow the British navy to interfere. In 1817 Britain succeeded in getting Spain and Portugal to agree to the navy's 'right of search' of their ships, with the right to capture them if slaves were found on board. This, however, was not satisfactory if empty slavers could get clear, so the 1835 'equipment treaty' with Spain allowed slave equipment found on board to be proof enough. Even then Portugal refused to sign a similar treaty, though Palmerston pressed for it for three years. Instead, Parliament passed an extraordinary Act unilaterally empowering the navy to seize Portuguese ships carrying equipment, which enabled the navy largely to destroy the Portuguese trade. Portugal afterwards signed an equipment treaty in 1842. The truth was that while most powers followed Britain quite rapidly in declaring the slave trade illegal, and Britain's role as the leader in this has been overstressed, they were not prepared to exert themselves much to enforce a ban, nor to allow the British to do it for them. Both Spain and Portugal accepted large gifts of money from Britain before they agreed to ban the trade, but in fact it continued on a greater scale than ever before. All the western European powers banned the trade quite soon after the wars, and even Brazil did so in 1831, but the two powers that could really have helped Britain speedily to stamp out the trade – France and America – were slow to do so. Condorcet, Rochefoucauld, Mirabeau and Lafayette were abolitionists, and their

group, *Les Amis des Noirs,* was similar to the British Abolition Committee. But the French Revolution proved no friend to the slave,
especially after the slave revolt in the West Indian colony of Saint
Domingue. During the wars the French slave trade was of necessity
abandoned, and towards its end the British abolitionists exerted strong
pressure. In 1814 the Bourbon government signed a treaty with Britain
agreeing to abolish the trade within five years; this was followed by
Napoleon's escape from Elba, when, hoping to gain British support, he
declared for immediate abolition. After Waterloo a defeated France was
obliged to repeat the ban, though only the Act of 1818 put it in satisfactory form, and then the penalties were mild. It was not until 1831
that effective penalties were introduced and France attempted enforce-
ment. At this time a British right of search was accorded, and two years
later an equipment treaty was signed, but Britannia's method of ruling
the waves was so disliked that the treaty was suspended in 1845, and the
two countries then agreed to maintain twenty-six warships each on the
West African coast. Abolitionist zeal was not measured in the same
quantities, however, and the number and effectiveness of the French
ships faded rapidly. By this time France was being hounded by British
humanitarian pressure in another area – for conducting 'free labour
emigration' from East Africa to the French Indian Ocean colonies under
virtually slave trade conditions. British protests poured in, until the
system was abolished in the 1860s. Britain herself had had some difficulty in curbing the East African slave trade to Mauritius after she took
that island from France in the war.

British pressure on France had achieved something, therefore, but
naval and commercial rivalry figured too largely to allow real co-operation. With America there was more willingness to agree on basic
principles, but even less desire to see Britain gain from her self-
appointed role. Of American sympathy with British humanitarian
ideals there is no doubt. Indeed these attitudes in the two countries
were closely related in their development, and there was a transatlantic
community of ideas which thrived, especially in the religious societies,
on a constant exchange of visitors, correspondence, pamphlets, methods
and money. Every missionary society, Frank Thistlethwaite has written,
every evangelical and humanitarian scheme in Britain had its corresponding scheme in the United States. The British and American Acts
abolishing the slave trade were passed almost simultaneously, and in
1820 the Americans declared slave trading was piracy and a capital
offence. But many slavers, especially those trading with Cuba and
Brazil, flew the American flag with impunity; and when it came to a

British right of search, America was strongly opposed to the idea, even though her own efforts to stop the abuse of her flag were clearly insufficient. In 1834 she signed the Ashburton Treaty with Britain, agreeing to maintain her own African Squadron, which she did, though with bases confined to Madeira and the Cape Verde Islands its effectiveness off West Africa was hampered. American commanders sent home indignant reports about British methods which appeared to be winning naval and commercial supremacy along the coast, and inroads into African territory as well. Naval rivalry precluded any real co-operation with Britain, and slavers of all nationalities hoisted the American flag merely to escape British warships. When Lincoln became President in 1861, the outlook changed and co-operation was at last achieved. The Anglo-American Treaty of 1862 granted a mutual right of search and established mixed commission courts, which marked a final triumph for the British policy of involving other nations in her own campaign, though it came too late to make very much difference to the trade in general, now in its last stages of decline. It did speed the end of the Cuban trade, however, the last main sphere in which American ships were involved. The Brazilian trade had already been stopped, partly due to Palmerston's intervention.

The American observation that Britain was gaining territory in Africa had some truth, and it is possible to argue that anti-slave-trade zeal was in some areas used as an excuse for territorial acquisitions, for example the Gold Coast forts in the 1840s and Lagos in 1861. Some humanitarians, led by Sturge and Clarkson, in any case declared in the late 1830s that the use of force at sea was unjustified and ineffective, and they favoured a 'positive policy' in Africa itself. From 1838 the British government responded by making anti-slave-trade treaties with African chiefs, with the aim of cutting off the trade at its source. Legitimate trade was to replace the slave trade; Europe would eagerly buy Africa's raw materials and produce in return for manufactures. Commerce would bring civilisation, and this, coupled with Christianity, would render the slave trade and slavery things of the past. No-one seemed to question whether legitimate trade would squeeze out the slave trade, and the fact that the two had been carried on side by side for a long time troubled few people.

Buxton's Society for the Extinction of the Slave Trade and for the Civilisation of Africa was confident, however, as the grand name implies. Buxton followed earlier suggestions of Sharp and the geographer M'Queen in not only encouraging legitimate trade but fostering cultivation on a new scale in Africa. His book *The African Slave Trade and its Remedy*, published in 1840, set out the aims of the society to end the slave trade by the spread of trade, Christianity and treaties, and to support a government-aided expedition up the river Niger. Africans themselves must be involved in the process. The chief means was to be new types of cultivation with the participation and assistance of Europeans. All Christian powers should unite to 'call into action the dormant energies of Africa', but if this unanimity was not obtained, Britain should do it, and he assumes that Britain in fact would have to proceed alone, claiming that Africans from Senegambia to Benin already wished to have the British as neighbours. Neighbourly help would take the form of establishing plantations where Britons could teach modern methods of agriculture and raise new crops. The British neighbours would not declare sovereignty over these areas, but one does note that the British government was to supply a police force sufficient to protect persons and property. To elevate the African mind was the first aim, then to persuade Africans to sell their productive labour instead of themselves. The coastal peoples had been ruined by the slave trade, but Buxton followed the accounts of Denham, Lander, Clapperton and others in asserting that peaceful agreements for agricultural settlements could be made further inland. Christian teaching, along with technical training of all kinds, would also be a feature, and here he suggested utilising the new wave of missionary zeal among Christian Negroes of the West Indies who expressed keenness to go to Africa. One may perceive many naïve assumptions in Buxton's proposals, especially over questions of sovereignty and African co-operation. He was evasive about the difficulties of the scheme. Nevertheless the government responded to the vigorous public campaign, and the Niger expedition set sail in 1841. It proved to be a disaster, with the climate taking a heavy toll of the personnel; and even though many casualties ought to have been expected, the fiasco meant an end to Buxton's schemes, and a very severe blow to the prestige and influence of Exeter Hall, the great humanitarian and missionary meeting centre.

Public opinion was turning against the anti-slave-trade campaign by the late 1840s, and disillusion with the Niger expedition, and with some of the consequences of slave emancipation in the West Indies, led to a decline in humanitarian fervour. The cost of the naval patrols was especially criticised. It needed the discoveries and widely publicised revelations of David Livingstone to rouse public opinion yet again to support an anti-slave-trade campaign, this time against the Arab trade in East and Central Africa. Since about 1812 Britain had been exerting some pressure on Arabs in the Indian Ocean, and successive sultans of

Zanzibar were obliged to restrict the trade in order to retain British support. A few British warships attempted to patrol vast areas up to the Persian Gulf. It was a minor repeat of the West African story, but on a smaller scale, with slower progress. In 1871 Parliament pressed for it to be speeded up, and in fact the final anti-slave-trade treaty was forced on the Sultan of Zanzibar not only by the consul's skilful persuasion but by threat of naval bombardment. British humanitarian zeal did not hesitate to press the Sultan beyond the point where he could control his subjects, and he had to rely on British aid in quelling rebellions among the habitual slave-traders. As a result his power and authority in East Africa was partially destroyed, and the last remnants of the slave trade in the interior provided an excuse for the British to extend their sphere of influence in East Africa just when the 'scramble' for Africa was on. As in West Africa, the anti-slave trade campaign led to the acquisition of territory, whether by design or not.

Meanwhile humanitarian endeavour had reached out to the victims of the slave trade – the slaves themselves. The great missionary zeal which burst forth at the beginning of the nineteenth century was closely linked to the anti-slave-trade movement, and the same leaders were the promoters of both. Most of the British Protestant churches, Anglican, Methodist, Baptist, Presbyterian and others who supported the anti-slave-trade campaign, formed missionary societies at the same time, and sent out pioneers to evangelise both slaves and free inhabitants in the West Indies, South and West Africa, India, Ceylon, Australia, New Zealand and the Pacific. The size of the task, the hazards and the casualties were on a heroic scale. Often enthusiasm outran prudence, and the societies can be criticised for sending mission families out with inadequate training, resources and supplies. We are concerned, however, with one particular aspect of this great outflow of missionaries – the humanitarian content of their message. Were they solely concerned with the spiritual condition of the people they evangelised, or did they try to temper colonial rule with humanity? Certainly they did a great deal more than teach the Gospel, and they set up as physicians (albeit usually untrained), vocational instructors and agriculturalists, bringing material improvements to those they contacted. Education also formed a major part of their work among both slave and free populations. In the case of the West Indian slaves their work was greatly opposed by the planters, who saw it as a danger to a slave-owning society. To teach the slaves was to imply that Negroes had intelligence which might measure up to the Whites'; and Negroes who were both educated and Christian could hardly continue to be slaves. The missionaries might be thought to be emancipists therefore, from the start; but in fact they were not. This was partly because they depended on the good will of the planters in allowing them to work among the slaves at all; it seems that missionaries might have some humanitarian motives, but these did not necessarily include an abhorrence of slavery. The Moravians, a mixed German and British mission, actually owned a slave plantation in Jamaica, and many of their other stations had a few slaves. As late as 1827 the Moravians in St Kitts were still buying slaves for domestic purposes, and they were not pleased when the home board said this was unwise in view of the imminence of emancipation. Methodist missionaries also owned domestic slaves in most of the West Indian islands, and the 1807 resolution of the Methodist Conference in Britain against this was hotly disputed by them. Missionary societies tried to avoid being associated with British emancipists by instructing their missionaries to concentrate purely on religious instruction, without reference to the slaves' civil condition. Indeed, many missionaries held that a Christian convert would be a better *slave*. Certainly there was no great rush to carry the humanitarian banner to the slave-owning colonies, and many missionaries on the contrary emphasised that their efforts helped to preserve the social order, the *status quo*. The Methodist missionary J. Shipman expressed what many thought: 'Were I to be questioned respecting the condition of the slaves, relating to temporal things, I think I should not hesitate to say, that many of them are in far more comfortable circumstances than the labouring class at home.' True, in some respects this statement illustrates the blindness of some, who would normally be classified as humanitarians, to the fact that slavery was a basic affront to human dignity. But many missionaries realised that Christianity had its revolutionary aspect, and that the conversion of thousands of slaves was bound to arouse discontent with their lot. Though missionaries were compelled to play it safe with the planters, some were prepared to lead the way to a better order.

At first this took the form of demanding amelioration of the slave laws, and missionaries on the spot worked with humanitarian groups at home to this end. The British slave code was a harsh one compared with the Spanish, French or Dutch codes, and although many British planters treated their slaves comparatively well, there were many, especially in Jamaica, who did not. Planter-dominated legislatures tried to pass Bills denying religious toleration and freedom of worship to slaves, and penalising missionaries. This issue was the first to arouse Parliament to urge amelioration of the slave code and, later, emancipation of the slaves. In 1815 both Houses addressed the Crown to recommend colonial legislatures to promote the physical, moral and religious improvement of their slaves; this was the beginning of a political struggle between Britain and the West Indian colonies which ended only with emancipation in 1834. Wilberforce and James Stephen in the Colonial Office worked hard in the first stages, but by 1818, after little progress had been made, Wilberforce knew that the only real answer was complete emancipation. He helped to found the Anti-Slavery Society, again with Quaker participation, but unlike the Abolition of the Slave Trade Committee, this society had a royal duke as its president, five peers and fourteen members of Parliament as vice-presidents. The humanitarian cause was assured of infinitely more official and political support at this stage. Buxton took over from the ageing Wilberforce, and a flood of pamphlets backed up his campaign, along with his *Anti-Slavery Monthly Reporter*, and many articles in the *Edinburgh Review* and the *Westminster Review*. Petitions to Parliament from town and country poured in, and when Buxton introduced a motion in 1823 that slavery was repugnant to the principles of the British constitution and the Christian religion, he must have felt that success was certain in the end. But he knew that emancipation would be a dangerous and tricky process in the colonies, and he suggested that amelioration of the slave laws could be the first step. In this he was immediately supported by the government, and Canning, the Foreign Secretary, put forward a series of resolutions to 'prepare the slaves for freedom' as early as was compatible with their welfare, the safety of the colonies, and with due regard to the interests of private property. Any one of these three considerations might engender enormous difficulties, but in fact the planters knew they were fighting a rearguard action from now on. They obstructed such measures as the restriction of punishment by the whip, the admission of slave evidence in civil and criminal cases, easier conditions for the manumission of slaves, for their marriage, acquisition of property, greater leisure, etc., all of which were urged by successive colonial secretaries. The slaves, conscious of the fact that they were being denied a better deal, indulged more frequently in revolt, and looked to the government in Britain and the missionaries in the colonies as their champions. The latter had already produced a martyr, in Smith of the London Missionary Society, who was imprisoned and died as a result of the revolt in Demerara in 1823.

The story of emancipation is well known, and it was a battle in which the government, the Colonial Office and Parliament were all firmly on the side of the humanitarians. There is one aspect of the campaign which must be noted here, however, because it affected the humanitarian

approach to other problems in the rest of the century. One assumption
of the society which had sanctioned slavery was that the Negro, 'Black
Quashee', was racially inferior to the Europeans, morally and intellectually, and so it was quite fitting that slavery should be his appointed
station in life. Europeans in West Africa before this period had been
shocked to encounter what appeared to them degraded cultures and
barbarous practices, and although the 'noble savage' might exist in the
interior away from the corruption of the slave trade, further exploration
revealed much to horrify the traveller, and the 'myth of the interior'
died out. Yet in the first decades of the nineteenth century a few genuine
anthropologists from Britain began to study African cultures scientifically, and the African Institution questioned travellers on the nature
of African society. A reaction against the racial and cultural chauvinism
of the European was just beginning. Wilberforce wrote in a pamphlet
of 1823: 'The day, I trust, is gone forever, in which the alleged inferiority
of intellect, and incurable barbarity of the African race were supposed to
extenuate their oppression.' Buxton held that the slave was lazy and
deceitful only because slavery had made him so: Europeans who had
been enslaved showed the same characteristics. British missionaries in
the West Indies supported this stand, and their writings, as well as
British anti-slavery writings, were full of the potentialities of the Negro
and his fitness for emancipation on the grounds that as a human being
he was the white man's equal.

The stage was set for Britain to lead the colonial powers in emanci-
pating the slaves in their colonies. Some effort was needed to arouse
sufficient public feeling: Wilberforce complained that people wished
only to be assured that slaves were well treated – a question equally
appropriate to cattle – and that they were blind to the slaves' social
condition. But the numerous slave revolts, especially the 1831–2 revolt
in Jamaica, had a cumulative effect and helped to make the British
realise that the West Indies could not be held indefinitely under this
system. Emancipation should not be viewed as exclusively the achievement of humanitarians in Britain: a revolutionary situation in the West
Indies helped to precipitate it. Since Canning's resolutions of 1823,
however, it was clearly official policy in Britain to bring about emancipation, and the Clapham Sect had firm allies in high places, especially
in James Stephen, legal counsel in the Colonial Office and later Permanent Under-Secretary, and son of an early anti-slave-trader. The link
between government and evangelical interests was never closer. The
missionary societies became bolder, especially the Methodists in 1824,
in declaring for emancipation. A great humanitarian had arrived in

Jamaica at this time: William Knibb, Baptist missionary. Though, like other missionaries, he had to keep his views on slavery to himself at first, when persecution of the missionaries and obstruction of the amelioration schemes became really flagrant, and when the slave revolt had been ruthlessly put down, he and his colleagues, Burchell and Phillippo, went to Britain to lead an emancipation campaign throughout the length and breadth of the land. In an atmosphere of reform at home, such vivid accounts as they gave fell on sympathetic ground, and missionaries from the West Indies provided the cutting edge to the emancipists' weapon. The Emancipation Act of 1833, albeit softened with a grant of £20 million as compensation to slave-owners, put Britain right in the forefront of humanitarian endeavour among the colonial powers. Children born of slaves had been freed before this time in northern U.S.A., and in Ceylon and St Helena (then territories of the British East India Company), but these were minor measures. Emancipation by other powers followed only slowly: Uruguay in 1842, France and Denmark in 1848, Argentine in 1853, Peru in 1854, U.S.A. and the Netherlands in 1863 (though the Dutch continued 'compulsory labour' until 1873), Cuba in 1880–6, Brazil in 1883–8, and Spain in 1886. Not all these powers owed much to Britain's example, though America was again a close follower, and in the 1830s American emancipists adopted much of the British campaign apparatus for themselves. In Africa and India the situation was more complex, because in many cases the slaves were owned not by colonists but by natives. Humanitarians tended to confuse colonial plantation slavery with indigenous domestic slavery, which could be an altogether different kind. The Boers in South Africa trekked out of British territory partly to avoid the consequences of emancipation, but Britain persuaded them to free their own slaves in the Sand River Convention of 1852. In British protected areas in Africa where slavery was customary, the Colonial Office was very cautious in pressing for emancipation, until Lord Carnarvon, Colonial Secretary in 1874, moved by a fresh wave of humanitarian protest, declared the time had come to lay aside a timid attitude and remove the dishonour and moral taint which any toleration of slavery incurred. Gradually the legal status of slavery was abolished, and the acquisition of new slaves in such areas as northern Nigeria was prevented by some of the last anti-slave-trade campaigns – those of Lugard and Goldie, which extended into the twentieth century. Such activities in these decades were not confined to the British, because in the scramble for Africa the participating powers, in the Berlin Act of 1885 and the Brussels Act of 1890, had all pledged themselves to suppress the slave trade and slavery. Britain was a major instigator of such agreements, however, and tended to be more attentive to these obligations. The Germans, for instance, never abolished slavery in German East Africa, though they declared slave children free; it was left to the British, in taking it over as a League of Nations mandated territory, to abolish slavery as late as 1922. In British India and Malaya the legal status of slavery had been abolished in 1843.

The British claim to have led the anti-slave-trade and emancipation campaigns out of disinterested and purely humanitarian motives has had its detractors, and few historians would not share some of this scepticism today about these 'perfectly virtuous' pages of British history. Eric Williams attacked the claim in his *Capitalism and Slavery* (1943). He admits that humanitarians were the spearhead of the onslaught which destroyed the West Indian system, but considers their influence has been exaggerated. Instead, economic motives were of prime importance in persuading government and Parliament to act. When the slave trade was abolished, British participants had been losing ground anyway; and, afterwards, West Indian slave-grown, tariff-protected sugar came under attack from the East Indian interest and from Free Traders, and emancipation was their victory. Williams was right in asserting that many emancipists were also Free Traders, but a consensus of opinion now prefers the conclusion that, while economic conditions in Britain facilitated and no doubt encouraged the abolition of the slave trade and slavery, they did not require it to be carried out as an economic necessity. The Williams thesis could perhaps be better applied to the similar campaigns in East and Central Africa towards the end of the century, where humanitarian motives were assuredly mingled with motives of expanding trade and capturing territory, though naturally this was seldom admitted at the time.

If humanitarian concern combined with economic interest at the time of emancipation, yet the former persisted afterwards in taking close account of the welfare of the free slaves, and in doing so aroused Britain to a certain awareness of the concept of trusteeship for colonial subjects. The West Indian Negroes were not entirely freed by the emancipation Act, but were made apprentices to their former owners for a period of adjustment to a free-labour system. Missionaries there soon aroused humanitarians at home to make new efforts on behalf of the Negroes, as conditions for the apprentices were extremely harsh. Phillippo's prophecy that they would rebel unless the system was ended was read by Lord Brougham in the House of Lords. Knibb supplied his humanitarian friends in Britain with a stream of stories about oppression.

As so often before, the Quaker response was especially strong, and Joseph Sturge was induced to tour the West Indies with Harvey to see for themselves, and write a report. They supplied powerful propaganda against the cruelties of the system and the harsh punishments at the workhouse and the treadmill. (One may notice even here, however, the element of prudery and moralising that went with British humanitarianism: they seemed, for instance, more concerned with women's exposure to indecency on the treadmill than with the barbarity of the punishment itself.) Public pressure succeeded in obtaining the end of apprenticeship in 1838, two years earlier than its due date.

Nor did British concern stop with the ending of apprenticeship. The smooth transition to a system of free labour, with fair wages, education for the children, and village settlements for a new class of Negro peasants, was to a large extent the work of the missionaries, backed up by their societies at home and in particular by Quaker money. The missionaries who for so long denied that they wished to influence the civil state of the slaves, now became the champions of the free Negroes in asserting their rights. Knibb was called 'the Dan O'Connell of Jamaica' by the planters, for his pains to procure decent working conditions for his followers. Phillippo wrote that he was ready to sink with the fatigue of riding from estate to estate, where properties and attorneys submitted wage scales to him for comment. In all the islands it was the same story: an awareness of the Negro's status was gradually aroused, sometimes with the help of sympathetic governors. Above all, the missionaries called on British philanthropy to finance schools and 'free villages' for Negroes who moved away from the sugar estates and set up as peasant farmers, the 'noble free peasantry' that Knibb said he hoped to create.

The education of the Negro, slave and free, received considerable attention from British humanitarians. By the 1820s all the missionary societies regarded education, both secular and religious, as part of their work, and organisations in Britain such as the Ladies' Negro Education Society, the Society for the Furtherance of the Gospel, the British and Foreign Bible Society, the London Association in aid of Moravian Missions with its Negro School Fund, all supplied aid to schools in the West Indies and parts of Africa. With emancipation, Parliament saw the urgent need to expand this work, and voted £30,000 per annum to the ex-slave colonies for the support of mission and charity schools. Lord Glenelg, the Colonial Secretary, who was closely linked with humanitarian groups at this time, wanted adult education for free slaves to be included in this scheme. But some missions were suspicious of this subvention, and the way to state-aided education in the colonies was still fraught with hazards, as it was at home. Nor may the government's interest in Negro education be attributed solely to humanitarian motives: Lord Stanley, Colonial Secretary in 1845, urged the expediency of making this education largely industrial, so as to increase the prosperity of the colonies and, as some alleged, to keep the Negroes in a low place. It was not until after Crown Colony government was established in the West Indies in the 1860s that a state-aided education system came to be accepted by missionaries and philanthropists, now less distrustful of colonial authority.

Before mid-century, humanitarian interest focused not only on the Negro, in the West Indies or West Africa, but on Indians, Africans in Southern Africa, Red Indians in North America, Maoris and Aborigines in New Zealand, Australia and the South Seas. At a time when 'the high-water mark of humanitarian dominance in British colonial affairs' was reached, as one writer puts it, when successive colonial secretaries, such as Lord Glenelg (1835–9), Lord Normanby (1839), Lord John Russell (1839–41) and later Earl Grey, were all willingly compliant, people were aware that colonial expansion had caused hardships to natives everywhere, in the shape of the loss of land, disruption of culture, forced labour, new diseases and new evils connected with such novelties as European liquor and firearms. The 'fatal impact' of western man on primitive peoples had to be softened by humanitarian ideals of fair dealing, and the 'improvement' of natives by imparting western civilisation and Christianity to them. Since Britain was pre-eminent in the quest for new markets, and her traders and colonists appeared likely to come into contact with more natives than those of any other power, Britain had a world-wide role to play, a great moral responsibility, it was claimed. The corollary, of course, followed very closely: British trade could expand only if natives were civilised, at peace and imbued with western habits of industry which would promote wealth. From 1835 to 1837 a parliamentary select committee on aborigines was chaired by Buxton, and its aims were supported in public by the Aborigines Protection Society. The committee set about examining the injustices inflicted in every part of the empire. The combination of 'civilising zeal' with commercial endeavour is most marked in its deliberations, though this was partly of course to persuade Parliament and government to follow its recommendations. A fair and better treatment of natives would 'promote the civil and commercial interests of Great Britain', they declared. The depredations of colonists in Australia and New Zealand and the depopulation and demoralisation of the Pacific Isles by British seamen were clearly to Britain's disadvantage. By contrast, a civilising mission would induce gratitude and show a profit. 'Savages are dangerous neighbours and unprofitable customers, and if they remain as degraded denizens of our colonies, they become a burden upon the State.' The most effective remedy was the propagation of Christianity together with the preservation of the civil rights of the natives. Christianity and civilisation were inseparable, and could only be introduced together. Much missionary evidence was adduced in support of this. The committee condemned settler control of natives, the vagrancy laws in South Africa and the purchase of any new lands or territory without the approval of Parliament. Instead the accent was to be on religious instruction and education of the natives, and on their political, social and economic improvement.

Buxton intended this report to be 'a sort of manual for the future treatment of aboriginal nations in connection with our colonies', but historians differ as to its real effect. There can be little doubt, however, that the committee, with its supporters in Parliament and the Colonial Office, and with the continuous activity of the Aborigines Protection Society thereafter, did mould colonial policy, if only at certain times and in certain areas. In South Africa the Rev. Dr John Philip of the London Missionary Society had already managed to achieve some success for these principles, and continued to do so. As superintendent of the mission in South Africa from 1820 to 1850, in close touch with Buxton and the evangelical humanitarians, he provides perhaps the most prominent example of successful action in this field. He was partly responsible for the Fiftieth Ordinance of 1828, freeing the Hottentots from oppressive laws, and he also persuaded the colonial government to modify its frontier policy. In 1835 Lord Glenelg responded by actually forcing the abandonment of the newly annexed Queen Adelaide's Territory (though Philip would have preferred a type of protectorate), and by condemning the 'commando system' of retaliation against thefts of stock. He forbade the extension of Cape Colony by conquest or cession. It was admittedly a period of retrenchment in colonial policy anyway, and Philip could not get the government to go a stage further and take native areas into British protection against colonial encroachment – this type of 'humanitarian imperialism' did not yet appeal sufficiently to Britain. Again Philip had earlier secured by treaty certain safeguards for the lands of the Griquas, peoples of mixed descent who had left Cape Colony, but in the 1840s this did not prevent the overrunning of their land by colonists. Robert Moffat, Livingstone, the French Protestant missionary Casalis and others kept up the struggle to curb Boer and colonial encroachment on native lands, but the Basutos, the Bechuana and the Natal tribes had to suffer just the same. In the 1850s, when Britain decided to recognise the independence of the Boer republics, humanitarian influence was at a low ebb. When British protectorates were later declared over Basutoland and Bechuanaland, the humanitarian element of 'protection' of native interests was only one of several motives: the scramble for Africa was beginning. In West Africa humanitarians fought against retrenchment in the early sixties with rather more success. Missionaries (many Swiss and German as well as British) initiated a powerful campaign against withdrawal, which evoked strong support from the British public and Parliament, making it in the end impossible for the government to withdraw from the Gold Coast or Sierra Leone. When the Gold Coast Colony was established in 1874, the Aborigines Protection Society persuaded Lord Carnarvon to abolish slavery there, as we have seen. This change would require much supervision, and so the government found itself taking on more burdens in the name of humanitarianism, not fewer. The annexation of Lagos in 1861 was also a late victory for the anti-slave-trade campaigners, as well as for Palmerston's African policy 'to encourage and extend British commerce and thereby to displace the slave trade'.

In Australia and New Zealand the British government strove, with only moderate success, to keep relations with the natives in their hands rather than in the settlers' hands, but could not prevent a series of wars breaking out over land disputes. In New Zealand missionaries were again the instigators of the idea that natives had rights, to be defended against the incursions of colonists. The Church Missionary Society loudly protested that New Zealand was not under British sovereignty and was inhabited by Maoris who would be harmed by colonisation. Lord Glenelg was a vice-chairman of the C.M.S., and his under-secretary, Sir George Grey, was a committee member; it is small wonder that the Colonial Office responded, and sent an officer to make the Treaty of Waitangi with the Maoris in 1840. The treaty provided a model to delight the hearts of the Aborigines Protection Society: British sovereignty was acknowledged, but Maori land rights were safeguarded, and sales of land were to be conducted through the Crown. The colonial government when it was established did its best to carry out the intention of the treaty, supported by Colonial Secretary Lord Stanley, who was much in sympathy with the humanitarian view. It was a chimera though, to believe that Maoris and colonists could exist as separate nations side by side, with colonial administrators as the only link between them. Both sides committed violence, and the parliamentary select committee preferred 'amalgamation' to the clearly impractical ideas of the Aborigines Protection Society. It was left to Sir George Grey, Governor of New Zealand for two spells, to blend these ideas together. While safeguarding Maori interests as best he could, respecting their customs and traditions, and establishing a benign personal influence over the chiefs, he took steps to 'westernise' them, with schools and hospitals, resident magistrates to spread British law, and with agricultural assistance, etc. This was a step far ahead of the ideas of earlier humanitarians concerning Australasia, of leaving the natives in their pristine purity, many missionaries having advocated the least possible contact with western civilisation so as to avoid corrupting and demoralising influences.

In India various East India Company officials had a concern for the millions of Indians under their rule, and Parliament had on several occasions nudged the Company into an awakening to its responsibilities. Missionaries in India and evangelicals at home were not the only leaders in this cause: rationalists and utilitarians such as James Mill and his son, John Stuart Mill, also wished to 'humanise' British rule in India and take western civilisation and 'improvement' to the people. Humanitarian pressure speeded the reform of the harsh Indian criminal codes, and the abolition of practices held to be evil and barbaric by the British, such as suttee and female infanticide; and where British rule was extended into new territories, these motives often played a part. Missionaries began to make their influence in India effective on a small scale in the first decades of the nineteenth century, just when Parliament, in its successive Acts renewing the Company's charter, started pressing for a greater degree of responsibility to be shown towards native welfare. 'It is the duty of this country to promote the interests and happiness of the native inhabitants of the British dominions in India,' stated the Act of 1813; and a modest annual grant was made towards education. Inevitably the education offered to the Indian was western. Modernisation would now proceed apace, and this would lead at some time to irresistible demands for self-government; but many of the reformers and humanitarian sympathisers gladly acknowledged such a result. However, the Indian Mutiny of 1857 was a severe set-back to the popular acceptance of such ideals, and the wisdom of westernising and modernising a foreign race was questioned. Indeed, British attitudes towards race were inevitably affected. The atrocities of the Mutiny, the increasingly lurid revelations of explorers penetrating deeper and deeper into Africa and the apparent indigence of the West Indian Negro, all contributed to a rising racialism in the fifties and sixties, and a feeling that British humanitarianism overseas was misdirected.

The doctrine of racial superiority, common to all the colonising powers, had its protagonists in Britain. Darwin's *Origin of Species* (1859) was used by them to boost the idea that the white race was destined to conquer and rule the inferior races, and it was followed by *The Races of Man* (1862) by Robert Knox, who has been called the real founder of British racialism. In a confused but influential book he justified imperialist expansion and poured scorn on humanitarian efforts to lessen the shock of colonialism for subject races. 'A wish to serve Africa forms the excuse for an expedition to the Niger, the real object being the enslaving of the unhappy Negro, dispossessing him of his lands and freedom. I prefer the manly robber to this sneaking, canting hypocrisy.' He laughs at the 'mock philanthropy' of England, and at attempts to protect aborigines, when the annexation of New Zealand, for instance, was merely a cool piece of aggression, in which the Colonial Office certainly did not wish to give the Maoris rights as British subjects. Inferior races were destined to be subject races. The new imperialism which grew soon after Knox's book had a definite basis on this type of racialist assumption, and the humanitarians' case against it was weakened, as Curtin points out, because they persisted in confusing a supposed cultural inferiority, which they tended to acknowledge, with a basic racial inferiority.

More moderate racialists took the very common view that the primitive races were 'children' who needed to be fathered. Many humanitarians indeed took this view themselves, and urged on Britain the duties of a father: humanitarianism could in many cases be said to have sprung from a belief, not that all races were equal and should be treated equally, but that some were inferior and needed special treatment. Often this notion of cultural and racial superiority arose out of sheer ignorance of the complexities of the societies and cultures which empire-builders met. (There were exceptions in India. A few Britons had a knowledge of and a high regard for Indian culture.) Even missionaries, supposedly the most open-minded on this question, regarded African tribes, for example, as living degraded lives, with evil customs and pagan beliefs which hardly merited study. Curtin suggests that missionary societies deliberately stressed this barbarism in order to stir philanthropic hearts into donating more money to *change* African society. For the missionaries and humanitarians believed that all races went through progressive stages of civilisation, and if some had been held back for various reasons, it was Britain's duty to bring them forward. Buxton explained, in *The African Slave Trade and its Remedy*, that 'what we found the African, the Romans found us'. The Romans improved our culture and introduced theirs: we must do the same in Africa, 'to raise Africa from the dust'. When the time came for the scramble for Africa, the public were thoroughly prepared for British intervention, especially in East and Central Africa, on humanitarian grounds.

Livingstone may be seen as a key figure here, in bringing about a change in attitude in the fifties and sixties, just when racialism was at its height. His accounts of his travels were very widely read, and he inspired many explorers, missionaries and administrators to modify their views and bring more patience, sympathy and humility into their approach to Africans. He established close personal relationships with them: he had a keen curiosity concerning their customs and beliefs, and though he too spoke of white superiority, he was convinced that Africans could speedily be elevated to a 'higher' level of civilisation by the elimination of the slave trade, which he now revealed as widespread in East Africa, and by the introduction of Christianity and commerce. Britons, he thought, could be 'harbingers of peace to a hitherto distracted and down-trodden race'. Though this may not seem very different from the pious outpourings of previous decades, Livingstone initiated a second phase of the anti-slave-trade campaign, a new period and a new area of missionary endeavour, and a trust in the intermingling of white settlers and traders with Africans in a new colonial society, which was different from the 'treaty policy' or the isolation of Africans in protectorates advocated earlier in southern Africa. When H. M. Stanley (whose own attitude to Africans had been considerably transformed by Livingstone) made his famous appeal in 1875 for missionaries to go to Buganda, it was not only the dark side of the picture that he painted but also the high level of civilisation, the rich and elaborately organised Buganda monarchy which he cited as an inducement. Towards the end of the century Britons in positions of responsibility in Africa all had their 'favourite tribes', whom they positively admired for various manly characteristics: the humanity of Livingstone was inherited by the wielders of trusteeship.

Trusteeship was the last and most sophisticated notion of the humanitarians in the nineteenth century. From the private empire of the Brooke family in Sarawak, to the new protectorates in Africa, there was a permeating idea of British rule as a trust for the advancement and enlightenment of subject peoples, leading ultimately to self-sufficiency of a new type. Not that this idea was new. The word was applied to Sierra Leone in its early days, and the ultimate advance to self-government was mentioned as the goal of British tutelage in the Gold Coast as early as 1852 by Earl Grey. By the time Britain had acquired the willing or unwilling co-operation of the world in banning the trans-atlantic slave trade, she felt she had the power to be the moral guardian of civilisation everywhere. Not only British Christianity, culture, industrial and commercial life, but also democracy and law were con-sidered to have reached a perfection hitherto unknown: to export them to less fortunate peoples was a moral duty. Chamberlain, Colonial Secretary in the nineties, believed that the British race was the greatest of the governing races that the world had ever seen, and that the *Pax Britannica* always brought clear benefits to those under its sway; the 'undeveloped estates' of the empire must be developed and advanced by a positive colonial policy, aiming not only for power and profit but also for welfare and justice. In other words, imperial expansion, involving military conquest as it frequently did, could yet be linked with humani-tarian causes in the minds of contemporaries, though few would have stated it thus. Such a process of thought was engendered by the long tradition of a paternalistic, civilising, evangelising mission which we have already seen. The famous *Punch* cartoon about the acquisition of Uganda shows Uganda as a baby, a foundling on John Bull's doorstep, requiring, like the other colonies, to be brought up. The days of informal empire, the possession of 'spheres of influence', where missionaries and traders plied without the British flag, seemed over in the eighties and nineties: John Bull had the responsibilities of a father, not a distant cousin. The father-and-child analogy was also useful in that it provided a satisfactory excuse for the wielding of colonial authority, if necessary of a harsh disciplinary type. Punitive expeditions were sometimes regarded as necessary to teach a salutary 'lesson'. Humanitarianism could easily shade into authoritarianism.

If trusteeship now became more positively a political matter involving the *Pax Britannica*, it must not be thought that the evangelising mission had become any less intense. The missionary was still an agent of humanitarianism: he might carry civilisation and material advance more directly to colonial peoples than the administrator. Christianity and civilisation were to advance together; this was a Buxton tradition and it was still in vogue. Material progress had to be linked with spiritual, and the proportion of missionaries who were not ordained ministers but lay helpers, teachers, artisans and craftsmen was high. Moravian missions always included craftsmen; Livingstone was a medical missionary who also did not hesitate to include irrigation schemes, etc., in his work; Mackay went to Uganda as an 'engineering missionary'. In the South Seas the great majority of the early missionaries were artisans, while in Australia and New Zealand they preferred to regard themselves as the sole custodians of civilisation, to the exclusion of settlers, in elevating the aborigines. Livingstone, on the other hand, fondly hoped that British settlers, when they came to Central Africa, would bring both Christianity and civilisation to Africans by their example; so did the organisers of the missions from the West Indies to West Africa who sent 'exemplary' West Indian families there. The Morant Bay rebellion of 1865 in Jamaica had been partly caused by missionary concern for the oppression of the Negro peasantry by a colonial government which was not fulfilling the role of trusteeship according to the ideas of the mother country. E. B. Underhill, Secretary of the Baptist Missionary Society, exposed this oppression after his visit there, and gave a very full account of the Negroes' plight, suggesting a wide range of social and economic reform. When a Crown Colony government was established after the rebellion, it showed a fairly keen awareness of the trusteeship role, and a new system of state education, better medical services, tax revisions, legal reforms, road improvements, etc., followed. It cannot be said that this enthusiasm lasted, however; royal commissions of enquiry into West Indian conditions at the end of the century revealed that colonial rule had been paternalist but inert; the pressure of humanitarians at home always tended to be focused on newer areas of interest. The West Indies had had their day.

Africa was the last area where contact with new peoples still excited them, and where anti-slave-trade fervour could still exercise itself. Britain led the Brussels Conference of 1889, in which seventeen nations took part, to pledge themselves to suppress the trade by taking control of areas where it originated and setting up European administrations there. Nothing suited the current British mood of 'humanitarian imperialism' better. But this mood was affected by a number of other more material considerations, and the humanitarians were only half successful in their wishes. In South Africa, Cecil Rhodes was bent on Cape colonial expansion, but humanitarians fervently advocated protectorates rather than Boer or Cape colonial rule. Missionaries and explorers usually assumed that their activities would sooner or later usher in colonial rule, and hoped that this would be British rather than Boer, Portuguese or any other; some of them actually helped to promote it, and argued that it was humane to put an end to inter-tribal warfare by imposing white rule. Humanitarians at home, notably the Aborigines Protection Society, W. E. Forster in the cabinet and later Chamberlain's 'South Africa Committee', supported by a considerable group of Members of Parliament, met with only limited success, and saw the government hand over 'native administration', affecting many tribes, to the Cape and to the Boers in the Transvaal. The Pretoria Convention of 1881 was supposed to give Britain a watching brief over native rights, as a sop to the humanitarians, but they knew it was not worth much. Strategic and economic rather than humanitarian considerations guided the government's determination to keep an imperial suzerainty over southern Africa. In Bechuanaland the struggles of the missionary John Mackenzie have been well chronicled, and he ranks with Philip as one of the great humanitarian champions of native rights. In the 1880s, when either Boer or Cape expansion into the area seemed inevitable, Mackenzie, backed by the London Missionary Society, made his plea for a British protectorate. Vigorous support came from Britain and, when a protectorate was declared, Mackenzie was actually made resident commissioner. But even then the Cape dominated it, and succeeded in paring off South Bechuanaland from British control ten years later. Rhodes in any case used Bechuanaland as a jumping-off point for his annexation of Rhodesia, and here again humanitarians fought for native interests against his South Africa Company, in a losing battle. Rhodes's request for a royal charter for his company to administer and develop the area was too great a temptation for the British government to refuse. They could get occupation on the cheap, and all the efforts of the South Africa Committee and the Aborigines Protection Society were of no avail. When it came to declaring a protectorate in Nyasaland, however, all these interests could combine: missionaries in the area urged it, so did humanitarian groups in Britain; the government desired to keep Portugal out, and, a reason which probably weighed more than any other, Rhodes offered to subsidise a protectorate government. Only after Sir Harry Johnston began imposing taxation by force, with harsh penalties, did the missionaries realise that perhaps they had been too ready to call in the forces of colonialism to redress the evils of the slave trade and tribal warfare. Even so, they felt a glow of righteousness in keeping out the Portuguese, who were much criticised for ignoring the duties of trusteeship in Africa. The idea that 'humanitarian imperialism', and even Christian evangelism, might not be welcomed by Africans at all was discounted by the missionaries.

Some have argued that in the 1890s humanitarians and missionaries had in any case lined themselves up much more with the colonialist school, and that in the new age of imperialism, humanitarianism had bowed itself out. Perhaps it would be more accurate to say that colonial policy and its administrators had come closer to the humanitarians' point of view; there was less difference between them. In East Africa humanitarians had long campaigned for British intervention to stop the slave trade and support missionary work, and when British agents did penetrate inland, first in the employ of the Imperial British East Africa Company, later of the protectorate governments, they pursued roughly the same ends that the humanitarians urged. They were concerned not only with the exclusion of rival European powers and the possibilities for settlers, but also with the elimination of the slave trade and slavery, of the arms and liquor trades and with the 'advancement' of the Africans. The I.B.E.A. Company was not even seriously equipped to make a profit out of trading, and it spent a lot of its money on freeing slaves. Similarly the British government built the Uganda Railway at enormous cost, primarily for strategic reasons in order to command the Nile headwaters, but it was far from convinced that there would ever be much economic profit from it, and the chief reasons for it advanced in Parliament were that it would help to eradicate the slave trade and speed the advance of civilisation into the interior. In what later became Kenya there was a mixture of aggression against unco-operative tribes combined with a consciousness that protection was supposed to mean something and not merely to provide lip-service to humanitarians at home. Some officials genuinely tried to rein in the punitive expeditions and to concentrate on the benefits which colonialism was supposed to bring. Sir Charles Eliot, in charge there at the end of the century, was typical in thinking that British rule was a change for the better: 'If East Africa is not yet a paradise,' he wrote, 'we may at least congratulate ourselves on having changed this scene of human suffering. The slave trade is at an end . . . massacres are equally a thing of the past . . . Africa has not yet become civilised, but it has become possible to think of civilisation.' The arrogance of the colonialist combined here with the classic assumptions of the humanitarian.

In Uganda, when the company announced that it could no longer afford to administer the country, a public debate took place in Britain about her role in this part of Africa. Most missionaries there were firmly wedded to the idea of British control, and the Church Missionary Society definitely wanted to see a British protectorate supporting British evangelism. Lugard, too, who had made treaties of 'protection' or alliance in Uganda on behalf of the company, campaigned ardently in Britain against disowning such promises. If the British withdrew their presence from Uganda, the slave trade would revive, Islam or paganism would triumph over Christianity, and the company's allies and friends would be overrun by their traditional enemies, he argued. All these appeals were to the humanitarian public, and it was on these lines that the question was debated, though the government in finally declaring a protectorate was concerned with strategic interests primarily. Yet the fact that the public had strongly supported the humanitarian cause was bound to be reflected in the behaviour of the administration, and the Uganda Protectorate provides one of the clearest examples of the trusteeship ideal moderating the more dominating tendencies of colonialism. It was no accident that the Uganda Agreement of 1900, while securing tight political control, attempted to respect native king-ship, tribal authorities, religious freedom and the rights of different communal groups.

Nineteenth-century British humanitarianism had been a strange mixture. It rose quickly to its zenith in the anti-slave-trade campaign, and in the emancipation campaign. It mingled with missionary zeal. After a mid-century decline it rose again with more comprehensive ideas of trusteeship, though these became clouded with 'humanitarian imperialism', which at times did not seem very different from territorial imperialism. In this present century, however, when imperialism has gone, one may still note many emanations of the last century's humani-tarianism, which shows how deep its roots must have been.

SUGGESTIONS FOR FURTHER READING

There is no general book on British humanitarianism. Sir Reginald Coupland, *The British Anti-Slavery Movement* (1964) is a good short account, and if out-dated it may be corrected by G. R. Mellor, *British Imperial Trusteeship, 1783–1850* (1951), which attempts a synthesis between Coupland and Eric Williams. S. Neill, *Colonialism and Christian Missions* (1966) draws very interesting com-parisons, K. Ingham, *Reformers in India* (1956) is a good short account. P. D. Curtin, *The Image of Africa* (1965) is of vital importance regarding British attitudes in West Africa to race, culture and the civilising mission. W. M. Macmillan, *Bantu, Boer and Briton* (1963) discusses John Philip and native policy. H. A. C. Cairns, *The Prelude to Imperialism: British Reactions to Central African Society, 1840–90* (1965) is a highly critical analysis of humanitarian aims in that area. A. Holmberg, *African Tribes and European Agencies: Colonialism and Humanitarianism in British South and East Africa, 1870–95* (1967) gives a valuable Swedish outlook over this wide field. Lastly R. Robinson and J. Gallacher, *Africa and the Victorians* (1965) has much to say on the links between humanitarianism and imperialism.

In writing this chapter I would also like to acknowledge my indebtedness to two cyclostyled collections given at seminars held by the Edinburgh University Centre of African Studies, *The Transatlantic Slave Trade from West Africa* (1965) and *The Theory of Imperialism: the European Partition of Africa* (1968).

7. Imperial Britain

DONALD SOUTHGATE

As the editor emphasises in the first sentence of his introduction, it is gravely misleading to think of Britain Pre-eminent mainly, still less wholly, in terms of a British 'empire' much of which seemed to policymakers in London an embarrassment rather than an asset. It is true that even before the Scramble for Africa the British Empire had become the vastest ever known and that most of it was acquired in the hundred years after the loss of the American colonies. But the acquisitions were not made as part of some single and central policy. The 'empire' was never a unity except in the narrowly legal sense that the 'Imperial Parliament at Westminster' could, if it wished, legislate for any part of it. And whether one thinks in terms of acquisition, real or supposed economic value, constitutional status, population patterns or apparent destiny, it consisted of highly disparate elements, which came only accidentally to constitute parts of an anomalous whole.

Within the British 'empire' of the nineteenth century were now unwanted relics of its eighteenth-century predecessor. The Caribbean colonies had once been economically, strategically and prestigiously important, but now, because of the abolition of slavery in the 1830s and of imperial preference in the 1840s and 1850s, they were unable to adjust to the new conditions of international economy or to attract either immigrants or investors. Even those other relics of the old Atlantic empire, the colonies of British North America, had a limited attraction for immigrants and investors, and were little prized in Whitehall. The vast preserves of the Hudson's Bay Company beyond the settled areas of the St Lawrence and Toronto began, by the middle of the nineteenth century, to receive settlers up the natural geographical routes from the American Mid-West and West, and were saved from absorption in the great neighbouring republic rather by the pressure of the St Lawrence colonists on London than by the wishes of Whitehall. But what was known from 1867 as the 'Dominion of Canada' was distinctly part of the 'empire of settlement', like Australia, New Zealand and (with obvious distinctions) South Africa. These four were in the early twentieth century to be known as *Dominions*, a term which was shorthand for 'the self-governing Dominions beyond the Seas'. Canada and Australasia provided a picture, whether in terms of population or constitutional progress, in sharp contrast to that of India. There a viceroy and a select band of British administrators exercised a despotism under the lax control of a parliament at Westminster which preened itself as the mother of 'free' (though still subordinate) constitutions in the Dominions, yet which required to be assured by Morley, the Liberal Secretary of State, that the beginnings of representation in India early in the twentieth century did not augur progress towards a parliamentary system of government, though both British Tories and the Indian National Congress could see that it did. In addition to the Caribbean relics, the empire of settlement and India, there was the chain of strategic points encircling the globe whose function was partly to protect the empire of settlement and the British raj in India, but partly to serve the Royal Navy in its performance of a role far wider than that.

While the survivals of earlier Atlantic empire were retained reluctantly by Whitehall, a new Pacific empire was acquired reluctantly when intrepid settlers made it inevitable. British North America and Australasia were the beneficiaries of a great and fruitful experiment in self-government and growing self-government. Very different was the constitutional fate of the West Indies. Beset by the strife of classes closely linked with distinctions of colour and racial origin, they suffered the abrogation of long-standing, if not very reputable, representative institutions accorded to them more or less as a matter of course at settlement in the seventeenth century or conquest in the eighteenth. After the explosion in Jamaica in 1865 (and the questionable 'whitewashing' of Governor Eyre), Britain, unable to abandon the Caribbean incubus, as utility would have dictated, had to assume full responsibility for administration and legislation in colonies all of which (except Barbados, Bermuda and the Bahamas) became *Crown Colonies*, despotically governed because Britain would not permit the domination of non-whites by white minorities and could not trust the non-whites (mainly ex-slaves and their descendants) to work institutions tailored in the seventeenth century for planters. Thus by the 1870s the British West Indies had fallen into the same constitutional pattern as the stragetic posts, of which Malta, Mauritius and Ceylon (unlike Heligoland, Gibraltar, St Helena, the Falklands, Singapore, Aden and Perim) involved Britain in responsibility for considerable populations. So, more importantly and vexatiously, did the possession of the Cape and Natal, for here the British presence meant involvement in the frantic interplay

of Boer and Bantu, burdening the Exchequer with the cost of Kaffir
Wars, unwanted annexations and military precaution. The Cape had to
be kept, not for its commercial importance, but because it commanded
the route to India and Australasia and to the trade routes of the Orient.
Whitehall (though granting representative government in 1853 and
responsible government in 1872, as soon as Cape Colony could afford it)
had to bear among the resident Britons, Burghers and Boers the stigma
of 'Liberalism' for seeking more status for Hottentot and Bantu than
the settlers approved.

That British governments regarded much, perhaps most, of their
great and ever-growing empire as both an encumbrance and an irrele-
vance was difficult for foreigners to understand and is, perhaps, difficult
for posterity to accept. But it is true. Some public men deplored the
growth of the empire of settlement; they were Separatists. Many more
felt, as Seeley put it, that 'it does not grow for us'; they were Pessimists.
The confederation of the North American colonies (except Newfound-
land) to form the Dominion of Canada in 1867, to which the territories
of the Hudson's Bay Company were transferred, was the political pre-
condition for the construction of a railway from the Atlantic to the
Pacific to defy geography and the annexationist aspirations of the
United States. Separatists, who saw in the imperial connection with
Canada only a burden and an embarrassment balanced by no advantages,
sharply regretted it, though hoping that if it prevented the absorption of
Canada into the United States it might expedite its independence of
Britain. That the Australasian empire would in due course go the way of
the thirteen colonies was widely thought inevitable. If Lord John Russell
was to be congratulated for telling the French in 1839 that all of
Australia was British, it was not for Empire's sake, but because he
prevented a juxtaposition of British and French territory in the Pacific
which would have been inconvenient and expensive. Australia, becoming an important source of gold as well as wool, was very little trouble or
expense to Britain, having, unlike the North American complex of
colonies, no international frontier but the sea and, unlike New Zealand,
no Maoris to be cheated and maltreated and disturbed into rebellions
which demanded the presence of imperial troops.

If it were hoped by some and expected by many that these colonies
of settlement, reluctantly retained or acquired, would 'fall away',
nobody of importance thought that Britain could abdicate her principal
colonial responsibility, India, no part of which was technically a colony
and no part of which was, until 1858, when the East India Company
disappeared, directly under the Crown. The possession of India gave a

special shape to Britain's foreign relations and raised most serious problems of policy and intent. Conquest had begun, and been renewed, as
a by-product of the world-wide struggle with France. But the conquest
had been completed, in the generation *after* Waterloo – though mainly
with Indian troops and at Indian expense – because Lords Wellesley,
Hastings and Dalhousie had the spirit of conquering proconsuls (if
benevolent ones) and regarded British paramountcy over all of India as
a duty, and indeed as predestined. To some the government of India,
officially dedicated to the interests of the peoples of India, was the
proudest achievement of the British race, evoking, because it was a
'true' empire in the line of historic empires, comparisons with the
Roman Empire in a way that neither the old nor the new empire of
settlement could do. To others it was a vexatious and bewildering responsibility. But by the second half of the nineteenth century all agreed
(they had not done so before) that India could not be given up except
in some distant future, the shape of which could hardly be glimpsed.
The British must govern India as though they were to be there for ever.

    And yet the rulers of Britain Pre-eminent, the overrulers of the
rulers of India, mostly professed, and with sincerity, a positive distaste
for empire. Not for them the theme 'Wider still and wider, shall thy
bounds be set', but only 'Britannia rules the waves'. The last great
French war having confirmed Britain's command of the oceans, she
could chart for the trader the seas and channels of the world, harry the
slavers in the Atlantic and Indian oceans and the pirates of the Arabian
seas and the Far East, and intervene decisively at some points in
Europe and at most points outside Europe – her pre-eminence being
due to a combination of this sea power with a competitive superiority
in industry, commerce and credit. This superiority was such that she
did not need to command, less still to own and govern, her principal
markets and sources of raw material, which were, indeed, the United
States and Europe. She did not need to monopolise the trade of the less
developed regions of the world, for if these were opened to all on equal
terms she would secure the superiority wherever her merchants exerted
themselves adequately. To have sought monopoly would have roused
the other Powers against her. Monopoly not being necessary, and being
profoundly unfashionable (not least because it would encourage other
Powers to stake out monopolistic claims), Britain's competitors were
obliged to her for her efforts to secure 'the open door' for Western
commerce, and sometimes they helped her to secure it. But the foreigners
were not exactly grateful. They were jealous of Britain's 'informal empire
of commerce' and suspicious of the gospel of Free Trade which, from

the middle of the century, she preached to them. She had surely embraced it for her own convenience, and only to prolong a pre-eminence achieved by a combination of power, invention and expertise under the precisely opposite system of monopoly which had been abandoned.

It follows from the above that for most of the century Imperial Britain was not 'imperialistic' in the old-fashioned sense. She did not deny to the less developed communities of the earth the right to political independence. When in the 1880s the Western states began to vie for paramountcy in most of Africa and much of Asia, Britain's rulers sincerely deplored this novel development, though by occupying Egypt in 1882 (with the object of withdrawing speedily) they initiated it. Because they deplored it, they were dilatory as well as parsimonious about participation in it. They won paramountcy on the Niger, but only because they thought that they had discovered in Goldie's Company a cheap way of pre-empting one of the two principal avenues to a populous and productive interior. Everything had to be done on the cheap, for the British taxpayer knew that the government of white men and Africans on the coast brought involvement in the hinterland and was not profitable to the Treasury. Outside South Africa (where the trekking Boers were first pursued and then, in the early fifties, allowed to go their own way under a vague suzerainty) the single annexation of Britain in Africa up to the 1880s was Lagos.

When the Imperialism of Mercantilism was abandoned, and the Imperialism of the Scramble was not foreseen, 'the Imperialism of Free Trade' prevailed. Where it operated, political independence was allowed. But political independence was not allowed to mean abstention from the mainstream of international commerce, which Britain as the biggest customer, producer, creditor and factor commanded as surely as she commanded the seas. The Spanish empire in the Americas was assisted to liberate itself from Spain and enter this mainstream. The Celestial Empire, self-sufficient, exclusive, disdainful of Western barbarians, was broken open brusquely (in the wars of 1839–42 and 1857–60) that the Indian opium-grower and the British manufacturer (with, of course, his European and American rivals) might have access to what was erroneously imagined – because China's population was 200 million – to be a vast market. The Ottoman Sultan was forced to open his dominions – including Egypt – to the trader and investor, partly because the alternative to the modernisation and stabilisation of his hateful regime would give Russia Constantinople and a Mediterranean fleet and perhaps bring her down to the Tigris and Euphrates. This was too high a price to pay for a British Egypt. Palmerston's attitude to Egypt is a classic exposition of the preference for effective access to formal rule:

> We want to trade with Egypt, and to travel through Egypt, but we do not want the burthen of governing Egypt, and its possession would not, as a political, military and naval question, be considered, in this country as a set-off against the possession of Morocco by France. Let us try to improve all these countries by the general influence of our commerce, but let us abstain from a crusade of conquest which would call down upon us the condemnation of all the other civilised nations.

and, again,

> We do not want Egypt any more than any rational man with an estate in the north of England and a residence in the south, would have wished to possess the inns on the north road. All he could want would have been that the inns should be well kept, always accessible, and furnishing him, when he came, with mutton chops and post horses.

Latin America, China and the Turkish Empire were opened to Free Trade, largely by British initiative and entirely in accord with British policy, with only two colonial acquisitions – Hong Kong and Aden. And in the vast island-strewn seas which stretch from the Indonesian archipelago (handed back to the Dutch by Castlereagh) round to Canton (the principal door opened into China) there were only two acquisitions – Singapore and Labuan. That Europe had a civilising mission in the world was the simple corollary of the assumption that the world must be opened up to the agents of the highest civilisation, most of whom would be British. But the agency was 'legitimate commerce' (so called to distinguish it from slave trading). It was hoped that the flag would not have to follow trade (though gunboats might have to protect traders and sometimes open the way for them). Only slowly was it learned that the impact of the merchant (especially where he followed the slave trader) and of the missionary (where he was allowed to precede, accompany or follow the trader) might be so disruptive as to impose on the European an obligation to end the chaos he had done so much to create. The impact of the investor might be worst of all, as the bankruptcy of the Sultan of Turkey and the Khedive of Egypt in rapid succession were to show. But in these particular cases natural, if unintended, results could always be blamed on the French, who held the greater part of the Ottoman and Egyptian debts.

We must now confine ourselves to the formal empire and, for reasons of space, to the Empire of Settlement and the Empire of India. We will ask what were the British attitudes towards them and what the influence of Britain upon them.

That the Empire of Settlement constituted a unique and important example of the spread of British influence throughout the world is at once evident. Throughout it thousands of place-names indicate a British (often a Scottish) origin, and governmental, parliamentary and judicial institutions are essentially derived from those the British bestowed or those the settlers chose of their own accord to copy. English-speaking, the nineteenth-century settler populations looked to Britain for their reading-matter, including their school textbooks, and as they developed a higher degree of literacy than the population at home and their newspapers were full of 'News from Home' and comment on British events and controversies, one can go too far in emphasising the in any case diminishing effect of distance. There was in Britain widespread ignorance of the colonies, mitigated by the specialised knowledge of businessmen who knew that they were *per capita* Britain's best customers and that they were an increasingly attractive field of investment. But it was galling for an Australian visitor to Britain to be regarded as an 'ill-informed colonial' when he had followed in his newspapers not only the limited home coverage of events in Fiji, New Caledonia and New Guinea (of which those newspapers were full), but a Russian threat to India (e.g. the Pendjeh affair, 1885) and news from Egypt and the Cape, which much concerned his continent, and also the Home Rule controversy, in which, though he lived so far away from Ireland and Britain, he might well feel emotionally involved.

Irish-Americans, of course, were emotionally (and sometimes financially) involved in the Home Rule matter, but the tendency to write of the United States as though it differed from the British Colonies only in being independent (with the implication that this distinction had hardly more than juridical importance) can go too far. In America, indeed, a sort of English was the official language and the lingua franca, and a common literary heritage united the intelligentsias of the United Kingdom and the United States. But when all the constitutional links had been broken by a War of Independence, Americans had tended to emphasise rather their departures from than their acceptance of British models. They had rejected, with hereditary monarchy, that principle of responsible cabinet government which had hardly crystallised by the time of the Independence War, but which formed Britain's most important nineteenth-century constitutional export. Americans, even

when of recent British origin, showed comparatively little interest in
Britain's affairs unless Canada or Ireland was involved. Those late-
nineteenth-century British publicists of the 'kith-and-kin school' who
sought to embrace the achievements of independent America with those
of the British race – the colonisation of 'empty' lands now being followed
by the domination of lands less unpeopled but economically undeveloped – were sometimes making a valid historical point which was highly
convenient for its suggestion of Anglo-Saxon racial superiority. If they
went on to suggest a special relationship between the United States and
a 'Federation of Greater Britain', as twin harbingers of progress and
freedom in a benighted but evolving world, they begged a dozen questions and must be credited with sleight-of-hand rather than informed
foresight. What they could foresee was that the United States and Russia
were destined to become super-Powers, and that Great Britain, as
distinct from a somehow unified British Empire, could not continue to
be a first-rate Power, still less pre-eminent. That was why Joseph
Chamberlain advocated imperial union and the 'development of the
imperial estate'. At the very end of the nineteenth century he spoke of a
Triple Alliance of Great Britain, the United States and the German
Empire. This was diplomatic nonsense, but is worth citing here because
it betrayed a hankering after the superintendence of the human race by
the superior Anglo-Saxons and their Teutonic cousins, which could also
be an entente between Britain, diplomatically isolated and, in comparative
terms, economically declining, and the two Powers which were most
clearly rising in the scale of states.

The successful revolt of the Americans and the expansion of the
United States after independence featured in British public thinking for
most of the nineteenth century as a warning of the folly and evanescence
of empire and a proof that the prosperity of British settlers, and of the
large British interests which flourished by trade with them, did not
depend on the maintenance of formal ties with the Mother Country.
Pessimists, regarding themselves as realists, thought the Canadians and
Australasians would emulate the Americans. Separatists thought that
the sooner they did so the better, as they were a burden on the British
taxpayer who had to pay for their defence. Once Britain had ceased to be
protectionist, the Retentionists had only one material advantage to cite
in favour of keeping colonies in the 'empire' – that the overriding
authority of Westminster committed them all to Free Trade. But this
argument lost force as early as 1859 when the upper St Lawrence colony
of Canada asserted its right to impose discriminatory tariffs, if necessary
even to protect its nascent industries against British goods. Britain,

which had lost the heart of her old Atlantic empire partly because she would not allow colonial enterprise to compete equally with home enterprise under the policy of mercantilism, was in effect warned that she might now lose her Empire of Settlement by seeking to impose Free Trade to the disadvantage of the colonial entrepreneur. The Duke of Newcastle was told by the Canadian minister Galt that 'the Government of Canada, acting for its Legislature and people, cannot, through those feelings of deference which they owe to the Imperial authorities, in any manner waive or diminish the right of the people of Canada to decide for themselves both as to the mode and the extent to which taxation shall be imposed'. If the British ministers used their legal power to disallow the tariff acts they must be 'prepared to assume the administration of the affairs of the Colony irrespective of the views of its inhabitants'.

This dramatic confrontation is too little known. There could be but one reply – that Britain would not impose Free Trade on the 'self-governing' colonies against their will. But the strongest critic of Newcastle's surrender was that dogmatic Free Trader, Earl Grey. And it was none other than this Lord Grey – the third earl – who, on becoming colonial secretary in 1846, had implemented Lord Durham's proposals of 1840 for the grant of 'responsible government' to the North American colonies and in due course to all colonies of similar character and, by doing so, won at least equal claim to the title sometimes conferred rather extravagantly on Durham – 'principal founder of the British Commonwealth of Nations'. The grant of 'self-government', by the application to the colonies of many of the conventions of the British Constitution, was intended to solve in the colonies the problem it had solved at home – the problem of deadlock between the representatives of the electorate and an irresponsible executive, at home the monarch, in a colony the governor legally representing the monarch, but in fact the agent of the British cabinet. It was hoped, by this grant, to avoid clashes between colonial opinion and Whitehall. For, *where the internal affairs of the colony were concerned*, the Governor would in future act on the advice of local ministers responsible to a colonial assembly from which most of them were drawn. It was at least half-understood, moreover, that Whitehall would not use the monarch's undoubted lawful power to disallow Bills passed by a colonial parliament and that Westminster would not make laws for a colony which a colonial parliament was competent to make. But Durham called what was granted 'municipal' self-government. It was not meant to imply, as in the twentieth century it implies, that independence was round the corner.

Durham and Grey and the few other enthusiastic supporters of the policy were not Separatists but 'Colonial Reformers' or 'Radical Imperialists', intent on avoiding separation by granting freedom. Grey's opposition in 1859 to extending this freedom from the strictly 'municipal' field to that of tariffs, which could not appear to the Colonial Office wholly an 'internal' matter, shows that the original concession was *not* meant to be what it in fact became, the beginning of a process of encroachment by the colonial authorities and unavowed or only half-avowed abdication by the imperial authorities, of which the final effect would be the virtual independence of the colonies. If that keen Colonial Reformer, Sir William Molesworth, had had his way, a list of 'municipal' affairs delegated to the colonial authorities and of 'imperial' affairs jealously excluded from them would have been statuted and ordained and the whole process by which the British Empire (or part of it) became the British Commonwealth of Nations (or part of it) would have been rendered impossible.

The successful Canadian ultimatum of 1859 had very small practical effect. And yet it really determined that in the long run the British Empire would have no common economic policy. And it was the first conclusive sign that Britain had stumbled uncomprehendingly upon a long-term solution to the constitutional problem of how to avoid colonial wars of independence.

In 1887 British ministers met in conference with the premiers of self-governing colonies to discuss matters of common concern. If the Separatists and Pessimists of the middle of the century could have foreseen this and later Colonial Conferences, they would have been very surprised, for to them the great dilemma was how to part from the colonies in amity rather than anger. This dilemma never had to be faced, for the colonists, so far from asking for independence, became angry at any hint that the British government would be obliged to them if they did so. When Gladstone's ministry, which came into office in 1868, seemed not to dislike the idea that the newly created Dominion of Canada might join the United States, its prime minister, Sir John A. Macdonald, threatened to appeal to the people of Britain against the government of Britain. He was to fight his last election twenty years later on the slogan 'A British subject I was born, a British subject I will die'. The grudging attitude of the colonial secretary, Granville, towards the New Zealand settlers whose Maori wars had not only delayed but reversed the policy of withdrawing imperial garrisons from self-governing colonies, aroused to vehement articulation anti-Separatist emotions previously submerged. Solidarity with, and generosity towards, kith and kin across the seas was demanded by intellectuals and working-class newspapers and memorials, and 'with a rapidity and completeness which seem almost incredible, the Separatist school in England practically vanished from the face of the earth and the Pessimists dwindled into an insignificant minority'. Senior ministers might pretend that nothing of importance had occurred, but the whole tenor of the dialogue with, and about, the colonies had been transformed. An imperial guarantee of £1 million loan to New Zealand for immigration and public works was described by Granville himself as 'proof of the deep interests which [ministers] feel in the welfare and prosperity of this great possession of the Crown'. It was left to a junior, Knatchbull-Hugessen, to state that it was government policy to 'retain and preserve the connection between the Mother Country and the Colonies, basing always that connection on the sure and sound foundation of mutual understanding and the promotion of mutual interests'. Ten years later, at the Mansion House, on 7 August 1881, Gladstone described the business not only of founding but of *cherishing* these 'distant, but not less dear, portions of the great British Empire' as 'distinctly ... entrusted by Providence to the care of the people of this country'.

There seems no reason to think that this 'new' Imperialism which advocated the strengthening of ties with the colonies of settlement was really new. It was now discovered by the politicians to be a powerful popular prejudice to which, however logical the Separatist argument that from the formal ties the British people derived no tangible advantage while incurring material liabilities, policy must defer. Disraeli, a dyed-in-the-wool Pessimist, so far from creating the sentiment, merely recognised it and sought to exploit it when he told the Conservative working-men at the Crystal Palace on 24 June 1872 that Conservatism meant the maintenance of the Empire and accused cosmopolitan Liberalism of a forty-year conspiracy to destroy it, which had been frustrated by the loyalty of the colonists themselves. As it ceased to be practical politics to think of dispensing with those dependencies that might have been able to look after themselves in independence, Gladstone could only hope that they would voluntarily undertake more of the burden of their own defence. This was Lord Salisbury's principal interest at the 1887 Conference. The problem had become not of how and when to disengage, but of how to co-operate. Some there were, especially in the Imperial Federation League, who sought to substitute for constitutional disintegration (which was, in fact, in progress as it became more and more unthinkable for the imperial government or parliament to exercise lawful powers to override the colonial will) an institutionalised partnership. In his notable lectures on the *Expansion of England*, published in 1883, Professor Seeley had urged that with the defeat of distance by steam and electricity the Greater Britain to which the British at home and the British in the colonies living as British subjects under the Crown all belonged could be federated as effectively as the United States. The trouble was that such a scheme would offer the colonies no advantages which they did not already enjoy and would limit or hamper the process of emancipation from Britain's leading strings. Britain, as the senior and predominant partner, might gain, not least in enhanced prestige among the Powers, but in proportion as she gained the growing Canadian and Australian sense of nationality would be affronted. Hofmeyr, the Afrikaner leader at the Cape, suggested in 1887 an Empire-wide tariff on foreign goods to create an Imperial Defence Fund. But progress in the matter of colonial contributions to imperial defence could be made only by agreements between the British government and such colonies as were willing to make them, followed by legislation in the colonies. Even treaty-like commitments of this nature could be dangerous, as the premier of Queensland discovered on his return to his chauvinistic and faction-torn colony; he was defeated on his 'Naval Tribute Bill'. The elder statesman of the premier Australian colony, Sir Henry Parkes, so strongly opposed the notion of a federation between the strong and the weak that New South Wales would participate in the 1887 Conference only on the understanding that the subject was barred from the agenda. And so it was that the Conferences themselves became the principal visible 'organic' link of Great Britain and Greater Britain. They were apt to be embarrassing to the British ministers involved. Salisbury, who had tolerated French and German encroachment in the South Pacific, found himself criticised with Antipodean directness of speech for neglecting the imperial and imperialist interests of the Australasians. Ten years later the colonies, led by Canada, urged Britain to abandon her policy of Free Trade in order to reciprocate colonial preferences in favour of British goods (the duties on which might nevertheless remain protective). Joseph Chamberlain came to urge this course of action by 1903, because, as he himself confessed, all other avenues to imperial unity had been barred by the colonies.

This proposal of Tariff Reform (i.e. Protection with Imperial Preference) does not belong to the story of Britain Pre-eminent. It arose from Chamberlain's keen awareness that because the British Empire was neither a political nor an economic unity, and because the British were falling behind the Americans and Germans in technological

innovation and technical education, drastically new programmes of
imperial co-operation and development were called for. He was thinking
in the terms of twentieth-century geo-politics. Very different was the
habit of mind of Salisbury, calm, sceptical, detached, rooted in the
older concept of Britain Pre-eminent, but doomed to preside, with
reluctance, over Britain's part in the Scramble – a distasteful business
of chartering companies run, he suspected, by 'bounders' among whom
Mackinnon had not even, like Rhodes and Goldie, the virtue of audacity;
of 'pegging out claims'; of declaring protectorates and, too often, of
taking these over as colonies requiring grants-in-aid from the Imperial
exchequer. Thus it was that much of Africa, and part of Asia, became
red on the map at the same time as, and partly because, British naval
superiority had become suspect and British commercial hegemony was
challenged. By now the future markets and sources of raw materials for
the industrialised nations, unless guaranteed open to all equally by
international treaty (and sometimes, as in the case of the Congo, even
if they were) were apt to be closed to 'fair competition'.

Chamberlain and his old Radical colleague of the days of the second
Gladstone administration of 1880–5, Sir Charles Dilke, were unusual
in being willing to look on colonial politicians as exemplars for British
politicians. The colonists had, of course, taken to their new homes many
of the prejudices they had learned in the old, and they took their religious
beliefs and organisations with them, so that Catholics, mainly of Irish
origin, and Protestants of English and Scottish origin disputed in
familiar terms about voluntary education and sectarian instruction
in the Australian colony of Victoria. But the emigrant population was
not a cross-section of the British population. The comparatively light
influence of Anglicanism had made possible a state system of education
unattainable politically at home. The absence of aristocracy and the
weakness of oligarchies, Whig or Tory, had permitted in the colonies
a rapid growth of democratic local government and a comparatively
rapid access to political democracy at the centre too. The problems of
development demanded more state activity than was politically practicable at home, similar to that reforming activity of Chamberlain as
Lord Mayor of Birmingham which was dubbed 'municipal' or 'gas-
and-water' socialism. But these radical developments in the colonies,
and the Protectionism which accompanied them (and led to the 'White
Australia' policy as well as to tariffs) were not due merely to the absence
of traditionalist impediments in a 'new' country. They were due to a
positive spirit of radicalism. To have left home for a distant land to
better oneself, because it was so difficult to better oneself or even to

survive in the old country, implied a criticism of British society – and for many the old country was persecuted Ireland. The emigrants to the colonies were apt to be Chartists or Fenians and so far from being, as the Colonial Office often seemed to imply, 'mere colonials' running in a rather amateurish way imitations of the British system of government (and Heaven knows that was amateurishly run!) they were Radicals framing their own policies with a freedom and power envied by Radicals at home.

Only when thinking in terms of strategy – the protection of Britain's world role and world-wide communications and commerce – could British public men think in the same context of the settler colonies and the dependencies, of Australia and India. Their co-existence made the British Empire the most extensive and populous ever known, and they were confusedly linked in the oratory of complacent Imperialism and hysterical Jingoism. But they were totally different in kind, in their relationship to Britain, their current position and their apparent destiny. India, especially, stood at an opposite pole from, for example, the colonies federated in 1900 to form the Commonwealth of Australia. In the latter the inhabitants, bound to Britain by affinity and sentiment, by moral obligation (for on Britain, in the last resort, depended their defence, and towards it they contributed little, and that little voluntarily), were few to the square mile (though much concentrated in capital cities). They were free, democratic, egalitarian, optimistic, confident of an expansion limited only by a calculated policy of maintaining a high standard of living by protective legislation. In India teeming millions scraped an inadequate living from tortured soil in villages 'which seemed to last where nothing else lasted'. By providing peace and good order and plans to deal with famines the British in India increased the burden of human and animal population on a deteriorating soil. They altogether failed to perform the task, prescribed for them by Marx, of stirring the villagers out of their inertia and obscurantism. They increased the inertia, for under the chain of command which linked the village via the district with the provincial government for purposes of taxation, order, justice and information, the village institutions decayed. The raj failed to enlist or elicit any spirit of co-operative self-help or to provide adequate incentives to better agricultural techniques. Even where Cornwallis's unfortunate Permanent Settlement was not imposed or copied, the taxes, though fixed and certain for a term, tended to be high, and where the principles of the Permanent Settlement operated, based on a misreading of the status of a Moghul official which converted him into a hereditary land-lord, the cultivator was subject to heavy dues without having the chance of benefiting from any improvements he made. Even the certainty of the fiscal obligation was balanced by dispossession for non-payment, by Westernised court process. The British created absentee landlords and landless labourers, while depressing, by the destruction of handcrafts, all but a few cities. The repair and construction of irrigation works which could produce, locally or (if large-scale enough, as in the Punjab) regionally, improved agricultural methods and yields were not extensive enough to balance the predictable, or even the actual, increase in population.

A few cities had grown and continued to grow as centres of adminis-tration and Western capitalist enterprise. Commercial investment was followed by steamships and railways and these by industrial investment. By Victorian standards it was an 'improvement' that an English traveller in 1866 should find the low villas and distant factory chimneys of the Hooghly at Calcutta reminding him of the Thames between Battersea and Fulham. (The same observer, Dilke, remarked on the inferiority of British-style nineteenth-century architecture throughout the Empire to that of other European colonisers and earlier Asian regimes.) The rail-ways were a visible symbol that India was being integrated into the world economy dominated by her alien rulers. The infrastructure of a twentieth-century Indian economy was being laid. Indian capitalists began tentatively to emulate British (especially Scottish) capitalists and invest in industrial enterprise. But if the British rulers understood that railways, though expensive to build, would yield returns of revenue by increasing trade, and sought by guarantee to extend the mileage begun before the Mutiny (and an invaluable help in suppressing it), the amount of construction was not, in the nineteenth century, very remarkable. Considerations of internal security, administrative convenience and external defence often had much to do with the planning of new lines. The strategic considerations which caused the British to oppose the construction of the Suez Canal (of which they were certainly the greatest beneficiaries) and to delay the construction of the Baghdad Railway naturally caused them to veto any idea of linking the Indian railway system via Persia or Afghanistan with that of the Russians in Central Asia. Similarly, the development of industry in India, whether by British or Indian capital, was viewed with reserve, for it would jeopardise the export markets of British industry, especially in Lancashire. British industry had been helped by British fiscal policy in India to destroy sooner, rather than later, the handcraft industries of India (hence the bones of the weavers whitening the plains!). It was then helped by British fiscal policy in India to compete with nascent machine industry in India. The Free Trade Britain which was reluctant to allow the self-governing colonies to enjoy the benefits of protective tariffs was reluctant to allow India to enjoy the benefits of genuinely free trade.

Since 1813, if not before, the British had been committed officially to govern India in the spirit of trustees for its peoples, as Burke had demanded in those attacks on Warren Hastings which were at once sublime, partisan and unfair. But in the nineteenth century it was advantageous when arguing that the British must govern in India indefinitely to be able to add to the concept of onerous duty – sometimes projected as honour and glory which both edified and exalted the character of the governing race (as Dilke argued) and gave to Britain a character as a Great Power which she would otherwise have lacked (as Disraeli argued) – the more sordid consideration of protecting the British investment and the British stake in commerce. For, said Seeley, if the formal British connection with Australasia ended, the channels of trade would be hardly affected, but if the British left India and Ceylon those regions would have no trade at all, for they would be left to anarchy or foreign invasion or both. India, it was said, had fallen to Britain's imperium because, on the decline of the Moghul Empire, she had become un-governable except by a Western Power, and India, it was implied, would remain ungovernable, except by the Indian Civil Service, until some distant time when a sub-continent which had never been wholly a political unity became a nation with a numerous and strong and responsible Westernised élite. This had not been the concept of early nineteenth-century notables such as Munro and Elphinstone, who combined a respect for native institutions with a sense of the serious limitations of alien rule, but their outlook was overborne by that of Bentinck and Macaulay. These Utilitarians were not lacking in benevolence towards Indians, but they had come to the conclusion that the Orient had nothing constructive to offer for the future welfare of Orientals. The road of progress lay through the introduction of 'English literature and science through the medium of the English language', which became the language of government.

The inauguration of this policy in 1835 has been described as 'perhaps the most far-reaching single measure in the whole nineteenth century' (Spear). From it was to spring an Indian nationalist movement led by an élite literate in English and citing the teachings of Western political science to confound the validity of the continuance of an alien despotism however benevolent its intentions. British policy in nine-

teenth-century India created the beginnings of this élite, but denied it
participation in the government of the country except in a menial role.
The Queen promised in her proclamation of 1858, when the East India
Company's governing functions were transferred to the Crown, that
there would be no discrimination on grounds of race, colour, religion,
etc., in official employments. This was a hollow mockery, as Lord
Lytton admitted – the Viceroy who attempted to curb those signs of
racial arrogance which had reached a crescendo when the cold-blooded
atrocities which accompanied the suppression of the Mutiny were
blessed in British pulpits, and which had a more routine existence
betokened by the public notices asking gentlemen not to strike their
servants. Lytton, like Ellenborough before him and Curzon after him,
regretted the Westernising policy and deplored the disrespect for the
best achievements of Indian culture and the neglect by the British of the
old ruling class. Curzon said bluntly that the British held India by the
allegiance of its martial races, not 'hothouse Babus', and that the main
cause of their difficulties in India was 'the lavish distribution of the
resources of culture and knowledge'. As a matter of fact the distribution
was not all that lavish, and the quality of the culture assimilated was
suspect, as became clear by the time of the Hunter Commission of
1882, when higher education was described as 'a sterile exercise in
obtaining useful knowledge rather than a real culture of the mind'.
Many of that select band of dedicated and efficient policy-makers and
supervisors of Indian administrative assistants, the Indian Civil Service,
did not perhaps regret that the Western education provided in India
was unlikely to turn out many Indians who would have been able to
compete with the products of British public schools and universities
in the entrance examinations even if they had been held – as they were
not – in India as well as in England. For they thought that Britons
could rule India, and that no other men could, and that they knew the
interests of Indians of all classes – and especially of the inarticulate
masses for whom they felt a genuine responsibility – better than Indians
themselves. Yet it was surely ironical that the senior scholar of the
Madras College could find in British India, because he was an Indian,
no public employment worthy of his calibre, but should find it as
Prime Minister of Travancore, one of those princely states where, after
the Mutiny, British interference was kept to a minimum, and which
were, consequently, generally so backward as to be worthy of preservation as a back-handed advertisement of the superiority of British rule.
It was also dangerous, for, as Dilke saw, 'under our present system of
exclusion of natives from the Indian Civil Service, the more boys we

educate, the more vicious and discontented men we have beneath our rule'.

The future in India was not to lie with unrepresentative savants like the Hindus Ram Mohun Roy and Swami Vivekananda and the Moslem Sayyid Ahmed Khan, who saw the superiority of Western rationalism and attempted to reinterpret their own creeds, essentially so different, in terms compatible with that rationalism. Such endeavour was not unimportant, as it provided a bridge for the Nehrus and Jinnahs of the twentieth century to 'think Western' without becoming entirely *déraciné* and without becoming inseparably divorced from the masses whom they were to mould into the rank-and-file of a nationalist host. But the really important product of Western education in India was the professional man who, arguing on the hypotheses of the Western system of representative and responsible government, civil liberties and political democracy, demanded participation in the government of India and the phasing-out of British rule. As early as the sixties and seventies Dadabhai Naoroji (1825–1917) lived in Britain for a decade with the aim of explaining the truth about discrimination and lack of opportunity for Indians in India, convinced that the truth, if known, would prevail. Did not Lord Lytton himself say that 'both the Government of England and of India appear to me up to the present moment unable to answer satisfactorily the charge of having taken every means in their power of breaking to the heart words of promise they have uttered to the ear'? The ear of Gladstone, more attuned than most politicians to nationalism in Ireland or Europe or the colonies, caught Dadabhai's message. Gladstone declared it a weakness and a calamity that 'we have not been able to give to India the benefits and blessings of free institutions'. His viceroy, Ripon, added to the municipalities and town committees inaugurated under Canning in 1861 municipal committees and district and local boards, as 'a measure of political education'. He failed, in the following year, 1883, to pass the Ilbert Bill, which would have made Europeans in certain circumstances amenable to Indian judges!

If Lord Ripon's talk of 'political education' meant anything, it meant that there would be a progressive advance in self-government, and when the Indian National Congress was formed (1885), under the inspiration of certain unusually liberal members of the I.C.S., its aim was to promote by constitutional means 'those sentiments of national unity which had their origin in our beloved Lord Ripon'. When the second Congress met in Calcutta Lord Dufferin thought it proper to entertain the delegates at a garden party. After all, he said, the Indian middle class was a 'microscopic minority', but 'now that we have educated these people, the desire to take a larger part in the management of their own domestic affairs seems to be a legitimate and reasonable aspiration, and I think there should be enough statesmanship among us to contrive the means of permitting them to do so without unduly compromising our imperial supremacy'. The Indian Councils Act 1892 was followed by another of 1909 (the key measure of the Morley–Minto reforms) which seemed both to British Tories and to Congress to make it a question not whether, but merely when, and by how many stages, the goal stated by Congress in 1908 – 'a system of government similar to that enjoyed by the self-governing members of the British Empire' – would be reached. But this was not admitted by the authors of the Morley–Minto reforms to Parliament, to the Indian Civil Service, to one another or, probably, to themselves. They did *not* envisage India undergoing, at least within measurable time, the process of evolution via internal self-government to that something wider (though still short of technical independence) which was christened at the Imperial Conference of 1907 'Dominion status'. They denied that the British parliamentary system, presumably in a federalised form, was appropriate to India. They aimed to 'maintain British supremacy clear and unchallenged at the top'. They claimed to be practising 'government by durbar' in contrast to Curzon's remote if reforming and beneficent despotism. They wanted the first Indian nominee on the Viceroy's Executive Council to be not a civil servant and 'not a Congress wallah or leader of opposition, but a representative of moderate Indian thought, who would assist us in dealing with extremists and in many native questions, as to which we are now dangerously out of touch'. But Indian nationalists did not see in the admirable Mr Sinha the precursor of anybody, because he was a Government nominee. Even to the moderates the precursor was the leading Congress figure in the Viceroy's Legislative Council, Mr Gokhale, for he or his successor was surely destined to become a prime minister as representing the majority of an elected Indian assembly which the British would not be for ever able to withhold. The British had told the world that *their* system of government was the best. The Westernised Indians took them at their word. Nothing but the best was good enough for them.

The most pregnant British introductions into India were railways and Western education. Together they produced sufficient economic growth and sufficient political consciousness, though in a small minority of the population, to develop a sense of national self-consciousness which rendered the continuance of an autocracy dominated by aliens increasingly difficult and at last impossible. The emphasis which has been laid upon the defects of that autocracy – its remoteness from Indian opinion, racial superiority, increasing rigidity as one professionalised generation of the I.C.S. followed another – should not obscure its virtues, which fair-minded Indians will allow it. But these virtues have been so often sung that it is well to remember the other side of the coin. Paternalism was marred by the national self-interest of the British, as the fiscal story shows. The professionals were not very good at dealing with the by-products of their own successes – with the problems of over-population and the problem of the Westernised élite. And though it is true that the Indian Civil Service was the most incorrupt body of its kind ever known, and was to be more effective than might have been expected in passing on its standards to its Indian recruits, its ill-paid Indian subordinates were more susceptible to corruption of the deeply ingrained oriental kind the lower down the official ladder one looked, and those who had most contact with the people most susceptible of all. And while the British gave India law, of an enlightened kind for all the alien elements, especially procedural, which made it bewildering and sometimes oppressive where there was no intention of oppression, and the concept of the Rule of Law, the Indian policeman would not have secured the commendation of the International Commission of Jurists. The British raj was at its weakest in its contacts, through subordinate Indians, with the very people whom the Indian Civil Service sincerely professed to protect against Indian, and sometimes against European, malefactors of power and wealth. And this only the excellence of the European district officers concealed from the British people and the world.

SUGGESTIONS FOR FURTHER READING

C. A. G. Bodelsen, *Studies in Mid-Victorian Imperialism* (1961 repr.); A. L. Burt, *The Evolution of the British Empire and Commonwealth from the American Revolution* (1956); C. W. Dilke, *Greater Britain* (1868) and *Problems of Greater Britain* (1890); R. L. Schuyler, *The Fall of the Old Colonial System* (1945); J. R. Seeley, *The Expansion of England* (1883).

G. D. Bearce, *British Attitudes towards India 1784–1858* (1961); R. Coupland, *The Indian Problem 1833–1935* (1942); M. N. Das, *India under Morley and Minto* (1964); M. Edwards, *British India 1772–1947* (1967); S. Gopal, *British Policy in India 1858–1905* (1965); Sir P. Griffiths, *The British Impact on India* (1952); P. Spear, *The Oxford History of Modern India 1770–1947* (1965 repr.).

8. Statecraft, Power and Influence

C. J. BARTLETT

THE nineteenth century was the era *par excellence* of British diplomacy. At least four British statesmen achieved world stature. Even an illiterate Russian peasant was vaguely aware of the existence of Lord Palmerston. The name of George Canning was lauded and abused in two worlds. In their quieter ways, but with equal skill, Lords Castlereagh and Salisbury likewise made their impact. Domestic politics may have been the true forte of Gladstone and Disraeli, yet Bismarck was as much exasperated by the one as he professed to be impressed by the other. Lesser figures such as Lord John Russell and Lord Clarendon also knew their moments of influence, while even a British ambassador, Lord Stratford de Redcliffe, could earn a European reputation. The achievements of British diplomats and statesmen have been minutely examined by historians, so that the intricacies of most of the crises in which they were involved are well known. Yet it may be useful to pause and reflect upon the international environment in which they operated, and try to measure both the influence that Britain herself could exert upon other countries, and the degree to which she was indebted to favourable and fortuitous circumstances. In this bird's eye review it will be necessary in most instances to omit the personal contributions of British statesmen: we are concerned here mainly with the forces which they tried to manipulate rather than with the men themselves.

Clearly to be entrusted with the foreign relations of the world's richest power was a head-start in itself for any politician. Yet certain disadvantages have also to be taken into account. Possession of a world empire, together with a range and variety of interests in excess of those of any other nation, made Britain's foreign and defence policies the most complex of all. Much of history is a cautionary tale of the perils that attend and usually befall pre-eminent empires – the grudges, fears, hostility and jealousies that they provoke. In this respect Britain seemed peculiarly vulnerable since her activities impinged upon those of so many other peoples. Yet, unlike Spain and France before her, or Germany later, she provoked no long-term coalitions bent on her destruction or humiliation. Her escape from such a fate was a result of her own restraint, physical isolation from Europe, and sheer good fortune in that possible rivals were usually divided among themselves. British statesmanship was able to play upon this last condition in particular, it being found practicable to enjoy reasonable relations with one or other of Britain's main rivals – Russia or France – for much of the nineteenth century. The refusal of the United States to become entangled in European rivalries also played into the hands of the Foreign Office, though Washington did at times try to turn British difficulties with other powers to its advantage. British statesmen showed much awareness of both these dangers and opportunities, even if over-confidence or arrogance occasionally led to forgetfulness and embarrassment.

Britain's power and influence in international politics were also limited by the nature of her political constitution and society. Paradoxically the statesmen of the world's richest state were often troubled by want of funds. Throughout the century advocates of economy could usually be sure of a favourable hearing in Parliament. A small group even preached the virtues of a non-interventionist foreign policy, and in the 1860s came near to seeing their ideas implemented. Although there were occasions when, as over the Crimean War, public opinion outran the government in favour of action, more usual was the situation in which a minister had to weigh with care the pros and cons of an appeal to Parliament for additional funds with which to execute his desires. Thus Richard Cobden, John Bright and Joseph Hume sought, in their continual campaigning against the estimates for the armed services, to reduce the freedom of action of the Foreign Office. As Molesworth pointed out in 1849, large naval estimates enabled the Foreign Secretary to 'meddle in every squabble that took place on the terraqueous globe – to teach constitutional maxims in Portugal – to contravert the "divine right" of kings in Sicily – to lead on a crusade against the slave trade in Africa – and to do, he knew not what, in the Rio de la Plata'. Certainly Palmerston found that his ability to conduct a foreign policy of his own choosing was enhanced when he did not need to confront Cabinet or Parliament with a demand for increased naval estimates. Public opinion influenced foreign policy in various ways, but most persistently through parliamentary control of the purse.

It was thus both a great achievement and a blessing for British statesmen in the nineteenth century that they were able to play so large a part in world affairs at a cost to the nation in defence expenditure, until the late 1880s, of rarely more than £1 per head of the population, or 2 or 3 per cent of the national income. This provided them with a small army, whose main tasks lay outside Europe, and the world's largest navy. In proportion to their responsibilities they appeared absurdly small, and hardly outstanding examples of fighting efficiency. The armed services are usually portrayed as the victims of political neglect and professional conservatism. Certainly the politicians spent as little as they dared, and many senior officers strove to keep innovation to a minimum. Nevertheless the British Empire not only survived; it expanded. And at times, too, Britain was able to exercise a remarkable degree of influence over the affairs of Europe. Britain's armed strength was thus not so inadequate as it might appear, especially in view of the enormous reserves that could ultimately be mobilised given sufficient national will. This was to be strikingly demonstrated during the Boer War. But save in the Crimean War no real mobilisation was necessary between 1815 and 1899. Although potential as well as actual strength can influence the conduct of international affairs, there were occasions when Britain gained successes that were in excess both of the effort made and of any extra effort she might have made in pursuit of such objectives.

This disproportion is particularly interesting with respect to Europe, where Britain was always short of that currency so respected among continental powers – large numbers of trained soldiers. Influential as British subsidies might have been in impoverished European capitals during the struggle against Napoleon, Wellington, as a successful land commander, gained for himself and his country a measure of influence and prestige that was not obtainable with mere cash. After Waterloo, however, the possibility of British military intervention became increasingly unlikely. The intervention in Portugal in 1826 was in a country which was widely regarded as being a special British interest. The attack on Sevastopol in 1854 was attempted only with the aid of France, and soon British military prestige had fallen so low that Bismarck jokingly promised to arrest with Prussian policemen any British force that interfered with his plans. Not until the 1900s did British military planners prepare seriously for a war on the Continent.

But if the British army became of little consequence in Europe there was always the Royal Navy. Here too, however, there was some loss of impact after 1815 until the writings of Admiral Mahan and the great colonial scramble at the end of the century. Europeans had not fully appreciated the contribution of sea power to the defeat of Napoleon, and in any case much of the Continent was not immediately susceptible to naval pressure. Even so maritime a people as the Dutch proved remarkably resistant to a British blockade in 1832, and a French army was needed to hasten the independence of the new state of Belgium.

The European wars of 1859–71 were all essentially military conflicts, and it was believed that the creation of a railway network over much of the Continent would greatly reduce the danger from amphibious operations. Even the great naval contributions to past wars – the blockade of hostile ports – seemed less relevant when railways and elaborate mobilisation plans were expected to decide a war before the strategy of attrition could make much impact. The importance of these developments must not be exaggerated. Clearly countries with long coastlines or poor internal communications remained vulnerable. The British navy was a prime factor in the Near Eastern Question for much of the century, and was crucial in any extra-European crisis. Only the slow conquest of deserts and mountains by the new railway networks towards the end of the century threatened its position in Asia.

Naval supremacy can therefore provide only a limited number of clues to Britain's nineteenth-century successes, especially in Europe. One must look for other circumstances that were helping to promote her basic interests at this time. What other forces favoured the maintenance of a balance between the powers, and the preservation of peace? What other states favoured the containment of France, the neutrality of the Netherlands and the Iberian Peninsula, and the maintenance of the Ottoman Empire? Although liberal and humanitarian feelings sometimes swayed British foreign policy, basically she was concerned with her cwn security, her commerce and her trade routes to the Atlantic, the Mediterranean and the East. These were objectives that could often be reconciled with the policies of cautious, defensively-minded statesmen in Europe; statesmen who doubted the strength and stability of their own countries; statesmen who neither feared a British hegemony, nor sought one of their own. These were the types of men who dominated European politics until the 1850s, and it was no coincidence that one of the great periods of British influence in Europe should approximate to the period of their rule. Difficulties arose with them mainly when British sympathy with liberal and national movements was to the fore.

Britain and her allies agreed in 1814–15 that they should seek to establish a Europe of satiated powers, governed by broadly conservative regimes. The other leading states similarly agreed that the principle of the balance of power must be respected, and if they differed in their interpretations of the balance, this did not lead to fatal clashes. Nor was Britain mainly involved in any differences over details. When she insisted on the independence of the Netherlands, this annoyed no power save France. She could similarly insist on the independence of

Spain and Portugal – so useful for the security of her shipping routes – without provoking the hostility of others, while she could see no strategic threat to herself in Austrian influence in Italy. These circumstances did not apply with equal force throughout the century, but by and large Britain's interests and position gave her a degree of detachment to which no continental state could aspire; a degree of detachment which could retain its validity so long as no power threatened to achieve a position of hegemony in western Europe.

No European state from 1815 until the end of the century possessed the resources to make a bid for such an hegemony. Furthermore, for the first forty years most powers were convinced that even the pursuit of lesser objectives could bring unacceptable risks. Territorial revision could precipitate a revolutionary landslide that might sweep away not only the Vienna Settlement but the existing political and social order to boot. Europe might return to the darkest days of 1793–1815. Wars for limited purposes might prove uncontrollable. Statesmen had become accustomed to consulting and working together in their efforts to defeat Napoleon and recast Europe, and the habit remained with them, and even to some extent with their successors. If no subsequent British foreign secretary was to achieve such intimacy with European monarchs and ministers as did Castlereagh between 1815 and 1822, the idea of a Concert of the great powers did not wholly lose its appeal. Castlereagh and the Austrian statesman, Metternich, even found it possible in the early stages of the Greek Revolt of the 1820s to restrain Russia by warning the Tsar of the grave dangers that might result from a breach in the unity of crowned heads of Europe. No other British minister was able to exploit this sense of monarchical solidarity in this fashion, but in a more general way the fear of war and revolution did play into British hands until the 1850s.

French policy, even when directed by the restored House of Bourbon, remained suspect. Modest French ambitions could excite profound alarm in the rest of Europe lest they should start off a chain-reaction of unknown and terrifying dimensions. True, Britain could find no allies when France intervened in the affairs of Spain in 1823, but the boundaries of the Netherlands, Germany and Italy were a different matter. Polignac in 1829 could evoke no interest when he suggested that the Greek War of Independence should be the occasion for other territorial changes in Europe. For France any significant revision must benefit her eastern borders, and this was unthinkable for others. Changes of regime in France helped to prolong this concentrated hostility which greeted almost any move, so that for much of the reign of the bourgeois king,

Louis-Philippe, and in the early years of Louis-Napoleon Britain alone was disposed to display any friendship towards the pariah of Europe. This was strikingly demonstrated in 1849–50 when Prussia, despite differences over Germany with Austria, ignored important overtures from Louis-Napoleon. French support, it was feared, would be bought at too high a price. Britain, from her insular position, with her more liberal view of the world, and encouraged by the knowledge that other powers would assist her if France seemed in danger of getting out of hand, could afford to be more generous.

This was admirably demonstrated during the Belgian crisis of 1830–2, when Palmerston's determination that Belgium should become an independent state was assisted both by French support of this policy, and by the hostility of the other powers towards France which ensured that the latter should make no individual gains of her own. To complete the expulsion of the Dutch from Antwerp Palmerston needed the assistance of a French army, a possibly dangerous ally. But French isolation in Europe left Palmerston the main manipulator of events. In contrast, in 1823, when it was Britain who was isolated, a French army was able to intervene in Spain and ignore the verbal expostulations of Canning. Palmerston in the 1830s was once again more fortunate, when cooperation with a friendless France worked generally to Britain's advantage in the Iberian Peninsula. Yet even he was to suffer in his turn in 1846–7 when Louis-Philippe, his regime having grown more respectable in Europe, risked British hostility with his marriage policy in Spain. The Anglo-French break occurred at a time when the other powers wished to extinguish the republic of Cracow. Metternich wrote in high glee: 'All her (Britain's) resources are inadequate for the purposes of her Government, since she cannot make war for any of the ends which she pursues.'

If France was not always isolated in Europe between 1815 and 1856, she was so often enough for it to prove a real asset to British foreign secretaries. At such times they were free to choose whether to throw their weight behind Paris or the fearful chancelleries of Vienna, Berlin and St Petersburg. It was a comforting thought in 1832, and in the early fifties when Louis-Napoleon was consolidating his position at home, and wild rumours were beginning to circulate concerning his intentions abroad. But, in addition to this, the foreign policies of Austria, Prussia and Russia were remarkably modest in these years, save in defence of the conservative order. At Vienna in 1814–15 the appetites of Prussia and Russia had seemed too large in the eyes of Castlereagh for the stability of Europe, but once the boundaries had been finally agreed, the desire for change was muted. Fear of war and revolution was again a great pacifier, while the settlement itself left no power profoundly dissatisfied. This was an era of cautious men, such as Metternich, or Nesselrode, the Russian Foreign Minister, who were deeply conscious of the internal weaknesses afflicting their countries, and of the dangers of tampering with a not unsatisfactory *status quo*. The revolutions of 1848-9 were a further reminder of the fragility of the existing order, and significantly, when Prussia tried to turn the post-revolutionary confusion in Germany to her advantage, Russia sided with Austria against change. Prussia had to await both a Bismarck and a more favourable international environment before launching herself on a new career of aggrandisement.

Even Russia, whom the British felt to be occasioning them too much trouble in the Near East from the 1820s, was acting with great caution. Though tempted at times to intervene in the Ottoman Empire as the champion of the Greek Orthodox Church, and to promote Russian interests and security with control of the entrance into the Black Sea, her more responsible leaders were only too conscious of the financial weakness of the country, and of the poverty of her resources should she attempt to engage in battle far from her own territory. Where were the means to carry a great army to Constantinople, and maintain it in the face of European forces ? This sense of inadequacy, as well as recurrent fears of France, help to explain why Britain and Russia were able to co-operate in dramatic fashion in the Near East on two occasions. The deaths of Castlereagh and of the Tsar Alexander I removed an important bond between the two powers, and when Nicholas I seemed resolved to intervene in the Greek crisis Canning decided to revive British influence by the institution of a new partnership. With French aid an armistice was to be sought between the Turkish and Greek forces. A combined fleet, it was hoped, would achieve this by its presence alone, but the destruction of the Turks at the battle of Navarino ensued. The decision of Canning's successors to dissociate themselves from his partners reduced British influence in the Near East to one of its lowest levels. The anticipated Russian seizure of Constantinople, however, did not follow, since St Petersburg calculated that the dangers that might result from such a move would outweigh its advantages.

The second act of co-operation followed a decade of mutual suspicion and gloomy introspection. Belief that Parliament would not approve increased naval estimates was in part responsible for the British failure to aid the Turks against the rebellious Egyptians in 1832-3. The Russians responded, and to Britain's dismay gained what was believed to be a very advantageous position through the Treaty of Unkiar

Skelessi. But Russia, too, felt weak, and feared that any ambitious move on her part would bring the British Mediterranean fleet through the Straits before she could despatch a sufficient force to Constantinople. The objectives of both were defensive, and they discovered their common interest in the survival of the Ottoman Empire in 1839–41 when it seemed menaced by the ambition of Egypt and France. For Palmerston, Russian sympathy and support were most opportune, since he faced a divided Cabinet and divided country over the question of his support of Turkey. It was essential to expel the Egyptians from Syria before the end of 1840 with the existing British naval forces in the eastern Mediterranean, but these were overshadowed by the concentrated French fleet. Russian and also Austrian support gave greater credibility to Palmerston's dispositions in this great game of bluff. This has often been acclaimed as his greatest success in power politics, and it is no reflection upon his conduct to emphasise his dependence on as well as his adroit exploitation of favourable and, in some respects, exceptional circumstances. The crisis reached its dramatic climax in the British naval bombardment of Acre, and the discomfiture of the Egyptians when their powder-magazine exploded after a chance hit. But the political ramifications behind this military flowering ran back at least to the French Revolution, with the consequent tsarist aversion towards the upstart Orleanists in France.

In the next great Near Eastern crisis Britain was again, in theory, free to choose between her two main rivals, Russia and France. In fact, of course, British interests and public feeling left her little choice, but of her need for an ally in the Crimean War there can be no doubt. Against Russia in 1854 three things were necessary for the capture of the great Black Sea fortress of Sevastopol. Command of the seas was the first essential, and this was secured without a fight. Secondly it was necessary to provide sufficient troops, and here Britain was heavily dependent on the French. Overall the latter were to provide about three times as many soldiers, and were to play much the larger part in the final assault. Thirdly, however, both Britain and France were dependent upon Russian incompetence and weakness, and above all their lack of railways. Sevastopol became untenable as much through the Russian inability to hold the fortress as the allies' efforts to expel them. When the initial allied assault failed it became essentially a struggle in logistics.

As it was, the Crimean War did much to tarnish the British military image in Europe, such glory and prestige as could be derived from this unfortunate struggle being mostly acquired by the French. Lord Clarendon had to protest to the French in 1855 that Britain was a principal and not 'a political and diplomatic contingent' of France. More disastrously for the British the war shattered the trance in which many statesmen had been walking since 1815, with their thoughts on the French Revolution and the possibility of a second Napoleon. Even the obscurantist Romanovs of Russia decided that Napoleon III might be treated as 'a brother' after all. That unlikely contingency of the post-Napoleonic era, the alliance of another European power with an ambitious France, thus became possible. The war had divided the two greatest bulwarks of the *status quo*, Russia and Austria. The imposition of the Black Sea Clauses had made Russia a 'revisionist' power. Franco-Russian co-operation had ceased to be impossible. It had been a basic rule of British foreign policy since 1815 to be on good terms with either Russia or France, the two states whose ambitions Britain had most cause to fear. Prussia, too, no longer had cause to be intimidated by the Austro-Russian alliance, and under Bismarck was to join the 'revisionist' ranks in the 1860s. Between them these three states were to redraw the map of central Europe between 1859 and 1871, and Russia was to revoke the Black Sea Clauses. Only the latter was an immediate blow to British interests, but overall – and not solely due to her own choice – Britain's influence in Europe had fallen sharply. In particular there had occurred the humiliation of Palmerston over the question of the Danish duchies in 1864, when he had shown only too clearly his failure to appreciate the change that had come over Britain's relationship with Europe. In particular he could no longer work with France now that the brake on French ambitions provided by the three Eastern powers no longer existed.

If British inclinations, with political and strategic circumstances in Europe all combined to lessen British influence in continental affairs after 1860, there was not a total loss of interest. For instance, British diplomats were not wholly inactive during the succession of crises between France and Germany in 1870-5. Apart from the well-known Hohenzollern Candidature and 'War in Sight' crises of 1870 and 1875, they also tried to remove Franco-German differences that arose from the Spanish Civil War in 1874. Less marginal was the continuing British interest in the Mediterranean, where the policies and alignments of bordering states could seriously affect the naval balance on this vital route to the East. Here Britain's Mediterranean fleet remained her key instrument, a fact most interestingly demonstrated in governmental discussions in 1912. These arose from the need to recall the battleships of that squadron to the North Sea to maintain a sufficient concentration of strength against Germany. The Foreign Office feared that, in the absence of a strong naval presence in the Mediterranean, Italy and Spain might draw or be drawn nearer to Germany. It was feared, too, that British influence in the Ottoman Empire would decline still further.

As we have already seen, the Mediterranean fleet was far from omnipotent even in its hey-day. This was particularly so with respect to the Near Eastern Question. In the winter of 1877–8 Britain and Russia were once more in danger of coming to blows over the future of the Ottoman Empire. From the British point of view, at this time, it was by no means clear how Constantinople and the Straits were to be defended by the Mediterranean fleet, aided only by limited British land forces and such troops as the Turks could still muster. Austrian aid seemed essential, but the latter remained singularly unimpressed by the scale of British preparations for war. Fortunately it was the Russians who lost their nerve in view of their own financial and military weakness, the apparent revival of the Turkish army, and the possible support of Britain by both Austria and Rumania.

As after the Crimean War, British statesmen in 1878 sought advantages beyond the strength and will of the nation to support unaided. In particular Lord Salisbury insisted that the Straits should remain closed to British warships only so long as Britain was convinced that the Sultan was acting of his own free will. This attempt to menace southern Russia with British naval and amphibious forces almost at will was doomed to frustration. When Britain and Russia once more came to the brink of war in 1885 the Straits did not provide the hoped-for highway. Turkey, as well as Russia's partners in the *Dreikaiserbund* were all hostile to the opening of the Straits, and Britain was powerless to act in this theatre. Ten years later, and faced by yet another Near Eastern crisis, Salisbury found the British Mediterranean fleet neutralised by the recently concluded Franco-Russian alliance. Turkey was still hostile. Reluctantly Salisbury concluded that British strategy could no longer be based on Constantinople and the Straits: Egypt must become the key to the safety of the eastern Mediterranean and the route through Suez. The practicability of this policy was demonstrated in 1898 when, only three years later, a French effort to intervene in Egyptian affairs was to be frustrated at Fashoda. Egypt was of no interest to Russia, so that France could be isolated. Naval supremacy in the Mediterranean, and a local superiority on the ground at Fashoda sufficed to win a bloodless victory. It was one of the last great independent coups achieved by British diplomacy.

By the end of the century, however, Britain's freedom of action outside Europe was becoming constricted by the reappearance of naval and colonial rivals, following the spread of industry to Europe, the United States and Japan. The Franco-Russian alliance was not always dormant – as in 1898 – and in the early 1900s the British government was to make some striking decisions. An alliance was concluded with Japan in 1902 to try to contain Russia, and also France, in the Far East. The dominance of the United States in Central America was acknowledged, and the friendship of Germany assumed for the purposes of naval planning. The diplomacy of the Ententes followed in 1904–7 as Britain strove to bridge the gap between her global interests and her resources. The 1900s also witnessed the modernisation of the Indian army to meet a possible Russian attack, launched from the new railways of Central Asia. Fear of these self-same railways led Britain, the great nineteenth-century builder of railways, to discourage rail construction in the border states between Russia and India in the hope that this would impede an attacker's progress.

Britain's position in global politics for much of the nineteenth century had been very different. As Professor Arnold Toynbee described it: 'The United Kingdom had managed to corral all the wolves formerly infesting her sheep-run in one pen with a single entrance.' This meant that all the great powers could gain access to the wider world only by recourse to the sea, so that British command of European waters could, to a great extent, safeguard her interests elsewhere. This was largely true. The only power with a land route to the East was Russia, but neither for purposes of war nor trade could it compete with the sea. Until the opening of the Trans-Siberian railway in the next century a march of eighteen months lay between Russian troops and Vladivostok. Maritime nations were further aided by the fact that most of the riches of the East lay within fairly easy reach of the sea. Great, therefore, had been Britain's inheritance when she became mistress of the sea in the eighteenth century.

One qualification must be made to Toynbee's metaphor. One 'wolf' was indeed outside the European corral. This was the United States – fortunately for Britain a young and immature wolf. Admittedly here was a dynamic people, with a gift for enterprise and land and sea transport. But the States also remained comparatively weak and divided within themselves until the 1870s. The impact of the early American expansionists remained limited, while rapidly growing economic power in the late nineteenth century was not immediately accompanied by a positive foreign policy. Nevertheless it was perhaps fortunate for Anglo-American relations that the Caribbean had ceased to be one of the most coveted regions in the world and that Britain's interests were moving eastward. Clashes did occur between them – in Mexico, Central America and Cuba – in the 1820s and again in mid-century. But the War of 1812 had taught that conflict was likely to prove costly and inconclusive, and neither state, basically, was anxious to repeat the experience. Circumstances, reinforced by some good sense, thus conspired to prevent a collision. Nevertheless the naval strength of the United States, actual and potential, did influence British thinking down to the 1860s. It was seen in the perspective of European naval conditions, where France and Russia were Britain's main rivals. There were several occasions before 1865 when British politicians and admirals feared that a Franco-Russo-American combination might not prove impossible, and considered that a three-power naval standard might be needed in reply. The United States certainly tried to exploit British distractions during the Crimean War, but had no wish to become directly involved in European alignments. The American navy was of little importance from the late 1860s until the 1890s, and on its reappearance the British soon decided that it must be treated as a friend.

The strength of the Russian navy also varied considerably during the century, and the chief periods of British concern were limited to the 1830s and 1890s. In contrast, French naval strength was usually sufficient to cause concern. At times, indeed, especially during the period 1840–65, the French ran the British a good second. But in any competition between them the odds were all in favour of the latter. Britain's advantages in resources, whether in terms of money, industry, raw materials or personnel, were so great that only a failure of national will or political and professional ineptitude on a massive scale could endanger her position. France was further weakened by internal political problems, and by a much greater degree of involvement in European affairs. Her challenge to Britain outside Europe was thus hesitant and intermittent until the last two decades of the century, and until she was strengthened in particular by the alliance with Russia. Even then she was to fail at Fashoda.

Until the 1880s, therefore, it was not difficult for Britain to protect her extra-European position against other powers without any real strain on her resources, and without the need for allies. There were times, it is true, when she co-operated with others outside Europe, but never with the degree of necessity occasioned by crises in the Near East or on the Continent. The fact that Britain pursued her overseas interests with a certain measure of restraint may to some extent have lessened the incentive of others to compete with her. This must not be pushed too far, for the jealousy and hostility of other states quickly mounted once they looked to the Afro-Asian and Latin American regions for new markets and other openings. But if Britain added a considerable area to her colonial empire between 1815 and 1874, when the anti-colonial currents were running strongly, some efforts were made to control the process, and prevent, for instance, China becoming a second India in the 1860s. Britain's economic strength also meant that she had no need to imitate the colonial trading monopoly practised by Spain in previous centuries.

The British prided themselves on their self-restraint, but even came to see themselves as an international policeman, employing their navy for the benefit of all seafarers. This supposed disinterest was not recognised or appreciated by all. Some French merchants feared that the British anti-slave-trade patrol would be used to hamper legitimate French commerce, and consequently opposed any concessions on the right of search claimed by the Royal Navy. German historians and economists spent much time trying to uncover the reasons for Britain's phenomenal trading success in the nineteenth century, and many concluded that the navy was the key instrument in the development of markets outside Europe. Nevertheless there were some who saw that British naval power, while too great to challenge, might serve their interests to some extent. Thus Thomas Jefferson insisted in 1823: 'Great Britain is the nation which can do us the most harm of anyone, or all on earth; and with her on our side we need not fear the whole world.' John Quincy Adams, not a great friend of Britain during his active career, concluded in more reflective mood in 1840 that Britain was rendering an international service in the 'Opium' War by forcing China to open her doors wider to foreign trade. Much of American policy towards China in mid-century, though often bitterly hostile to Britain, was based on the presence of the latter's coercive power.

To measure the role of the Royal Navy in the protection of British interests against other powers one is really forced to ask what would have occurred had it been less strong. It is hardly conceivable, for instance, that other European powers would have remained so inactive during the Spanish American struggle for independence early in the century had it not been for the British naval veto. Certainly the Latin Americans themselves had no doubts. Bolívar insisted: 'Only England, mistress of the seas, can protect us against the united force of European reaction.' It is true that between 1815 and the 1820s there existed among European statesmen only occasional flights of fancy rather than real plans for intervention in Latin America, either in support of Spain, or in pursuit of their own interests. But there were undoubtedly individuals

in France who aspired to do more, and who were frustrated by British
naval power and diplomacy. The Monroe Doctrine must similarly be
related to British strength at sea. Assertions that the United States
should not meekly follow Britain's lead like 'a cock-boat in the wake of
the British man-of-war' must not be allowed to hide the essential truth
that, if the Americans had untied the painter, they were still sailing in
the same direction and under the cover of British guns. Latin American
efforts to probe behind the verbiage of the Monroe Doctrine found
nothing tangible, and in Mexico in 1826 it was to Britain that the new
leaders looked for protection against the 'machinations' of the court of
Versailles.

The role of the British navy could be demonstrated from many other
incidents. It was, for example, no coincidence that the policy of the
United States towards Britain over certain Central American questions
moderated when the ending of the Crimean War released British warships for service in North American waters. Similarly British sea power
discouraged Russian attempts to seek naval bases south of Vladivostok
in the Far East until the 1890s. British negotiations with the Dutch over
certain problems in the East Indies in the 1820s were supported by the
ultimate threat of naval power. As Castlereagh warned the Dutch in
1819, should they seek too exclusive a position, 'the day cannot be far
off when naval stations in those seas will involve both in unnecessary
expense . . .' Less direct, but still significant, was the despatch of
British squadrons to keep a watchful eye on the activities of other powers
overseas. The purpose behind these moves was not necessarily to
frustrate the operations in question, but to serve as a reminder that
British interests should not be ignored.

This was a move much employed by Palmerston, who believed in
making a fuss over quite small issues lest the other party should be
encouraged to seek greater success, and thereby precipitate a real crisis.
Thus in 1836–7 the Mediterranean fleet was used to remind France that
Britain's reluctant acceptance of her intervention in Algeria did not
imply a similar disinterest in Tunis. French activity in Latin America
likewise prompted Palmerston to send ships in the hope that their
ambitions would be moderated. Other British foreign secretaries acted
similarly, though none with quite the same relish or consistency. Nothing
pleased Palmerston more than to draw verbal pictures of the navy and
its officers as peace-keepers, international policemen, or as his most
infallible agents. Upon occasion special efforts were made to maintain
a clear superiority over French or American squadrons in certain parts
of the world. In Chinese waters, for instance, Aberdeen argued in the

1840s that Britain must maintain a larger force than any other power to impress upon China the fact that Britain was the world's greatest maritime state. Tangible proof was essential, given Chinese ignorance of the world.

'Showing the flag', however, was not always enough in British eyes. If relations with other powers were more peaceful than in any previous century, those with the peoples of Latin America, Africa and Asia were often difficult. By and large the British wanted trade, not territory, and sought to create the necessary conditions with existing governments. But a satisfactory relationship often proved elusive. The local regime might be reluctant to trade or have dealings with the West; its legal concepts might differ, or it might prove unable to protect aliens on its territory; it might be overthrown and its agreements broken by a successor; it might be friendly yet ineffectual, or hostile and obstructive. The situation was further complicated by the unscrupulous conduct and ruthless ambition of many British traders and adventurers. Differing cultures might collide from intent or through sheer incomprehension of each other. This is not the place to discuss the rights and wrongs of such conflicts, but it is necessary to try to gain some idea of the efficacy of the use of force in these circumstances. Even at the time there were critics such as Cobden and Bright who believed that trade could and should expand without aid from the flag, whether in the form of limited wars or 'gunboat diplomacy'. MacGregor Laird, in contrast, described a naval gun in the hands of British seamen as a 'moral power'.

The moral justification for the use of force was founded on the spreading belief that barbarous peoples could not claim equality with civilised states, and that the latter had a right to coerce them into acceptance of higher standards. The *Edinburgh Review* went so far as to assert:

> The compulsory seclusion of the Japanese is a wrong not only to themselves but to the civilised world . . . The Japanese undoubtedly have an exclusive right to the possession of their territory; but they must not abuse that right to the extent of debarring all other nations from a participation in its riches and virtues. The only secure title to property, whether it be a hovel or an empire, is that the exclusive possession for one is for the benefit of all.

Palmerston provided the pragmatic justification:

> These half-civilised governments such as those of China, Portugal, Spanish America, all require a dressing every eight or ten years to keep them in order. Their minds are too shallow to receive an impression that will last longer than some such period and warning is of little use. They care little for words and they must not only see the stick but actually feel it on their shoulders before they yield . . .

Nor was this view typical of Palmerston alone. Lord Stanley, noted for his non-interventionism in almost all aspects of foreign policy, sent the Mediterranean fleet to Cadiz in 1867 to demand, as *The Times* put it, 'a plain answer to a plain question' concerning a shipping incident. Aberdeen, for all his distaste of violence, also made much use of 'gunboat diplomacy'.

These lines of thought played into the hands of the many Britons who were trying to carve out commercial empires for themselves in various parts of the world. Not all were guilty of trying to call in the navy on the least provocation. Some, as we shall see, saw that in certain circumstances naval action might do more harm than good. At times both Admiralty and Foreign Office lost patience with the many suppliants for warships, either because the grounds were so trivial or because they distrusted their motives. Lord Clarendon complained in 1856: 'If in the remotest corner of the earth any Englishman gets a well-deserved, but uncompensated black eye, the newspapers and Parliament immediately demand an enquiry into the conduct of the bloated sinecurist in Downing St, who has no sense of British honour.'

The great era of British intervention in this fashion may be dated with some exactitude. It falls roughly between the fall of the Tories in 1835 and the end of the Second China War in 1860. True, the Barbary States had been coerced in 1816 and several times thereafter. The British navy had kept a watchful eye on events in Latin America during the struggle for independence. It is possible to conclude, however, that although there were some displays of strength by British warships, much restraint and understanding was shown by the officers on that station. One officer, Commodore Bowles, even persuaded the government of Buenos Aires in 1818 that a forced loan of $150,000 extorted from the local British merchants was illegal, quoting extensively from Vattel's works on international law in the process. Warships were at hand, but were kept in the background, and this discriminating use of force normally characterised British policy in the 1820s also. The leading historian of Anglo-Argentinian relations, H. S. Ferns, has indeed concluded that British interests were normally best defended by their indispensability to the local economies as creditors, investors and the main agents of international trade. It was only when local factionalism in, for instance, Buenos Aires was no longer restrained by economic rationalisation that gunboats became essential.

Circumstances, reinforced by a more aggressive mood of self-confidence – even self-righteousness – in the country, gave a more positive twist to 'gunboat diplomacy' after 1835. Several years of recession helped to increase mercantile pressure on the government, especially when the belief was strong that the vast Chinese market was ripe for exploitation if only the right trading conditions could be established. Wellington had coldly remarked in February 1835 that 'It was not by force and violence that His Majesty's government intends to establish a commercial intercourse . . .' but earlier hints that a Whig government would be less restrained crystallised with Palmerston's decision around 1837 to support British trade with China with regular displays of naval might. It was only a short step from here to the two China Wars of 1839–42 and 1857–60.

It is, of course, impossible to know what would have befallen Anglo-Chinese trade had the wars not been fought. Yet there are certain points that can be noted. In the first place it is clear that British trade did not grow as quickly as was expected afterwards, and certainly not to any marked extent until the 1860s. On the other hand there is wide agreement among western historians that the existing Chinese trading system – the Co-hong – had outlived its usefulness. It might also be argued that, given the determination of Britain and other states to trade with China, it was expedient for the latter to admit foreign diplomats to Peking and to recognise their countries as equals. From the British point of view it seemed that a new trading and diplomatic relationship with China was necessary, and that this would never be yielded by the latter save under duress. War was probably inescapable given the state of mutual incomprehension and the lack of common interests that existed on both sides. A *modus vivendi* might have been possible after the first war if the British had been content with limited trading concessions, and with no diplomatic representation in Peking. The British side was further confused by the lack of unanimity between the commercial and diplomatic elements, and since it was usually the more extreme parties that prevailed, a collision was unavoidable.

Direct experience of European arms was necessary before the Chinese leaders came to recognise the weakness of their country. Even minor victories tended to restore their self-confidence. Ignorance of the West was a major cause of their intransigence, and after the fall of Peking in 1860 a larger degree of realism began to permeate their governing class. As late as 1860, when Lord Elgin threatened to destroy Peking, Prince Kung replied that these were words which no 'subject' of the Emperor should dare to use. Although Chinese resistance in the second war was much stronger than in the first, British and French forces were able in time to prevail through superior weapons, discipline and organisation. The invaders were also assisted by divisions within China herself. There was the great Taiping rebellion; many Chinese merchants and inhabitants of the coastal towns were anxious to trade with the foreigners; the Manchu dynasty doubted the loyalty of the Chinese literati to itself, and feared that it could not rely on the obedience of the poorer classes. The situation did not exist in which the Emperor could mobilise a united people against the foreigner, safe in the knowledge that they would sacrifice all – or at least a great deal – for the regime. Once Peking was lost the prevailing opinion in governing circles was that terms must be made with Britain and France lest the process of disintegration in China should be carried further still.

A limited exercise of force was thus both practical and necessary in British eyes. It was rewarded for more than a generation with comparative stability in Anglo-Chinese relations, during which the British still used their gunboats as a deterrent and for punitive purposes, but only in so far as they felt such exercise of power to be compatible with the survival of the Manchu empire. Always there existed the fear that undue pressure on China might start a train of events that would lead to a second India. Fortunately the Chinese government was just sufficiently stable, as well as being sufficiently amenable to outside pressure, for this policy to succeed.

'Gunboat diplomacy' was even more effective in Japan. British power had begun to influence the Japanese indirectly long before the arrival of Commodore Perry of the United States Navy in 1853. It may even have eased his task for him. As early as 1808 a visit to Nagasaki by H.M.S. *Phaeton* is said to have inspired the eleven-year-old Takashima to begin his life study of western military strength and society in general. The First China War was followed with great interest by some in Japan, and led to a relaxation of the government's attitude towards foreigners. Dutch and American agents did their best to persuade the Japanese of the desirability of making concessions to their nations before the British arrived in force and extorted even harsher terms. On the whole the Japanese proved apt pupils, until the xenophobic south-western clans precipitated a number of incidents which led to international bombardments of their forts and towns in 1863–4. This direct exposure to western arms proved most salutary. At Kagoshima in August 1863, for example, the new and not wholly satisfactory British Armstrong breechloaders inflicted more than 1000 casualties; British losses numbered only sixty-three. The Japanese admired and strove to emulate such military prowess. The south-western clans were to provide many of the dynamic new men who were to bring about the Meiji Restoration, and rule Japan in the era of frantic modernisation from 1868. This was an unusual outcome to a first clash between an oriental state and the West. In contrast, the effective modernisation of Sikh armies had to await the imposition of British rule despite the efforts of Ranjit Singh to copy European methods.

In general gunboats served many British interests adequately in the Far East until at least the 1890s. They policed the Persian Gulf, but were not always so successful elsewhere. Along the coasts of Africa, especially of West Africa, they enjoyed much temporary success while operating both against the slave trade and on behalf of British merchants. The latter certainly gained in confidence from their presence, and at times abused it. But it was found in practice that temporary visits by warships were not sufficient protection, particularly when British traders began to push up the rivers. Nor could gunboats supply that permanent political authority that was needed when African society began to disintegrate in the face of the western impact. In time gunboats were adding to the instability, as they weakened African authority without supplying an adequate substitute, and thus helped to prepare for varying degrees of colonisation. Africa could not supply that measure of local governmental stability which was the necessary complement to gunboats. The limitations of gunboats were also demonstrated by the Kingdom of Dahomey in 1851–2 and 1876 when the King's preference for his prestige and independence as opposed to trade with the outside world rendered naval blockades unusually ineffective.

'Gunboat diplomacy' also experienced mixed fortunes in South America. Between 1843 and 1846 La Plata was the scene of perhaps the least successful of these operations. It is a confused story in which the policy of Aberdeen was neither consistent nor clear-cut. Broadly, British forces, with some French assistance, tried to prop up a weak Uruguayan regime against Argentinian-supported forces. They also tried to open the river Parana to trade against the opposition of the Argentinian strong man, Rosas. Militarily, both operations enjoyed short-lived success, but economically their results were unfortunate. The communities on both banks of the Parana were mostly hostile; the trade with Montevideo was declining, and British merchants in Buenos Aires found both policies detrimental to their interests. Indeed, British lives and property in Buenos Aires were several times in jeopardy, and Rosas claimed that only his authority stood between the British in that city and disaster. He also asserted that although Anglo-French maritime power might take his capital, he could still hold the countryside and its people against the Europeans. Ironically it was Palmerston who recognised the strength of Rosas's position, and introduced a policy of disengagement from 1846. The lesson was not wholly learned, as subsequent British efforts to browbeat another proud people, the Brazilians, were to prove in the early 1860s. Again official policy ran counter to and was opposed by British merchants.

Intervention in this fashion was a controversial instrument even in the mid-nineteenth century. One of its main forms, 'gunboat diplomacy', has never been properly explored by historians, and has remained an emotive phrase. According to political prejudice, people look back to it with nostalgia or a sense of outrage. Our concern here has been with its relevance to British needs in the nineteenth century. To argue, as was the wont of the Manchester School, that American trade flourished without the aid of a great navy was to overlook the American debt to British power, at least in China. On the other hand the cost of some of the naval squadrons hardly seemed justified by the profits from the trade protected. Equally, short-term and purely economic calculations could be misleading. But what is clear is that 'gunboat diplomacy' was a useful instrument only in certain conditions. This was a limited form of warfare which succeeded best against divided peoples, some of whom were attracted by western trade, capital and knowledge. If the internal weaknesses and divisions became too pronounced, the society would collapse, and a colonial solution result. The external pressures had also to be carefully controlled, and if more than one outside power were involved, respect for a common discipline was essential. The era of 'gunboat diplomacy' soon ended in the Africa of the later nineteenth century under the combined impact of international rivalry and internal decay. The upsurge of local nationalism was a contributory factor in the case of Egypt in 1882, when the successful bombardment of Alexandria really solved nothing. Local sentiment in Latin America repeatedly reduced the efficacy of naval action in the nineteenth century, and was to do so in China from 1919.

Nevertheless the overall story of British foreign policy in this period remains an impressive one. In 1871 Guido Verbeck advised the Japanese, who were engaged in an intensive search for the best possible western models for the modernisation of their state, that they should look in particular to the British example for instruction in the conduct of foreign policy. It is necessary, however, to acknowledge the British debt to the unusual conditions that prevailed in Europe from 1815 until about 1856, conditions that enabled her to exercise influence out of proportion to her current military and naval strength. Events in the 1860s underlined the nature of that debt. Fortunately for Britain great-power rivalries did not begin to challenge her interests outside Europe seriously until the 1880s, when the next generation found it necessary to inaugurate a revolution in arms expenditure and foreign policy. Between 1885 and 1914 naval expenditure increased fivefold. Even on the army, small though it remained, spending nearly doubled. By the twentieth century, too, the balance in Europe had moved so far in favour of Germany that Britain was being forced to concern herself more and more with the affairs of that continent, even to the point of limiting some of her commitments in the wider world. In the longer run still it would not be possible to maintain British influence in the under-developed world with the small military and naval forces that had hitherto sufficed. The day of small wars with 30,000 or so British troops was passing. Gunboats and Maxim guns ceased to overawe. As Jan Smuts had seen in 1899: 'The dominion that the British empire exercises over the many tribes and peoples within its jurisdiction rests more upon prestige and moral intimidation than upon true military strength.' The Boers were to be defeated, but only after a massive mobilisation of British strength which was wholly out of keeping with national experience of war since the time of Napoleon.

SUGGESTIONS FOR FURTHER READING

The early years are still dominated by the classic works of Sir Charles Webster, *The Foreign Policy of Castlereagh, 1815–22* (1963), and H. W. V. Temperley, *The Foreign Policy of Canning, 1822–27* (1966). The period of Palmerston from 1830–65 has now been comprehensively summarised by Donald Southgate, '*The Most English Minister . . .*' (1966). Much is to be learned from R. Millman's *British Foreign Policy and the Coming of the Franco-Prussian War* (1965) concerning Britain's changing relationship with Europe. The late-nineteenth-century challenge to British naval supremacy is admirably examined by A. J. Marder, *The Anatomy of British Sea Power, 1880–1905* (1964). The Anglo-Russian relationship during the Near Eastern crisis of 1875–8 is most interestingly illuminated by B. H. Sumner, *Russia and the Balkans, 1870–80* (1937).

A useful summary of Britain's extra-European relations is to be found in *The Cambridge History of the British Empire*, vols. ii and iii (1940 and 1959), while the restraint and consistency displayed by the Foreign Office in the promotion of British economic interests are portrayed in detail by D. C. M. Platt, *Finance, Trade and Politics in British Foreign Policy, 1815–1914* (1968). There is much to be learned concerning early relations with Latin America from the introduction to *The Navy and South America, 1807–23* (1963), edited by G. S. Graham and R. A. Humphreys, and for the period as a whole from H. S. Ferns, *Britain and Argentina in the Nineteenth Century* (1960) and A. K. Manchester, *British Pre-eminence in Brazil* (1964). On Africa one of the most revealing works is by K. O. Dike, *Trade and Politics in the Niger Delta, 1830–85* (1956), while many of the reasons for British success against China are explained by M. Banno, *China and the West, 1858–60* (1964) and I. C. Hsü, *China's Entrance into the Family of Nations* (1960). B. Bond has edited a useful collection of essays on some of the small wars fought by Britain in this period, *Victorian Military Campaigns* (1967).

Notes on Contributors

C. J. BARTLETT, Reader in International History, University of Dundee; author of *Great Britain and Sea Power: 1815–53* (1963) and *Castlereagh* (1966), etc.

KENNETH FIELDEN, Lecturer in History, University of Edinburgh; author of a doctoral thesis, *Richard Cobden and America* (Cambridge, 1966).

OLIVER FURLEY, Senior Lecturer in History, Makerere University College, Uganda; at present writing a book on the history of education in East Africa, and author of articles on West Indian and East African history.

S. G. E. LYTHE, Professor of Economic History, University of Strathclyde; author of *British Economic History since 1760* (1950) and *The Economy of Scotland in its European Setting: 1550–1625* (1960), etc.

D. F. MACDONALD, Professor of Modern, Social and Economic History, University of Dundee; author of *Scotland's Shifting Population: 1770–1850* (1937) and *The Age of Transition* (1967), etc.

DONALD SOUTHGATE, Reader in Modern Political and Constitutional History, University of Dundee; author of *The Passing of the Whigs* (1962) and '*The Most English Minister . . .*': *the policies and politics of Palmerston* (1966), etc.

PETER N. STEARNS, Professor of History, Rutgers University, New Brunswick, New Jersey; author of *European Society in Upheaval: social history since 1800* (1967) and *Priest and Revolutionary: Lamennais and the dilemma of French Catholicism* (1967), etc.

D. R. WATSON, Lecturer in Modern History, University of Dundee; at present writing a biography of Clemenceau, and author of articles on modern French history.

Index